||||||||||||||||||||||||||||||||||||

B54 000 147 0

NO MIDDLE

ROTHERHAM LIBRARY & INFORMATION SERVICE

RAW

RIG2

RAWMARSH

815

KIVETON PARK

- 2 NOV 2015

WICKERSLEY

ASTON

GRE 8/18

2 4 APR 2023

25/2/24

This book must be returned by the date specified at the time of issue as
the DATE DUE FOR RETURN.
The loan may be extended (personally, by post, telephone or online) for
a further period if the book is not required by another reader, by quoting
the above number / author / title.

Enquiries   774

www.rotherham   raries

||||||||||||||||||||||||||||||||||||

D1407434

Sanjeev Shetty began writing about boxing in 1994. He has reported from ringside on greats such as Mike Tyson, Lennox Lewis, Naseem Hamed, Ricky Hatton, Joe Calzaghe, Oscar de la Hoya and Manny Pacquiao. The majority of his reportage has been for the BBC, for whom he has served over three years. He lives in Cheshire with his wife Laura and their two sons, Rafael and Ruben. He is also the author of a detective novel, Mary's Work.

SANJEEV SHETTY

NO MIDDLE GROUND

EUBANK, BENN, WATSON
AND THE LAST GOLDEN ERA
OF BRITISH BOXING

Aurum
Press

First published in Great Britain
2014 by Aurum Press Ltd
74—77 White Lion Street
Islington
London N1 9PF
www.aurumpress.co.uk

This paperback edition published in 2015 by Aurum Press Ltd.

Copyright © Sanjeev Shetty 2014

Sanjeev Shetty has asserted his moral right to be identified as the Author of
this Work in accordance with the Copyright Designs and Patents Act 1988.

All rights reserved. No part of this book may be reproduced or utilised in
any form or by any means, electronic or mechanical, including photocopying,
recording or by any information storage and retrieval system,
without permission in writing from Aurum Press Ltd.

Every effort has been made to trace the copyright holders of material
quoted in this book. If application is made in writing to the publisher,
any omissions will be included in future editions.

A catalogue record for this book is
available from the British Library.

ISBN 978 1 78131 360 2
eISBN 978 1 78131 269 8

3 5 7 9 10 8 6 4 2
2015 2017 2019 2018 2016

Typeset in ITC New Baskerville Std by SX Composing DTP, Rayleigh, Essex
Printed and bound by CPI Group (UK) Ltd, Croydon, CR0 4YY

For Mick Watts – I'll keep writing them if you keep reading them

and

Richard Shepheard – it's not Sonny Liston, but I hope it will do.

Introduction

It seems the easiest thing in the world to say, but they didn't like each other.

If you were alive when Nigel Benn, Chris Eubank and Michael Watson attempted to settle things, you'll know a bit about what it was like. And if you weren't, then you have my sympathy. Because what we could not have realised then was how lucky we were. This was as good as it got and to quote my friend Glyn Leach, the editor of *Boxing Monthly*, 'there's been nothing to equal it since'.

It began under a tent, on a Sunday night, in a deserted part of north London and the scale of it all was summed up by where it finished. At the home of the English football champions, Old Trafford, with over 40,000 people crammed into a venue nicknamed 'the Theatre of Dreams', the unlucky ones without tickets were forced to watch it on television. If Saturday night square-screen viewing defines us as a nation, with the masses now drawn to the finals of *Strictly Come Dancing* and its ilk, then what did it say about us twenty years ago when we'd give up our evenings for blood, sweat and violence? Did we evolve, did boxing become less compelling or was it down to the quality of what was in front of us?

I'm not sure there are any easy answers to the question. Except that, when it reached its height, on that otherwise tranquil evening in Manchester, I was there, part of a quartet of people from contrasting backgrounds and diverging futures, united by one thing. We all had our favourites. One day, we'd all admit that if at times we wanted one of them to win more than the other, when it all came to an end, when the final punches had been thrown, admiring all three of them wasn't a chore.

A two-man rivalry is essentially a pick-em. Him I like, him I don't. When there are three, we look to find one who we can identify with. During the 1970s and early 1980s, one of sport's most enduring rivalries could be found in tennis, with Björn Borg, John McEnroe and Jimmy Connors locked into something that all of us could relate to. Borg was the full vessel, or so it seemed, a man so at ease it seemed impossible to ruffle his feathers, even when others tried. Connors was the artisan, the blue-collar worker who played every week because he'd known hard times and knew the value of every cent. And then there was McEnroe, the volatile, magical and charismatic kid who begged you to be seated even as he warmed up. Given his privileged background, no one could ever work out where the anger came from. But to see those eruptions was more than just a voyeuristic occasion. It was also a precursor to something that you knew would find its way into the scrapbooks.

While Borg, Connors and McEnroe were all-time greats, among the twenty best men ever to hold a racket, Benn, Eubank and Watson would probably only feature in the best-of category when the discussion turned to British boxers. However, the similarities were in how they felt about each other. There was dislike which quite often bordered on contempt. And these were young, angry men who had reached the ring by following different paths, but each of whom had a point to prove, and that made for a dangerous cocktail with a pair of ten-ounce gloves.

Chris Eubank looked imperious, his body seemingly carved from stone, his visage impassive and, whether by design or not, he dared his opponents to dislike him. Michael Watson had known hardship, raised with love but without luxury. He fought because it was something he was good at but also because he needed something other than faith and fresh air to live on. And then there was Nigel Benn, who could charm you outside the ring, but harm you inside it. The anger within was a mystery to those who didn't know him. Even after years as a professional boxer, he didn't know why he'd wake up and want to hurt people.

Born within two and a half years of each other, all of West Indian immigrant parents, and raised in London, their rivalries did not begin in the amateur ranks. It was only when they started to earn money that the dislike came to the fore. When they started fighting for financial reward, Britain was a haven for quick-buck artists. And when one of them made easy money, the other two were left wondering why their pockets were empty. They all wanted to be champions, but also wanted to be paid more than the other. They all sought independence from the men who managed their careers. And they all thought they were the best. Most attempts to settle things in the ring provoked more arguments.

Their contests sometimes reached genuine sporting greatness and at other times promised more than they delivered. But the tension was always there. These were three men who, at various times, genuinely despised each other – sometimes the hate appeared manufactured, but we didn't know that, nor did we know how much that personal venom would both shape and destroy them. All we knew was that it made for some of the most unforgettable boxing this country has ever played host to.

In their own way, they'd all pay a high price for their endeavours. History tells us that ring wars, when fuelled by personal animosity, can have tragic consequences. In 2013 we mourned the passing of Emile Griffith, a superlative boxer of the 1960s, who spent the last fifty years of his life in a state of torment because of one of boxing's most gruesome moments. Griffith, a humble welterweight from the Virgin Islands, became a popular figure in his adopted New York because of his classic style and easy-going attitude. In 1962, his demeanour was disturbed when an opponent, Cuban Benny Paret, grabbed his buttocks before a bout and called him a *maricón*, the day before they were due to fight at Madison Square Garden. The word *maricón* is Spanish slang for homosexual, something that no man would admit to being then and even less so if he was a boxer. It was the kind of thing one man could say to another in the 1960s without fear of the authorities interceding. Fast forward fifty years and the British heavyweight Tyson Fury can expect a fine from those who run the sport in this country for making homophobic comments on his Twitter account. Times have changed for the better, with even boxing, as old-fashioned a sport as any, doing more than before to eradicate prejudice.

But back to the 1960s, being called a *maricón* provoked a fury in Griffith which had not been evident before, perhaps because he had been harbouring doubts about his sexuality that he would struggle to come to terms with throughout his life. If those who managed and trained him regretted their fighter's lack of anger, they had no idea of the consequences once that fuse was lit. Paret and Griffith had fought twice before, the Cuban winning the second bout after being stopped in the first. If only in terms of combat there had been honour in those bouts, there would be no such thing in the third and final episode of their rivalry. Griffith had been told by his trainer, Gil Clancy, to keep throwing punches if he got Paret in trouble. And in round twelve that's exactly what he did. Paret, hurt in a corner of the ring, was subjected to an attack of unmistakable hostility and fury. More than twenty punches landed on his chin and upper body before he slumped to the canvas, unconscious. The images were captured live on American television and even the most optimistic viewer would have been able to tell that Paret's life was in danger. The Cuban slipped into a coma from which he would never awake, dying nine days after taking his final punch. It was the first ring death ever recorded on live television and its memory still brings a shudder to those who saw it in the flesh or on celluloid. Boxing disappeared from television screens in America for ten years, so haunting were those final seconds of Paret's life. In the course of Benn, Eubank and Watson's rivalry, there was a reminder of how close a boxer's life comes to a premature end when the reason to fight becomes personal and not professional.

That kind of fury between fighters didn't disappear because of one tragic bout. There would be countless other examples of men who didn't care for each other and didn't mind expressing it before, during or after battle. And, what's more, that feeling, call it dislike, animosity, or just pure hatred, wasn't discouraged. Gym gossip, the kind where one fighter lets a future opponent know by word of mouth that he wants to hurt him, continued. And promoters, sharks if you don't like them, smart businessmen if you do, turned a blind eye when one of their boxers opened his mouth and uttered the kind of words he'd never use in front of his mother. They knew that a promotion lived or died on quality and hype. You didn't need to manipulate the paying public when the match-ups were competitive and a belt was on the line, but if that wasn't the case then throw in some personal animosity and old-fashioned contempt and you definitely had a full house.

The era of Eubank, Benn and Watson was a time when boxing's place in the social landscape was much more prominent. Men had fought in what passed for a ring for centuries, long before football became this country's obsession. Its appeal had not diminished as the twentieth century drew to a close, as virtually every boxer was subjected to the 'Ali' complex – how could any of them match up to the most charismatic athlete the world had ever seen or heard? They couldn't, but 'the Greatest' had given them all the platform they craved. If his unique brand of braggadocio, bombast, beauty and brutality made him the most captivating boxer of any era, then those who followed suffered in comparison. Until it became apparent that you could market a fighter in different ways. In Britain, there'd be a Jim Watt, an Alan Minter, a Charlie Magri or a Maurice Hope. All of them world champions, but with qualities that were unique. Watt was durable, always finding ways to pull victory from the jaws of defeat. Minter was tough and tricky. Magri, with that flat nose, was everyone's idea of what a fighter should be, and Hope's silky skills were different from what we'd become accustomed to in British rings.

They'd come and go and there would be a period during the mid-1980s when Barry McGuigan's star shone so brightly you'd have thought him capable of unifying Ireland, such was his stature. 'The Clones Cyclone', however, never quite dominated the way we thought he would, a combination of tragedy in and out of the ring robbing him and us of more excitement.

And then, from nowhere, came Benn, Eubank and Watson. Not one of them began with the fanfare that had accompanied the professional debut of amateur star Errol Christie, and their rivalry wasn't something that you could predict. But as Benn began despatching what he called Mexican road sweepers, as Watson took the old-school route and beat some of America's best veterans and Eubank breezed into England with an act both unique and inflammatory, they became a threesome as exciting and flammable as any we'd seen for years. And the story they told us was that they weren't too keen on each other. Over the space of four years and five fights, there would be upsets, insults and tragedy. And it was hard to ignore. Whatever your background or sporting preference, you knew when a fight between any two of them was on. To see them live was a privilege but, if you couldn't get a ticket, terrestrial television was the alternative. Living rooms around the country were nearly as hostile as the arenas and stadiums where the fights were taking place. Boxing, by its very nature, doesn't encourage the half-hearted. You had to have a favourite. Was it the destructive force of Benn, who combined savagery with flash? His love of the good life and rags to riches tale resonated with those who believed that the best way to survive during the Thatcher era was to take your chances and maximise your income and profile. Or did you favour the hard work and honesty of Watson, who did things the old-fashioned way and rarely sought shortcuts? Never one to court publicity, he merely tried to be the best he could be and a vast percentage of this divided nation, who had seen Britain change so much during the 1980s, with huge swathes of working men rendered obsolete and unemployed, could relate to this humble Londoner who struggled to gain respect and adulation for just doing his job. And what about Eubank, whose eccentricities made him the boxer everyone wanted to hear from and who quite a few wanted to see lose. He'd become the darling of the chat shows, drawing a new breed of boxing fan to ringside – those who found preening and showboating as appealing as raw violence.

It seemed irrelevant that they were probably a level below the best at their weights. Eubank knew who he could beat and who he couldn't and showed little desire to seek fights against the likes of James Toney or Roy Jones Junior, two American boxers who were contenders for boxing's mythical title of best 'pound for pound' practitioner. Benn happily admitted he didn't mind being number two to Jones, while Watson's limitations were exposed the first time he fought for a world title. But these three Brits didn't need to go abroad to make their names or money.

As ever, someone had to miss out. Herol Graham's misfortune was to be born a decade earlier and also to be too good. If he'd been given the opportunities his talent deserved, there's an argument to say I'd have no book to write. 'He would have stood them all on their head,' one ex-fighter told me.

In describing the period between 1989 and 1993 as the last great era of British boxing, it might seem I'm dismissing the thousands of men and women who have pulled on gloves in the twenty years since. It should not be construed as such. It's recently been proposed that the calendar year of 2013 might be one of the best in the history of the sport. There have been top-quality skirmishes on these shores and elsewhere. Froch, Burns, Barker and Fury spring to mind, while the enigma that is Floyd Mayweather continues his journey towards recognition as one of the ten greatest fighters ever. I've watched them all, but the chances are the majority of you haven't. That's because in the twenty-first century, if you want to watch boxing on television, you have to pay. Your BSkyB subscription will get you only so far and then, after that, it's a list of channels on which you need to see the best of the rest. Of the names I've mentioned, Fury is the only one you can still get with your licence fee. If he ever does fight for a world title, however, you can be certain you'll need to pay a little extra to someone else.

I mention all this because the Herculean struggles between these three men, Benn, Watson and Eubank, were broadcast on television for a mass audience. And the timing of those bouts, on Saturday or Sunday night, meant they mattered, whether you liked it or not. So when one of these three won, it was a cause for celebration. And when something went wrong, it meant a degree of soul-searching and debate. When boxing was in the public eye, the morality of one man punching the other into a state of disarray and sometimes disability became a debate heard in the House of Commons. Its position now as a niche sport means that, if something similar happened today, an MP would have to ask for a tape of the fight before passing comment. Boxing has all but disappeared from free-to-air television. The biggest bouts are available only if you wish to pay extra. Both Benn and Eubank finished their careers on BSkyB, a fraction of the audience watching their last moments. Boxing can be found aplenty on satellite television in the 2010s and the die-hard fan has more choice than ever before. But it all costs. Old fans are prepared to pay but it's hard to believe new fans are being attracted to a sport which is as old as any. It's that exposure which made the Eubank, Benn and Watson era so special. Anyone and everyone could watch them. And the fights were so captivating and emotive that they competed in our consciences with the national sports of football and cricket. And during a period of our history when the Conservative government, led by Margaret Thatcher, divided the nation so spectacularly, the outlets for some of our woes and disagreements were the regular battles between these gladiators.

Act I
Scene I

The roads that boxers take, or are forced on, to stardom and glory are both similar and yet different. For every young Cassius Clay who becomes Muhammad Ali after being the victim of theft (the young man from Louisville, Kentucky, was directed to a boxing gym by a policeman after expressing his anger at having his bike stolen), there is a Mike Tyson who learns fear and rage when one of his pigeons has its head ripped off by a fellow teenage delinquent. The paths are similar because, somewhere along the line, there is anger, rage, fear or a need for revenge, emotions that boys struggle to understand and therefore turn to fighting. The difference comes when those boys become men and begin to understand their emotions. Some control them and use boxing as a profession and also a form of expression. Others use the anger and pain as part of their fighting DNA. The fire inside them burns and burns; when allied to talent, it is a proposition difficult to stop but easy to sell.

As one of seven brothers, there didn't seem anything exceptional about Nigel Benn, born on 22 January 1964, as he entered his ninth year. The second youngest of the brood, born to parents from Barbados who had emigrated to England, Benn had energy to burn and wasn't opposed to a healthy scrap with his brothers. The exception to the rule was his relationship with his eldest brother, Andy, who had been born in the West Indies before coming to England to be reunited with his family. Nigel described his relationship with Andy as being 'like a lion with his cub'. He idolised his big brother, who enjoyed a reputation as a genuine tough guy in the east London suburb of Ilford. To this day it's not known whether it was that reputation or his own arrogance that led to Andy's premature death. The bare facts are that he bled to death after falling from a house he should not have been in. According to Nigel Benn, the event was rarely discussed in the family household. Seventeen-year-old Andy Benn was buried in an unmarked grave, perhaps the biggest sign that none of his family knew how to react to his passing. It all left his eight-year-old brother with one overriding emotion.

'I lost my hero . . . and I was just angry,' says Benn of his early life as a restless teenager who roamed the streets of Ilford, looking for trouble. When he wasn't living the life of a petty thief, Benn would happily engage in street fights, where any unsuspecting youths would find out just how painful life could be when they were punched by a future world champion. Sensing that Nigel's promising career as a small-time criminal was about to take off, father Dickson insisted that his boy follow older brother John into the army, specifically the Royal Fusiliers. It was in the army that Nigel Benn, just sixteen and until then the consummate street fighter, learned how to put even more power into punches that were already blessed with a natural force. That blend of speed and strength may have been gifted to him from birth, but the desire to throw them emanated from the sense of loss and anger which had defined his life from the moment Andy died.

'I'd been throwing punches all my life. There was a lot of energy, a lot of anger in me, a lot of things that I couldn't deal with. I had to be able to channel it somewhere, without it consuming me. [Talking about fights in the army] I was fast and I punched hard. I didn't know what the first punch I'd throw was, all I knew was that there would be power going into it. I just had to make sure I was in shape – I knew if I was in shape, and if I connected with my punch, then the other guy was going to be out,' says Benn.

Fear seemed to play no part in any of Benn's early scraps, either on the street or in the ring, although those closest to him would testify that he would exhibit nerves before a bout – maybe those were the nerves of someone who just wanted the release of that aggression that swirled around his body. He'd happily fight heavyweights in those army bouts, inviting men with a five stone advantage to try and manhandle his then light middleweight frame (eleven stone), something they could never do. His trainers never seemed that concerned either; why would they be, given that Benn was, in their estimation, the most naturally gifted fighter they'd ever worked with? The fighter himself knew. 'I got it,' he told me. 'I just knew how to throw a right hand. It's in my genes,' he adds, having observed how well his teenage son, Conor, can fight.

According to Benn, that natural talent compensated for any tactical shortcomings he had in the ring. 'I knew I wasn't a great boxer . . . I couldn't box. I just didn't want to lose.' That may have been the case in the army but by the time he left the Fusiliers in early 1984 and joined the amateurs, fighting out of a club in West Ham, he had evolved. 'He was very well coached. He might have had that natural power, but he came from a strong amateur club where there were some good trainers who gave him some good schooling,' says Mike Costello, now the BBC's boxing commentator but back then a young coach working in amateur boxing in south-east London. Relying mostly on his power and ability to put punches together in sharp combinations, Benn secured notable victories against future professional stars: Rod Douglas – who gave Benn his one and only amateur defeat before losing the rematch in front of a packed crowd at York Hall – and future British middleweight contender Johnny Melfah. Knockout power is rarely appreciated at amateur level yet such was Benn's that he became the national light middleweight amateur champion. He had hoped to have earned the chance to make the 1986 Commonwealth Games as part of the English team; instead, it was Douglas who went. Benn, now tired of fighting for no money, and having to double up as a security guard to pay the rent, turned professional. His signature was coveted by all the top promoters in Britain. But rather than go with the established cartel, headed up by Mickey Duff, or even the emerging Frank Warren, Benn chose, initially, to be handled by Burt McCarthy, a boxing manager who seemingly loved boxing more than he did cash. McCarthy once gave up the contract of a Welsh heavyweight named David Price (not to be confused with the Liverpool heavyweight currently boxing) because he felt that the boxer's health would be in danger if he continued to fight.

Benn turned professional on 28 January 1987, his first fight against the much more experienced but smaller Graeme Ahmed from the north-east of England. Ahmed was essentially a light middleweight, while Benn had now, at the age of twenty-three, grown into a fully fledged middleweight. The bout ended seventy seconds into the second round; as a result, Ahmed would become a footnote in the Nigel Benn story. There was no disgrace in losing so quickly to Benn; by December that year, he would not be extended beyond the fourth round by any of his opponents. By then, Burt McCarthy's desire to do the right thing meant he wasn't opposed to letting Benn flee the nest, if he felt the boxer would be best served by a change of direction. That direction came in the form of Frank Warren, whose fights were a popular feature of ITV's programming, courtesy of a late-night show called *Seconds Out*. The programme would feature up and coming young fighters like Benn, who were building unbeaten records. In the case of Benn, the record was comprised of knockout after knockout, the perfect kind of material for that late-night showcase. Warren knew what he had. Many people, including Warren, believed that Benn was potentially the most exciting fighter seen in a British ring for many a year. Frank Bruno had excited and charmed millions on his way to two unsuccessful world title challenges, but he'd become a national treasure, less of a boxer and more a pantomime hero who occasionally fought. Benn was raw, violent and fast. There had been a buzz about Errol Christie just a few years earlier, but he was a pure boxer with style who moved with grace but not much menace. When Benn fought, you knew never to look away, such was the anticipation that fights could end with one blow.

'Nigel had a lot of power and presence. He was just an all-action fighter and I kept him busy. In his first year with me, he had fourteen fights. He was an exciting prospect and fighter – I remember Burt McCarthy had Errol Christie, who was considered the top amateur of the time. I said to Burt that Nigel will be ten times more successful than Errol as a professional. I thought Nigel would be a future world champion,' said Warren. 'However, he had a few problems. A lot of things happened outside the ring.' That's something I've heard many times while researching Benn's life. In the latter years of his career, many assumed those issues outside the ring involved drugs, but back in the 1980s virtually all of his issues stemmed from women and his inability to control his libido.

'I didn't care if the woman was eight stone, twelve stone, fifteen stone or twenty stone . . .' he told a therapist on television after he retired. Benn was an early starter with women, losing his virginity when he was twelve. Despite being in a series of long-term relationships, his love of women meant he was rarely faithful. The temptations and opportunities would only increase as his fame grew. A striking looking man, Benn still attracts women of all ages, although a mixture of maturity and his religious faith means he's better able to handle temptation. In his physical prime, however, there were few boundaries. Like many sportsmen starting out, he felt he could combine the demands of his job with extra-curricular activities, even while those around him were convinced it would cost him at key stages of his career and life. George Best's struggles with alcohol and women meant his football career at the highest level came to an end when he was only twenty-seven.

But from the moment Benn turned professional in 1987 through to that balmy night in Finsbury Park, the notion of failure seemed impossible. By the time he fought Watson, Benn had had twenty-two fights and won all of them by a knockout. The quality of the opposition was questionable, but the authenticity of his knockouts wasn't. He was good at his job because, in the words of someone who prefers not to be named, 'he was one of the few boxers I've ever met who seemed to genuinely enjoy hurting people. Most of the fighters I've met come from a life of poverty and are desperate to escape, or they're advised to channel their aggression by their parents. But not Nigel.' It's natural to assume that the surplus of aggression came from the death of his brother and a failure, until later life, to deal with those feelings of pain and loss. Now, Benn admits that the best way to avoid his issues was through training and then fighting. All those who have trained or managed him say that Benn was always able to remain professional in his dedication to training. And, through those wins, he had, like many boxers with unbeaten records, developed a 'Superman' complex.

That, no doubt, was enhanced by his acquiring the Commonwealth middleweight title from an African boxer named Umaru Sandu, whose toughness had been proved in twelve gruelling rounds with Tony Sibson, Britain's premiere middleweight for much of the 1980s. Whereas Sibson's left hook couldn't stop Sandu, Benn's put the champion on the floor on numerous occasions before the fight was stopped in the second round. That first title was won on 20 April 1988, in only his seventeenth bout, less than eighteen months after he had turned professional. Benn remembers, accurately, letting out a war cry after being awarded victory. But his rage, his thirst for more in-ring violence and a greater share of the profits, meant that the title was seldom enough.

His volatile nature, restlessness and impatience meant he wasn't satisfied with how his career was progressing. It wasn't that Benn had dark days of moodiness and introspection – he could have several moments on any given day when someone might trigger his temper simply by saying the wrong thing. He remembers feeling that Frank Warren wasn't showing as much interest in him as he felt he deserved, a point Warren would no doubt deny. It was at that time that he struck up a friendship with a fellow black man ten years his senior: Ambrose Mendy was involved in the careers of a number of black athletes, in football, athletics and boxing. In the words of Warren, who had once shared an office with Benn's new manager, 'Mendy blew smoke up Benn's arse'. Whatever Warren believed, Benn's recollection of events is a little different.

'I remember one day that I asked Frank to come and watch me train. For one reason or another, he didn't and I thought "Screw you! I'm showing you what you're investing your money in." Ambrose lifted me up, elevated me. I hold no grudges and I said I'd go back with Frank and I did [at the end of his career]. Ambrose Mendy and me did some incredible things – he was like the British Don King.'

The battle between Warren and Mendy over the services of the boxer reached the Court of Appeal – it would end in a permanent shift in the way boxers could handle their careers – but the partnership between Benn and Mendy would gain notoriety and success in equal measure for the period they were together. Even though the two men have no relationship now, a mutual respect was formed that exists to this day.

Mendy could bond easily with Benn because they had similar backgrounds. Both came from big families (Mendy was one of ten children) and were brought up in east London by immigrant parents. Like Benn, Mendy remembers there not being much money in his parents' house, but there was plenty of love and respect. His early life was based around sport – he was a talented footballer and knew plenty who could play better, including the late Laurie Cunningham. The likes of Garth Crooks, John Fashanu, Brendan Batson, Ian Wright, Paul Ince and David Rocastle, men who made their names during the 1980s, were all acquaintances of Mendy. All those players had one thing in common – they were talented, rich and black. Mendy's ability to get these men to talk to each other off the field gained him a strong reputation, for, strange as it seems, black sportsmen in England at that time were still something of a novelty. Even Liverpool, then the most dominant football team in England, didn't buy a black footballer until 1987. The man they did buy, John Barnes, was another friend of Mendy. The agent/manager presence that he generated, via the World Sports Corporation that he founded, meant that Benn was directed to Mendy when things started to turn sour with Warren.

'One day I got a phone call from Jake Panayiotou, the guy

who owned Browns nightclub [in London]. He told me that there's a boxer who badly needs some advice, some help. I asked who the boxer was and he told me it was Nigel Benn. I'd met Nigel a few times. I went to see him and he told me that he was never going to fight for Warren again, that he couldn't stand him. I told him he needed some legal advice. I introduced him to a lawyer and we set about trying to work out how to release Benn from his contract,' Mendy told me.

'In the beginning, all I wanted was for Nigel to have fair legal advice. If Warren was still interested in working for Nigel, I wanted the pair to patch it up because I knew Frank very well. Warren subsequently obtained an interim injunction preventing Mendy from inducing a breach of Benn's contract with him.'

That almost certainly increased Benn and Mendy's determination to work together. Their partnership seemed a perfect mix. The boxer wanted to fight, win, hurt people and get paid what he thought he was worth. Benn would always keep an eye on those people who did the deals in his career, but didn't entertain the notion of managing himself. Mendy believed he could make Benn rich beyond his dreams, with just a few tweaks in the way the boxer was marketed. Benn had only ever aspired to have what his father had – a house and a nice car. By making Benn wealthy, Mendy could draw more sportsmen to his stable. 'I use Nigel Benn, but he uses me,' he once told a television interviewer. What was also unique was the sight of two young black males working very publicly to make their fortune in a sport run by white men.

The pair ended up in the Court of Appeal, essentially seeking a release from the contract that Benn had with Warren. The case became known as Warren v Mendy, the point of the case being to allow Benn to fight for someone else. (Mendy was still only Benn's adviser and he still didn't have a licence with the British Boxing Board of Control to officially act as the fighter's manager.) All this was going on in 1988, with Benn now twenty-four and a middleweight boxer in his physical prime. Having fought so regularly since turning professional, he couldn't afford to be inactive, but the effect of the court case was quite distracting and nearly led to what might have been a very costly defeat.

In December 1987, Benn had been extended into the seventh round by the cagey American Reggie Miller. Mendy, who wasn't working with Benn at that stage, admits he watched that bout with a degree of edginess, because Benn was starting to look quite weary by the end. His power saved him that night, as it would do on more than one occasion during his career, but Miller's strategy of trying to box Benn, albeit dangerous given what could happen if he let his guard down for just a moment, had taken him close to victory. The winner admitted when he retired that he did consider, during the fight, that defeat was, for the first time, a possibility. The fact that Benn managed to avoid defeat, without looking very vulnerable, meant few people took note of his difficulties.

That wasn't the case when he stepped into the ring against Jamaican Anthony Logan. The 26th of October 1988 would be the night that Benn's cloak of invincibility was stripped of a little colour. Logan had a more than presentable record of fourteen wins from sixteen fights; also in his favour was that he talked a good game. The pre-fight verbal jousting, a feature of the sport since the days when the Marquess of Queensberry drew up the rules of combat, saw Logan score an early series of blows. He promised to hurt Benn, who admitted afterwards to fighting 'angrier' than normal. Any trainer will confirm that aggression only works when it is controlled. Without that, it can lead to ruin. Lloyd Honeyghan threw more than 400 punches in the first four rounds against Marlon Starling in a world welterweight title fight a few months later, Honeyghan admitting to boxing with such anger because Starling had 'slagged him off'. The problem was that Starling put his gloves to his own head and blocked most of Honeyghan's punches, before returning fire with interest, stopping the British fighter in nine rounds. Logan threatened to do much worse to Benn at London's Royal Albert Hall. He punched Benn to the canvas – the first knockdown of his professional career – and dominated the action in the opening round. The second started little better for the Ilford man. After being hit with twenty-two consecutive punches, it seemed certain the fight was about to be stopped. Benn, a fighter noted for always being on the front foot, was being forced backwards. His only hope was the kind of blow the boxing fraternity calls a haymaker – a punch you can see coming from the back of the arena but rarely believe will land. A fighter only fails to avoid it if the punch is thrown with too much speed or because he is too preoccupied. Both of those factors were in evidence when Benn missed with a right hand, but then rocked back on his other side and exploded a left hook onto Logan's chin, dumping him to the canvas for the fight-closing ten count.

The immediate problem for Benn was a domestic one – his mother. Mina Benn had come to the fight and had no doubt expected to see her Nigel deal with Logan as quickly as all the previous opponents. Seeing her son fall from one punch was enough of a shock but the twenty-two unanswered punches were something else. She told her husband Dickson to get in the ring and stop the fight. 'Stop that man hitting my son!' she is reported to have said. As his parents continued the discussion, their child found the fight-ending punch. As far as Nigel Benn was concerned, there was only one course of action.

'She got banned from that fight on. Banned!' says Benn. The story was one of the few back then that wasn't exaggerated in order to keep Benn's name in the spotlight. His PR and marketing machine in full working order, with Mendy pulling the strings in the background, meant he was seldom out of the headlines. But for the first time, the boxing press questioned the fighter's credentials. Rising contenders should not have so many problems with men like Logan. There was no doubt some fear that Benn might go the way of Frank Bruno, whose early reputation was built on a steady diet of opponents who would have struggled to keep Fort Knox safe. On the first occasion Bruno fought a man capable of taking a punch and hitting back – the American Jumbo Cummings – he ran into trouble. Like Benn, Bruno would find a way out, but the experts noted that the heavyweight was more vulnerable than previously thought. Subsequent defeats at the hands of two more Americans, James 'Bonecrusher' Smith and Tim Witherspoon, reinforced the notion that Bruno was a magnificent specimen of man, but his talent didn't favourably match his musculature.

Given the court case with former manager Warren that still loomed large for Benn and Mendy, the experience of near defeat was easy to explain away: a distracted Benn had taken his opponent too lightly and nearly paid the price.

The bout was also a rarity in that it was not televised that night. Previously, all Benn's fights had been shown on ITV, but, perhaps fearing repercussions if they broadcast the brawl, ITV passed on it and the BBC agreed to show it days later, on Saturday afternoon, on *Grandstand*. By then, the legend of Benn's miracle left hook guaranteed an expectant audience. Those who tuned in that Saturday were not to be disappointed. That chink of vulnerability would make him more popular, almost as it had the American Thomas Hearns, who, during the 1980s, was never in a bad fight, simply because he could brawl with the best and fall with them as well.

The Logan fight came after a period of inactivity for Benn – he hadn't had a bout for five months. During that time, his decision to seek camp with Mendy caused him to be ostracised by many in the boxing community. The consensus was that he should have stayed with Warren. The Logan fight appeared on a promotion by Mike Barrett, regarded as a member of the cartel of promoters that had run British boxing for most of the 1970s and 1980s. Benn was able to take the fight after a judge ruled in September 1988 that Mendy could act on his behalf. The British Boxing Board of Control might have refused to give him a licence to manage, but Mendy used his contacts within the game – notably Frank Maloney and former world champion boxer Terry Marsh – to get Benn on shows. All the while, boxer and manager were gearing up for the court case against Warren which had greater significance than their parting of the ways.

In January 1989, three judges on the Court of Appeal rejected Frank Warren's attempt to stop Ambrose Mendy from acting on Nigel Benn's behalf. Pivotal to the judgement was the notion that a boxer's career was not only short (Benn's would last less than ten years) but also a specialist one, requiring dedication, expertise and a high level of training. Warren had argued that Benn was reneging on a contract that still had time to run and also had further options. The verdict had echoes of a similar case in football just a few years later, when the Belgian player Jean-Marc Bosman broke free of a contract which would not allow him to move to another club, despite no longer being an active part of his current team. Like Benn, Bosman had to go to court – in his case the European High Court – in order to find a ruling that would help him. It would ultimately give players the power to decide how long their contracts with clubs would be, as well as sign lucrative deals with substantial signing-on fees. The ruling in favour of Benn changed a sport, which, in the opinion of another young promoter by the name of Barry Hearn, 'was a bit of a slave trade'.

Being Benn must have been more difficult than the man himself would let on. After all, as he has admitted on numerous occasions since he retired, his material desires extended simply to 'owning a terraced house like my dad and having a BMW'. Mendy, however, encouraged him to reap the rewards of his labour. Both manager and boxer remember driving past a Porsche garage on the day they won the court case and Benn admitting how much he wanted one of the cars in the showroom. Mendy told Benn that 'if he wanted one, he should get one'. Benn asked how he could afford such a car, to which Mendy responded by saying, 'if you believe you're going to succeed, you'll pay for it'. Benn drove away that day with the Porsche, a moment Mendy described as a 'major wake-up call'.

A wake-up call it may have been, but the sight of a boxer with a sports car, after just twenty fights and with no world title to his name, made him look, in the eyes of many, too flash and arrogant. This was still the era of old-school boxing, where respect had to be earned and the trimmings of success accrued with greatness. The decade may have begun with the era of the first million-pound footballer – Trevor Francis having joined Nottingham Forest in 1978 for that sum, a then record in the British Isles – but sportsmen and women were not yet millionaire celebrities. When Kevin Keegan returned to English football in 1980, having spent three years in Germany with Hamburg, he drew headlines for his new salary with Southampton of a thousand pounds a week, an unthinkable amount for a twenty-nine-year-old.

Benn's alignment with Mendy, which saw him join a group of ambitious, talented young black people (his post-fight parties would see not just boxers, but footballers, athletes and singers in attendance), may not have been to everyone's taste. Britain was still learning how to adapt to the wave of immigration which had made the country truly multi-cultural, and for most of the 1980s the most recognisable black sports star had been Bruno, whose affable and humble persona rarely offended much of white Britain, even if it jarred with many blacks. As the BBC's Mike Costello remembers, it was a clever move not to position Benn as Bruno's successor, instead choosing him as an alternative. In 1987, Michael Jackson had released the album *Bad* and had adopted a much rougher, tougher look than on his previous outings. Mendy encouraged Benn to adopt a similar image. Back then, Jackson's influence on modern culture was such that the *Bad* phenomenon lasted for the rest of the decade.

Being 'bad' meant lots of what is now called bling and Benn obliged, with gold bracelets and expensive watches almost always on display when he wasn't in the ring. He may have carried off the look with aplomb, to the amusement of others, but, privately, Benn wasn't always that easy with the direction in which he was going. His modest background and family leanings meant he'd sometimes prefer a little privacy, which he was struggling to find.

In the ring, the opposition was proving to be less than testing. The names of David Noel, Mike Chilambe and Mbayo Wa Mbayo will never be considered much more than padding on Benn's record. He learned to control his fury a little during these bouts, perhaps as a natural consequence of how perilously close he had come to defeat against Logan. Benn even admitted after knocking out Noel in December 1988 that '[I] let my emotions get the better of me' during the build-up and fight against Logan. It was easy enough to look controlled and sensible against his next three opponents. They posed no threat in terms of size and power. Only Mbayo would last past the first round – but only just. That bout took place in Scotland and, to the delight of the locals, Benn eschewed his black trunks in favour of red tartan. If there were smiles for the Scots, there were only scowls for ringside reporter Gary Newbon. The pair chatted about the ending of the bout before things got a little spicy.

'Are you not, in your career, in need of a real big test that's going to take you some rounds?' asked Newbon. It was the sort of question few had the nerve to ask.

'You're forgetting how long I have been in the game. I'm taking my time – I'm not here to rush for you or anybody. I'm here to secure my kids' future. It takes time and I'm

not going to be rushed,' countered Benn, his big brown
eyes, which could look welcoming or threatening, starting
to bulge.

'How much time, Nigel, because we're all behind you?'
asked Newbon.

'I'm not going over there [America] and fighting Michael
Nunn when I know I'm not ready!' replied Benn. Nunn was
a rising middleweight who held the International Boxing
Federation title and had just defeated the highly rated
Italian-based Sumbu Kalambay with a stunning first-round
knockout. The Nunn camp had made a $3 million offer
to Benn for a fight. At that stage of his career, the British
man was not ready for a test such as Nunn would provide.
The American was taller, moved well and boxed out of the
southpaw style, which was bound to make Benn look bad. He
might have got lucky and won by a knockout, but the odds
were that Nunn would have been too experienced and savvy
for a man who had only been a professional for two years.
But it was obvious, and not just to the likes of Newbon, that
Benn needed a real test. His world ranking was on the rise
(in America *The Ring* magazine had him in their top ten) but
there still hadn't been an opponent who could be considered
dangerous. After blowing away a string of African and West
Indian journeymen – Benn's 'Mexican road sweepers' – he
and Mendy assessed their domestic options.

Herol Graham had been the best British middleweight
for many years. His unorthodox style – hands by his waist,
his head a seemingly impossible target because of his
upper-body movement – meant he was rarely sought out
by rising contenders. The great Marvelous Marvin Hagler
should have defended his world titles against Graham, but

was spared the chore when Sugar Ray Leonard came out of retirement to fight Hagler in what was then the highest grossing fight of all time. That was in 1987 and when Leonard emerged from his dual with Hagler with the middleweight title, he showed little desire to fight Graham, the mandatory contender. Benn wanted the fight, though, realising that the easiest way to convince the sceptics was to take on the man no one wanted anything to do with. Those looking after him weren't so keen.

'As long as I was with Nigel, I would never let him fight Herol Graham. Nigel would tell me that he'd work his body and beat him that way, and that convinced me even more to make sure the fight didn't happen,' says Mendy. Given that Graham would be knocked out by another puncher, Julian Jackson, at the end of 1990, Benn might have had a better chance than his backers thought. Even so, Graham was overlooked in favour of another rising middleweight. Like Benn, this fighter was from London and had also come from a modest background. He didn't have the star quality of Benn, but anything Michael Watson lacked in charisma he made up for in terms of ability and dedication. The fight was set for 21 May 1989, with the poster for the fight asking the question: 'Who's Bad?'

More and more the public were finding out that Benn's perception of himself as being genuinely 'bad' wasn't far off the mark. He also told Newbon that he'd hoped Mbayo would have kept getting up, so he could keep knocking him down. That desire for violence was encapsulated in two ways. Around about that time, Benn gave a quote to an interviewer saying 'God put Steve Davis on this earth to pot balls, Diego Maradona to score goals and Nigel Benn to kick ass'. It was the kind of statement that marketing professionals like Mendy dreamed of and was even better because it was unprompted. The discipline of training may have satisfied part of Benn's psyche, but it was the violence that he truly enjoyed. It was why he spent his early years 'fighting the National Front' without ever taking a backward step and it's why boxing was only ever a forum for his rage, burning as brightly as it had when his brother died.

What almost certainly aided the violence was the nickname 'the Dark Destroyer', which he had acquired at the start of his professional career. A photographer at the *Daily Express* called Jack Kay was watching Benn and was reminded of the great heavyweight champion Joe Louis, whose nickname had been 'the Brown Bomber'. In the 1980s, such a blatant reference to a man's skin colour was barely noticed, although some, including Frank Warren, weren't comfortable with it. Nevertheless, it stuck and also became a part of Benn's make-up. Much of Benn's success had been down to his ability to produce the kind of action that others couldn't. That was designed and he was marketed as a wrecking machine – but the acquisition of the nickname was pure luck. Benn and Mendy took it and ran with it. Commentators were encouraged to use it as often as possible. In time, the nickname would also come to represent the other side of Benn's personality. He could be charming when he wanted, but when 'the Dark Destroyer' emerged, opponents and friends were best advised to run for cover.

Scene II

Michael Watson's family heritage belonged in Jamaica. His mother, Joan, came to England from the Caribbean in 1964; one year later, on 15 March, her first son, Michael, was born (she already had a daughter, Dawn, who was still in Jamaica). A few years later, the focus was on her second son, Jeffrey, two years younger than Michael, who was hit by a speeding car. So serious were the injuries to the toddler – he was seven months old at the time of the accident – that he was given the last rights. He had head injuries but he was too small to be operated on. He spent four months in a coma before beginning a remarkable recovery. The fighting spirit that would also become so obvious in his big brother in later years was evident in the younger sibling, whose only long-term repercussions from the accident would be a slight limp in the left leg and a slurring of his speech.

The Watsons, including father, Jim, lived in Stoke Newington. This north London suburb is now regarded as a fashionable area by young professionals, but in the late sixties life in a council flat was somewhat removed from that modern ideal. The Watsons did not have much money, but they had a rich sense of community. The family would move around on a regular basis, through Dalston and Islington. The church remained a constant – Michael, Jeffrey and their mother would attend up to three times a week and that faith would play a pivotal part in Michael Watson's later life. As a young boy and then a man, Watson was familiar to those in the area because of his strong ties to the church before his boxing career began to blossom.

If Nigel Benn enjoyed boxing because it gave him an outlet

for his restlessness, Watson's reasons were altogether more complicated. By nature quiet (but not shy, he assures me), the young Watson remembers an altercation with a peer when he was a boy. The outcome left him feeling inadequate. 'I didn't know how to deal with it,' he acknowledges now. Natural athletic ability meant he was already a member of a sports club but it wasn't until he turned fourteen that destiny found him. He had watched boxing on television and was transfixed by Muhammad Ali and Roberto Durán, the great Panamanian multi-weight champion. There was no obvious comparison between those two men and, as Watson developed as a fighter, his ability to box as the situation required suggested that here was a keen student of the noble art. But that love of the sport, combined with the need to learn self-defence, took him into the ring. As soon as he learned the basics of the game and was allowed to spar, Watson remembers the feeling of joy, the sense that he had found both his calling and an arena in which boys quickly became men. Gentle outside the ring, Watson's demeanour belied an inner toughness that revealed itself during the early stages of his ring career.

Glyn Leach, editor of the magazine *Boxing Monthly*, says, 'I had a friend in the amateurs called Jerry Hammond. He fought Watson twice, but the bouts were a few months apart. He lost them both, but it was the second fight he remembered. He said Watson had changed so much by the second fight, he barely recognised him. He'd grown physically and mentally so much.' Whether it was the onset of puberty or his skill, Watson was turning into an imposing physical specimen. And also one who knew his own mind. Perhaps aware of his potential, Watson moved gyms, from the local Crown and Manor gym to the Colvestone gym in Hackney. At the Crown, he was surrounded by fighters looking to pass the time and get fit. At the Colvestone, he mixed with the likes of Dennis Andries, a future three-time world light heavyweight champion and one of the strongest British fighters of any era, and Kirkland Laing, one of the most talented and eccentric. Laing had the ability to beat and lose to anyone – he once defeated Durán and then went AWOL, unable, it seemed, to control his love of alcohol, women and drugs.

The immediate goal for Watson was to be on the plane for the 1984 Olympics in Los Angeles. The north London teenager was one win away from securing a spot as Britain's middleweight hope when he lost a fight to Scotland's Russell Barker in Preston. A contentious decision had gone against Watson – historically, it would not be the last time he'd suffer such a disappointment – but his immediate response was to quit the amateur game and start earning money from the considerable amount of work he was putting into the sport. As a keen student of boxing, Watson knew that the promoter in Britain with the most clout and experience was Mickey Duff. A Polish Jew by birth, Duff escaped almost inevitable death when his father, a rabbi, conscious of the growing threat from the Nazi party in neighbouring Germany, emigrated to England from Kraków in the late 1930s. Duff had a brief career in the ring during the latter part of his teenage years and returned to the sport a few years later, initially as a matchmaker, before becoming part of the most powerful promotional alliance in British boxing history. The cartel, as the individuals who formed it became known, included Jarvis Astaire, Harry Levine, Terry Lawless and Mike Barrett.

Because of their links with television, specifically the BBC, most of the top fighters of the 1970s and early 1980s were represented by these men. Watson's decision to go with Duff was a logical one at that stage of his career; he would not be the star of the show by any means, but because of the nature of Duff's promotions, with established fighters headlining his shows, Watson would get good exposure on the undercards.

Signing as a professional did not bring about a dramatic change in Watson's day-to-day existence; he worked as a painter/decorator during the mornings and afterwards he'd go to the Colvestone gym, where his trainers, Eric Secombe and Harry Griver, would put him through his paces, managing his sparring and suggesting future opponents. Managing and training Watson wasn't the hardest job in boxing – he may not have trained as maniacally as Nigel Benn, but he understood the benefits of roadwork and honing his reflexes and stamina in the gym, on the speed and heavy bag. Aside from a love of nice clothes, there was nothing flash about Watson – he may have been developing as an artist in the ring, but outside it his was a strictly artisan lifestyle. He'd become something of a local star after winning his first seven fights as a pro; Winston Wray was his first victim on 16 October 1984. His next six fights took place over a period of around nineteen months. Such a number of bouts would be considered active today, but during the 1980s it was just about sufficient for a talent like Watson's. Perhaps mindful of that, Duff put Watson into another bout thirteen days after he'd gone the distance against Carlton Warren. All seven of Watson's bouts so far had been in London and number eight, against the experienced James Cook, was no different, Wembley Arena being the venue.

Cook had fought twice as many times as Watson when the pair met, but the bout still looked a formality for the unbeaten Watson. Cook had been knocked out in three of his previous five fights. The chances of an upset in the eight-round contest seemed remote, but Cook used his experience to good effect to win the decision of the referee, the only man who scored in non-title fights in Britain. 'It was just my time,' says Cook, now a community worker who, in 2007, was awarded an MBE for his outstanding work on Hackney's 'Murder Mile'. Cook would go on to win British and European super middleweight titles, although his inconsistency was typified by defeat in his next bout to Mbayo Wa Mbayo, a future victim of Benn. Cook remembers that his three consecutive defeats before the Watson bout made it easy for his opponents to underestimate him, and that's exactly what Watson did. Maybe believing Cook was a fading fighter and that he was on the rise, Watson didn't train as hard as he might have. The intensity he brought to the gym was missing and, as if to underline just how lightly he regarded Cook, Watson went nightclubbing in the week of the fight. That failure to prepare cost him, although there were long-term benefits: 'James Cook gave me a wake-up call – that fight made me the boxer I became.'

In the modern era, such a result for a young, undefeated fighter might have constituted a disaster, but Watson took it as a positive. He had become overconfident, seemingly unaware of his athletic mortality. In his previous seven fights, his size and strength, allied with solid boxing fundamentals, had been more than enough to see him through. Now he realised there was another level he had to go to. The day after the bout, his pride wounded more than his body,

Watson began training again, secure in the knowledge that his promoter was still with him but aware that the fan base he had built up during his victories had dwindled and would only return when he hit the big time.

He'd fight again in November 1986, a routine points victory over Alan Baptiste at Wembley. The following year would see Watson have five bouts, the opposition consisting of some of Britain's better journeymen. Cliff Gilpin, Ralph Smiley and Ian Chantler were boxers you could learn things from – although Chantler would become another footnote in Benn's career, lasting less than twenty seconds – and Watson continued his education without tripping up. By the end of 1987, Duff decided to up the level of Watson's opponents, matching him with a series of tough American fighters. Don Lee was the first of those – he had already met Britain's Tony Sibson, the tough Doug DeWitt and rising contender Michael Olajide. The Lee fight was shown on the BBC, and the venerable commentator Harry Carpenter remarked that some of Watson's best work was 'in the trenches, where American fighters are usually considered stronger'. The fight would end in the fifth round, stopped by the referee courtesy of a nasty cut on the American's mouth. Lee showed no disappointment at the premature ending, having been outpunched and outboxed for the entire bout. At six feet two and fighting out of the southpaw stance, Lee should have presented more problems for Watson. That he didn't said much for the British man's knowledge of the basics of the sport and his revived sense of dedication, which had been missing from the Cook bout. Watson thinks Duff didn't believe he could win the fight, one the boxer describes as one of his hardest.

Watson was also, like Benn, redefining the stereotypical image of the British boxer. For years, it was perceived, especially in America, that fighters on this side of the Atlantic preferred to box with a rigid, upright stance, chin high in the air with a jab pushed out in defence as much as offence. Watson worked from angles, in a crouch, unafraid of getting in close and using his strength to outmuscle his opponent. The wins began to build up in 1988 – Joe McKnight, Ricky Stackhouse and Kenny Styles all failed to hear the final bell, overpowered and outskilled by Watson, who would make his one and only foray into America that year, against Israel Cole. The fight was registered as a technical draw; stopped after one round because of a cut, under Nevada boxing rules – the fight took place in Las Vegas's Caesars Palace – this meant an automatic draw. The year would end with a fight against another American, Reggie Miller, who had tested Benn twelve months earlier. There would be no problems for Watson in this fight, which lasted five rounds and was one-sided from start to finish.

Nineteen eighty-eight was the year that Watson's potential started to take him places – but only in boxing circles. He was ranked in the top ten of the governing bodies, but his profile outside boxing remained minimal. Clive Bernath, editor of SecondsOut.com, one of the sport's leading websites, says of Watson: 'He was a bit of a throwback to the old days. He had good sparring with the rest of the Mickey Duff stable. But he was not box office.' Mike Costello says, 'Watson was a fighter's fighter. He was no-nonsense, old-school.' He was also starting to worry why it was the man from the east side of London, Nigel Benn, who was making the headlines. The kind of fan who'd read *Boxing News* would know just how good Watson was and the recognition he deserved, but in the 1980s, long before the age of self-generated, social media coverage, Watson's only form of publicity was his promoter and it's possible that Duff did not really believe in his fighter's ability. And maybe Watson, who lived by the creed that being good should be enough, didn't help himself. 'He didn't have much hype about him – he just worked hard and was very old-school. He didn't boast or brag and therefore probably wasn't as easy to market,' says *Boxing Monthly*'s Glyn Leach. It would come as no surprise that Watson would one day go to Ambrose Mendy for advice on where to take his career, having watched 'the Dark Destroyer' gain a reputation for constant excitement and value for money, two qualities he believed he also possessed. Building up inside Watson now was a sense of both resentment and envy – how could he, for all his dedication, have acquired so little, while Benn, a man whose skills he considered inferior, was making such a splash? Watson knocked people out and punched hard. But, while Benn did it with a snarl, Watson seemed to approach his job with the precision of a surgeon. To the casual fan, Benn's appeal was obvious: you wouldn't have to wait too long for what you were really after – violence. With Watson, there was a sense that you needed to understand boxing's scientifics a little better to really appreciate what he was doing.

As we have seen, at times Watson had taken a second job to supplement his boxing income – firstly in painting and decorating and then, latterly, as a minicab driver. He also had a family to support, a girlfriend, Zara, and two daughters. It all added up to a situation where he needed a moment to show the world how good he was and also get paid what he thought he was worth. Following two routine wins at the start of 1989, Watson, in a rare moment of bravado, told reporters he could beat Benn, because of his 'superior boxing ability'. Neither Duff nor his trainer, Eric Secombe, believed their man could do it, which gave Watson all the motivation he needed.

Watson could have continued fighting tough American middleweights for as long as he wanted, but they weren't going to give him the paydays or recognition he felt he deserved. There was one man he thought he *could* beat; one man whose name resonated throughout the British Isles and even further abroad. Victory over him would finally put him closer to where he wanted to be. For Michael Watson money was one thing, respect another. But he dreamed of becoming a world champion, and victory over Nigel Benn would take him closer to realising that dream. Watson had respect for Benn and his punching power, but was growing increasingly annoyed at the attitude of the Commonwealth champion, who didn't seem to rate him any higher than the calibre of opposition he'd been facing for the past eighteen months.

'I haven't got the recognition I deserve. I've been very underestimated. This is a great opportunity for me to go out there and box to my full potential,' said Watson after learning that he'd fight Benn. In his mind, Watson could hear Mickey Duff telling reporters that if he lost to Benn he would not be ready for a world title fight. 'This is a big break for me now – no one has really seen what I can do. Fair enough, people make a big thing about Nigel Benn, but let me tell you, Nigel Benn will be in for a painful experience and it will be an experience he'll never forget. If I don't get respect from Benn outside the ring, I'll certainly get it inside.' Behind the bravado and the braggadocio, the most telling thing Watson said was that he felt undervalued. After the Benn bout, he'd make moves to ensure he never felt like that again. But for now, he was merely a talented middleweight boxer, without a unique selling point – although he had by now acquired the nickname 'the Force' – and, more importantly, without a title. In the 1980s, there wasn't the proliferation of belts now available to fighters. There were four world governing bodies, the WBA, WBC, IBF and the emerging WBO. To earn a chance to fight for one of those titles, a boxer generally needed to prove he was good. A win over Benn was that chance for Watson. Until he won or lost, he would have, as many people told me, a 'chip on his shoulder'. In his mind, he knew he was the best, that he'd studied boxers and their techniques, copied the ones he thought most effective and refined all he'd learned into a smooth style. In Benn, he merely saw a straightforward brawler, a man without subtlety. Yet this boxing primitive had the money and limelight. Aggrieved and still exuding envy and resentment, Michael Watson could now also see clearly what he had to do. Win.

Scene III

'I'll do him, I'll smash him to pieces. I will do him – definitely,' Benn told Ambrose Mendy shortly after meeting Watson for the first time at a stage-managed occasion at the Royal Albert Hall. 'But Michael wasn't scared,' remembers Mendy. To put the fight together, Mendy, Frank Maloney and the lawyer Henri Brandman arranged a meeting with Mickey

Duff at the Phoenix Apollo at Stratford in the East End. When the fighters' representatives met, Duff refused to deal with Mendy.

'You're not a licence holder,' Duff told Mendy. While Benn's manager remained outside, negotiations began inside Duff's favourite restaurant and a contract was signed at around two in the morning, with Duff having held court for most of that time. Maloney says he kept himself sober, because the sums of money involved were large for such a Commonwealth title fight. In the end, both parties agreed that their fighters would earn £100,000, with the bout set to take place on 21 May 1989.

At the time, Watson's fitness was in part down to a friendship he had formed with another boxer who worked out at the same gym, a featherweight called Jim McDonnell, who is now regarded as one of the top trainers in British boxing. McDonnell's lifelong commitment to keeping in shape means that even today, in his fifties, he regularly runs marathons inside three hours. Both men were facing the challenges of their lives that summer. Ten days after Watson's fight against Benn, McDonnell would face Barry McGuigan, now making a comeback, in what was a crunch bout for both. If McGuigan lost, he'd almost certainly retire from the game for good, while a win for McDonnell, who'd start as underdog, would yield him a world title fight. Aside from each man facing a make or break challenge, both Watson and McDonnell were devoted Arsenal fans. And as the 1988–9 football season reached its climax, the Gunners went to Anfield, the home of champions and league leaders Liverpool, needing to win by two goals to secure their first title in nearly twenty years. Watson and McDonnell had a bet that both would win their bouts and their team would go to Liverpool on 26 May and win 2-0.

The football season was finishing later than usual that year because of an event which, only now, has finally received some semblance of an explanation. On 15 April 1989, ninety-six Liverpool fans lost their lives after being crushed at the Leppings Lane end of Sheffield Wednesday's Hillsborough stadium during an FA Cup semi-final between their team and Nottingham Forest. The match was abandoned with few aware of the scale of the tragedy. Liverpool's understandable reluctance to consider playing another until their players felt ready meant a fixture backlog for the Merseysiders. But such was the low standing of football supporters in the 1980s that many regarded Hillsborough as a tragedy of supporter ignorance, and not, as was subsequently proved by an independent report commissioned by the Conservative government in 2012/13, the culmination of a series of serious mistakes made by the police, who allowed too many supporters into an end of the ground in which there was not enough space and where fences prevented a quick escape, and other emergency services who were too slow to respond when the situation escalated dramatically.

Football hooliganism had been a problem that had blighted the sport in Britain. Fences, introduced during the 1970s to prevent supporters invading the pitch, were indicative of the low esteem in which fans were held by the clubs they supported and the authorities. Skirmishes inside and outside grounds were on the rise during the 1980s and if that meant that the ordinary supporter, who went to football simply to watch some sport, was maligned, then so be it. Football, which had become the preserve of the working class after the Second World War, when tickets were affordable, and boys spent many a Saturday afternoon sitting with their fathers in old-fashioned and often unsafe stands or crammed into equally antiquated terraces, was no longer the ideal venue for a safe day out. And nothing was being done to change that. You could go to any league match without a ticket, in the knowledge that one could be purchased before a game without any proof of identity, and that increased the chances of an opportunistic thug entering a ground and starting trouble. Elements of hooliganism, whether organised or spontaneous, could be found at virtually every stadium in the country. And there were basic safety issues – in 1985, a fire started at Bradford's Valley Parade stadium, destroying the main stand in less than a quarter of an hour and killing fifty-six supporters.

Neither did football have quite the number of stars that the Premier League would develop. The 1990 World Cup would make a household name of Paul Gascoigne, but he had to shed tears on a world stage before anyone really noticed him. It would not be until the start of the Premier League in 1992, backed by satellite television money and now family friendlier with the introduction of all-seater stadiums (introduced after the Taylor Report, following the Hillsborough disaster), that the sport began to find a new, more marketable identity.

It wasn't that football left a void for boxing to fill; it was just that the latter fitted more comfortably into an era when the working man felt displaced. Safety at a boxing event wasn't always paramount – promoter Frank Warren recalls a particularly brutal atmosphere at the Tony Sibson–Frank Tate fight in 1988 – but supporters making trouble at an event at which punching was legal was rarely as likely to make headlines in the way it did at football. Add that to the fact that boxing was almost always on television during the 1980s and you have a sport with a strikingly different outlook from the one you find in the modern era. While many bouts these days struggle to see the light of day because of problems about who will promote the contest and which television network will broadcast it, in 1989 there were considerably fewer such obstacles, certainly in the UK. There were only four TV channels – Channel 5 was a thing of the future – and two of those were owned by the BBC. Of the independent stations, Channel 4 had yet to show an interest in boxing, which left ITV as the logical home of the fight game. Apart from promotions by Frank Warren, the independent broadcaster would also be the place to watch top American fighters, including Mike Tyson, Evander Holyfield, Sugar Ray Leonard and Thomas Hearns.

America's love for the sport had dwindled during the eighties, in part because of one particular bout that ended in tragedy. In 1982, Ray Mancini, a very popular lightweight world champion, had knocked out a twenty-three-year-old South Korean boxer by the name of Duk Koo Kim in fourteen rounds. Four days after the bout, Kim died as a direct result of injuries he had suffered in the fight, which had been broadcast on terrestrial television. The World Boxing Council, under whose auspices the contest was fought, immediately ordered bouts to be shortened to twelve rounds. But the wider issue was the savage nature of the sport, which, according to long-time boxing writer Steve Farhood, meant boxing would appear on American television a lot less. The Tysons and Leonards would be seen on pay-per-view channels or closed-circuit television. An exception would be Benn–Watson.

Kevin Monaghan, then a leading executive at NBC, purchased rights to show the fight live on what would be a Sunday lunchtime slot in eastern America. The prime reason for the interest in the contest was Benn. 'He had a distinct presence,' says Farhood, who has edited *The Ring* magazine and has also commentated on boxing for television. 'He was completely different from the kind of British fighter we had been used to seeing.' Even given the quality of opposition Benn had faced, he'd caused a stir on the other side of the Atlantic, because of his 'crash-bang-wallop' style. The broadcasting of the Watson fight was the ultimate compliment. Commentating on the bout would be Dr Ferdie Pacheco, a familiar name to boxing fans as the man who had been Muhammad Ali's physician.

If America's interest in Benn was proof of his emerging power at the box office, it was the potency of his fists that most concerned Watson. 'If I had my hands down, I knew he could knock me out in the first round,' admits Watson now. The challenger was used to sparring with bigger men such as Dennis Andries. But in order to negate Benn's advantage in the power stakes, Watson had to think of a strategy different from any he had employed in his previous bouts. Normally a boxer who liked to go forward, Watson would have to adapt a defensive posture. His plan had echoes of one of the sport's most famous contests. In 1974, Ali had fought the hitherto undefeated wrecking machine, George Foreman, in Zaire, in a bout christened 'the Rumble in the Jungle'. For a number of reasons, Ali was a massive underdog. He seemed past his prime and was facing, in Foreman, a man who had destroyed the likes of Joe Frazier and Ken Norton in such brief and brutal fashion that there were genuine fears for the health of Ali, by now one of sport's most popular and admired figures. After an opening round during which he was happy to trade blows with the bigger and stronger Foreman, Ali retreated to the ropes, his hands and gloves protecting both sides of his head, allowing Foreman to target his lower abdomen. The younger man threw punch after punch at Ali, with limited success, until the eighth round, when, apparently exhausted, he was knocked to the floor by a short barrage of punches from 'the Greatest'. The strategy became known as 'rope-a-dope', yet another chapter in the enduring legacy of Ali. In order to pull off a similar tactic, Watson would need Benn to play the bull to his matador and, so far, there had been no evidence to suggest the champion knew another way to fight except straight ahead.

Not that Watson was especially fearful of his opponent. Lifelong friend Leonard Ballack confirms that his mate rarely, if ever, thought there was a better fighter around. 'We'd be watching guys on TV and I'd ask Michael what he thought of this middleweight or that and the answer was always the same: "He's OK."' His opinion of Benn, based purely on the evidence he'd accumulated from watching on television, was the same. Even so, he dedicated himself to a rigorous training schedule, after a final tune-up against American journeyman Franklin Owens, which Watson won in three rounds at the Royal Albert Hall. That bout took place on 8 March, leaving Watson more than ten weeks for preparation. He'd use his time wisely, sparring sixty hard rounds, some with Benn's amateur Commonwealth Games nemesis Rod Douglas, who was now a highly rated middleweight prospect, and also the tough American Wilfred Scypion, who'd once challenged Marvelous Marvin Hagler for the world title.

If Watson was quietly confident, then Benn was close to believing the hype that he generated. 'I was the best thing since sliced bread. I'd had twenty-two fights, twenty-two wins and twenty-two knockouts. So what can he do to me?' he says of that feeling prior to the bout. If he wasn't quite Britain's star boxer, he was close. Mendy's PR campaign had been breathless – he'd made sure his client's face was as familiar to the general public as possible. The extent of his fame was illustrated when, upon finding himself late for a flight from Heathrow, the police were persuaded to drive him and Mendy on the hard shoulder of the motorway to get him to the airport on time. 'Crazy, crazy. Wow. We got away with murder back then. Going to St James's Palace and Buckingham Palace and meeting Prince Charles and all.' Even with that stardom, Benn knew he had a problem with Watson, because he struggled to find anything to hate about the challenger.

'Good-looking guy, classic man. How could you hate him? Handsome-looking man, he was a gentleman. He just got on my nerves because everything about him was perfect. He was just lovely and you couldn't fault him. It was hard to look at him in any other way,' admits Benn, who also felt a little envious at the way Watson carried himself. Even so, the twenty-two knockout victories convinced him that Watson would pose no threat and he'd willingly use any form of verbal intimidation in the build-up to the bout, promising that Watson was going to get a beating like all the other men he'd knocked out. Even though the bout was billed as being for bragging rights in London, Benn's only concern was remaining unbeaten and winning the fight. Even so, his preparations didn't include much in the way of sparring. For years, boxers and trainers have sworn by sparring, the ritual of boxers fighting each other in the gym as part of training, in order to gain sharpness. Benn sparred just twelve rounds for the fight, hardly sufficient for an amateur contest. The venerable writer Colin Hart, who had covered the sport for decades for the *Sun* newspaper, questioned the preparations of the Benn camp and felt that Watson, who already, in his estimation, had a better chance of victory, would win in six rounds. Throughout his career, Benn's sparring would be a bone of contention – for the Watson fight, it was claimed that trainer Brian Lynch had limited the number of rounds the champion did, but it probably suited him to do less, given that he frequently admitted to not enjoying getting 'bashed up in the gym for free'. Sparring so little for the challenge of Watson indicated a touch of arrogance and also the fact that Benn probably had too much control over the way he trained. A stronger trainer would have insisted that Benn spend more time in the ring, conscious that Watson would pose problems the previous opponents hadn't. It wasn't just Colin Hart who felt Benn was making mistakes in his preparation. Frank Maloney, who was the official promoter of the bill, privately felt that Watson would win. 'Ambrose Mendy was so arrogant, he just didn't believe that his man could lose. But Watson was always more talented than Benn. He was a very clever fighter.'

Mendy had other things to worry about, namely how and where to stage the show. 'I'm driving home [after contracts for the bout had been signed] and the late Bernie Grant [back then, Member of Parliament for Tottenham] calls. Bernie was an amazing man, a mentor to me. He'd rung me to congratulate me on getting the fight signed and I said, "Bernie, where am I going to put it?" And he suggests putting the show on in Finsbury Park. I remember saying to him, "Bernie, how the fuck are we going to put it in Finsbury Park?"' Grant encouraged him to put the bout on in the open air and said if there was the threat of rain, why not go for a tent? 'You're the marketing man . . . Be creative! Don't put walls in front of yourself,' Grant told him. Mendy had already been thwarted in his attempts to get traditional venues like Wembley, the Royal Albert Hall or even at his beloved Highbury, the home of Arsenal. The idea of Finsbury Park crystallised further when he drove past a circus and enquired about how many people the covering tent held. When he found a company in Belgium could put together a tent which would hold 10,000 fans, at a cost of just over £40,000, a deal was done.

There were other hurdles to overcome, such as getting a licence from Haringey Council to show boxing, while the promoter, namely Mendy, incurred the wrath of Michael Jackson's representatives for using a poster showing Benn asking Jackson 'Who's Bad?'.(In the end, to avoid being sued for misuse of intellectual property, the Jackson party were offered ten ringside seats.) Finsbury Park turned out to be the perfect venue, being so close to where Watson was based and allowing his fan base – which was pretty sizeable – to attend in numbers, while Benn's supporters would also be there. 'He inspired a passion and loyalty in fans like no British fighter ever before or since,' says Glyn Leach. The support came from many social sectors – those who identified with Benn's combination of savagery in the ring and his style out of it. More and more, he was being marketed as a yuppie with boxing gloves, his face adorning the covers of men's fashion magazines as they bigged up alpha-male role models. The Benn image was also in keeping with the mantra of the Thatcher government – work hard, take your chances and you shall be rewarded. The yuppie revolution, albeit a short-lived one, had taken control during the final years of the decade, with young men taking advantage of a buoyant property market and displaying the fruits of their labour in the form of convertible cars, pinstripe suits, braces and the first mobile phones.

There were also hardcore boxing fans and fighters who jumped on the Benn bandwagon. Around that time, women's boxing was also finding a voice and Jane Couch, the first British woman to be granted a licence, was one of those who could be heard. 'He was all action. You knew he'd either knock someone out or get knocked out. He always wore his heart on his sleeve. He always seemed like he was in a real fight,' says Couch, who admits that one of Benn's most stirring victories, against Gerald McClellan in 1995, was one of the moments that ultimately inspired her to take on the British Boxing Board of Control who, until 1998, refused to license women to box professionally. Perhaps the other most prominent sector of Benn support came from the wide base of celebrities that Mendy courted. Sir Bob Geldof, at that time one of the most recognisable men in Britain thanks to his tireless efforts to help starving children in Africa, was at ringside, with his wife, the late Paula Yates. Other stars were in tow, while some of the most promising young boxers, such as recently crowned Olympic heavyweight champion Lennox

Lewis and middleweight sensation Roy Jones Junior, were also present.

What those people probably didn't know then was just how much Benn's corporeal vices could affect his preparations. The former soldier smoked, a habit that would have had a more obvious effect on his performances in the ring if his bouts had lasted longer. Before scientific research confirmed the negative effects of smoking on athletes, many footballers and other sportsmen could be seen smoking, but those days were coming to an end. If the odd puff was one of Benn's problems, another was his love of women – even though he was in a long-term relationship with Sharron Crowley – which would derail him in the final hours leading up to the fight. By this stage of his career, Benn had dispensed with the stark mohawk haircut and was now growing his locks. The day before the Watson bout, he went to get his hair 'styled'. The lady doing the styling was 'insanely pretty', says Mendy. It was yet another sign that Benn wasn't completely focused on the fight. Opinions vary on how long Benn spent getting his hair done. Some say three hours, others three or four times that. 'Just so he could smell it,' says Mendy. Either way, it meant trouble and someone should have got Benn to focus on the fight. To make matters worse, the fighter wasn't even happy with how it turned out. 'What in the blazes was I thinking? I went in a black man and came out looking like a Chinese man!' he recalls, laughing about how his locks had been pulled up so high that it seemed to tighten the skin around his eyes. 'You can't imagine Watson spending so much time on having his hair done the night before,' says Glyn Leach.

Whether or not Watson knew of Benn's distractions is not known, but the challenger was now exuding confidence. In the final press conference before the fight, he said to the champion: 'Nigel, I hope we can be friends after I beat you.' Benn smiled, perhaps taken aback by an opponent having such faith in his ability. It didn't shake his confidence or alter his preparations, however, for the Watson fight was to be Benn's coming-out party, the night he confirmed on live television in both Britain and America just how exciting he was. 'There almost seemed a belief from the Benn camp that he was so good, he could treat Watson with disdain, even though his boxing career wasn't nearly as expansive as Watson's,' says Leach.

Scene IV

'Watson couldn't fill a hole. They come to watch me'
– Nigel Benn

'Why should he be getting all the attention? I've lost only once in twenty-three fights and been in with better men'
– Michael Watson

Anyone who's spent any time in Great Britain will know that a typical May evening is neither dry nor necessarily warm. Sun, sleet, rain and snow have all been known in these isles during this most volatile of months. It goes without saying, therefore, that if you were thinking of staging a sporting event, such as a prizefight, you wouldn't gamble on an open-air venue. If you were going to stage a fight in London – and it would make sense to if both the main-event participants were from the capital – then Wembley Arena, or maybe even the Royal Albert Hall, would be your automatic choice. You'd need imagination, flair, bravado, not to say arrogance, to contemplate having it anywhere else.

For years, though, boxing promotion had been synonymous with exactly that – flair, bravado and arrogance. The flamboyant American Don King promoted 'the Rumble in the Jungle' in 1974 in Zaire because it was the only place where he could guarantee George Foreman and Muhammad Ali the enormous purses he'd promised them. Going further back in history, to the 1920s, the promotional team of Tex Rickard and Jack 'Doc' Kearns persuaded the town of Shelby, Montana, to build a stadium fit to stage a world heavyweight title bout between the pre-eminent fighter of the day and champion, Jack Dempsey, and an unknown challenger, Tommy Gibbons. Never mind that few paid to watch it and that four banks in the small western town went bankrupt – Dempsey got paid and went on to defend his title in bigger and better bouts.

Chances are that people would remember the night that Nigel Benn and Michael Watson first met whether the fight was held in a small hall or in an iconic arena. But Frank Maloney, Ambrose Mendy and Mickey Duff – the brains behind the event – had something a little more unique in mind. Finsbury Park, a part of north London which has always been associated with the staging of music concerts (the venue used to be called the Rainbow), was transformed for one night only into a location fit for this kind of fury. In order to combat the elements, all punches would be thrown inside a purpose-built red 'super-tent'. Nothing like it had been seen in British boxing before that night – and not much has come close to it since.

A whole host of notable football stars were in attendance – Paul Ince, then of West Ham but soon to join Manchester United, the Fashanu brothers, John and Justin, and future Arsenal star Ian Wright. Frank Bruno, the most popular British boxer of the time, was also there. People who saw it said it was the London equivalent of the Ali–Frazier 'Fight of the Century' in 1971, when everyone who was anyone was there, an occasion not to be missed. Even if it was easy enough to watch it on television. After all, in 1989, boxing was still free-to-air, available on either BBC1, or, in this case, ITV. And it was Sunday night – what could be more natural than switching from *Songs of Praise* to a couple of hell-raisers?

Boxing's pre-eminence on the screen in those days owed much to the endless supply of characters and stories that it generated. Kelvin McKenzie, the notorious former editor of the *Sun*, once told his staff that only three things sold his paper: 'Football, tits and boxing.' Certainly, there seemed little to dispute the health of the latter. February 1989 may have seen significant defeats for Bruno and another living-room regular, the former world welterweight champion Lloyd Honeyghan, but there seemed a surplus of men ready to thrust themselves into the limelight. In the three weeks after this fight, former world featherweight champion Barry McGuigan, multi-weight champion Duke McKenzie and rising cruiserweight Glenn McCrory would all make live appearances on both major channels.

Those three were involved in world title fights. Benn and Watson were to brawl for the former's Commonwealth middleweight title. As promoters have found in recent years, especially with the proliferation of spurious world titles, sometimes the prize is not as important as the bragging rights. In this case, the winner could only claim to be the best middleweight in London. Herol Graham was almost certainly the top British fighter in that weight class – the Sheffield-based boxer had just eleven days earlier lost a very debatable decision for the World Boxing Association title against Jamaican Mike McCallum. Graham's head and body movements were so unique that he often challenged visitors to his gym to try and hit him when his hands were tied behind his back. Such dares left Graham richer, but he would be studiously avoided by those at his weight and missed out on the bumper paydays his talents merited. It was his misfortune to have been born a handful of years too early. Graham would turn thirty later that year, and his reflexes were already starting to slow. Both Benn and Watson were still only in their mid-twenties.

With Graham at home nursing his bruises, Michael Watson of Hackney, a stone's throw from Finsbury Park, made his way to the ring. Watson walked to the squared circle like, well, like a fighter. There were no frills about him, no carefully manicured attempts to make him look more menacing than he was. The twenty-four-year-old, who had lost just once since turning professional in 1984, was flanked by trainer Eric Secombe and manager Mickey Duff. Depending on how you read body language, Watson was either nervous or confident. His handsome, black, mustachioed face seemed impassive enough, but plenty of people were looking for signs of nerves – after all, Watson was about to face the fearsome Nigel Benn, a man who had knocked out all twenty-two of his opponents, a man whose aura of intimidation had led people to christen him 'the English Mike Tyson'. Some believed that Watson was daft even to contemplate such a fight. The only possible salvation for him would be if his beating was swift, rather than prolonged. Benn had talked about 'hitting him with so many lefts, he'd be crying for a right.'

If you were a boxing fan in the 1980s, especially in the latter part of the decade, you'd have more than a passing knowledge of the phenomenon that was Mike Tyson. A juvenile delinquent apparently made good (the truth about his inner demons didn't come to light until the nineties), Tyson turned professional in 1985 after failing to make the Olympics and within twelve months was being talked about as the saviour of the sport's most storied division, the heavyweights. The New Yorker seemed to share many of the qualities of some of the great champions of the past – like Jack Dempsey, he entered the ring in the plainest of attire, no socks or robe, just black shorts and shoes, with a haircut that could only be described as severe. Like Sonny Liston or a young George Foreman, he exuded menace, his bleak stare, almost soulless eyes making men who would normally walk fearlessly around the toughest of neighbourhoods cross the street to avoid him. And there seemed genuine rage behind his blows. What else would you expect from someone who never had a father to speak of and a mother without the means to provide anything but the bare essentials?

Tyson benefited from a marketing strategy that was entirely of the time. His management team of Jim Jacobs and Bill Clayton, two experienced American Jews, matched Tyson against a series of opponents who would allow their man to show his talents. Tyson, still in his teens, would knock out or stop his first nineteen opponents in dynamic fashion and his management team would then send video highlights of these victories to some of the most influential journalists in America. Those montages, put together with such impact that they are still played in gyms around the world, generated both hype and aura. Before he was world champion, Tyson was already the sport's star in waiting, eclipsing the likes of Marvin Hagler, Thomas Hearns and Roberto Durán as a box-office attraction. He was that rarest of things: a fighter who delivered exactly what people wanted – violence. A boxing audience will seek reassurance that the finer aspects of the sport are still being practised, and those who attend big bouts in fancy casino locations want their action served fast and with maximum brutality.

Tyson's profile in Great Britain grew during 1988 and 1989, as a fight with national hero Frank Bruno was put together. The bout would be staged on 25 February 1989, with Tyson defending his undisputed world heavyweight title against 'Big Frank' in Las Vegas. Although Tyson would win in five, mostly one-sided rounds, the fight would have lasting significance. Such was the clamour to show the action, the BBC, ITV and the fledgling satellite company Sky would all bid to show it. In the end, Sky would secure live rights, forcing a small portion of the country to pay for a dish to be placed somewhere suitable on the outside of their house. The BBC would share TV rights with ITV to broadcast the recorded bout, while radio coverage gave those who didn't have Sky good reason for getting up in the middle of the night. The BBC's coverage was made all the more memorable by Harry Carpenter, who had by now developed a bond with Bruno, urging his friend on. 'Get in there, Frank!' bellowed Carpenter during a torrid opening round, which saw Bruno stagger the champion.

Bruno's defeat did nothing to dent the popularity of boxing in Britain. If anything, it encouraged a new generation of fans to fall in love with the sport. A trio of videos, with Tyson's name adorning the cover, were released, with the current champion invited to talk about the great warriors of the past. To his great credit, Tyson was able to discuss the merits of Ali, Louis and Dempsey, having watched their bouts on numerous occasions when staying with his mentor and first trainer, Cus D'Amato. His enthusiasm was infectious.

'I remember in 1986 [and for a few years after] that there was a period when Mike Tyson won the world title and Lloyd Honeyghan beat Don Curry – and we literally had kids outside the gym before it opened, waiting to train with us,' recalls Mike Costello of his coaching days. Honeyghan was a British welterweight who had done then what was considered unthinkable – gone to America and beaten Don Curry, the man then regarded as the best fighter in the world. He may have developed a reputation thereafter as being flash and brash, but his victory was a reminder of why people get involved in sport. 'Kids box because they want to win. It's not necessarily true that they go to gyms to get away from poverty and imagine a life of riches by becoming a boxer,' says Costello, who adds that 'boxing was massive in that time – just in the south-east of London we had at least fifty clubs or gyms.'

Around that time, Costello also remembers a buzz about

a young middleweight who had set the amateur scene alight with his ferocious punching power. This fighter had lost just once, had taken the coveted Amateur Boxing Association title and was about to turn professional, having missed out on a place at the Commonwealth Games in 1986. A former soldier who had served in Northern Ireland, the most dangerous place for a squaddie to be during the mid-1980s, much was expected of the apparently fearless Ilford-born Nigel Benn.

Having changed his hairstyle for the fight, Benn also arrived in the ring in a different manner. 'The Dark Destroyer' danced in wearing an all-in-one silver jumpsuit, having been announced into the arena by several members of his old Royal Fusiliers regiment. As he appeared from the entrance at one end of the tent, the sign 'Who's Bad?' glistened above his head. Mendy, by his side, was dressed in a similarly garish fashion, with Benn having insisted some time ago that if he was to look 'different' so should his manager. It seemed over the top then, but no one was willing to argue with a man who had knocked out his last twenty-two opponents. When he finally arrived in the ring, Benn began to shadow-box, as so many fighters do before the first bell. It can often be seen as a nervous reaction, the adrenalin kicking in as a fighter prepares for battle, but there was no such hyperactivity in the Watson corner. The challenger knew what lay ahead – in fact, he had predicted a sixth-round knockout to his closest friends, all of whom made sure to make a trip to the bookmakers before each Watson contest.

Once the two men disrobed, it became obvious to the neutral that Watson was the bigger man. 'He looked twice my size, built like a brick shithouse!' says Benn. Watson was taller and thicker and impassive when the two men were brought together before the first bell for their pre-fight instructions from referee John Coyle. The noise inside the tent made it hard for people to hear themselves speak and that included British commentating duo Reg Gutteridge, the voice of boxing on ITV for over twenty years, and his analyst, Jim Watt, a Scot who had held the world lightweight title during the late 1970s and early 1980s. The balance of support was overwhelmingly in favour of Benn. 'If I thought about it too much, I'd have frightened myself to death,' says Watson, whose core support came from those he'd grown up with – a sizeable number – and boxing devotees, who admired him for his diligence in the gym and the quality of his opposition prior to this bout. What neither man had were significant doubters who turned up merely to add their support to the one they disliked the least. You were either in one camp or the other.

In America, Dr Ferdie Pacheco told the TV audience, 'The excitement here is crackling', as the first bell sounded. In the UK, Gutteridge told viewers it was 'one of the hottest domestic showdowns I can remember. It's really like sitting on the red alert here, waiting for the bomb to explode.' Both Gutteridge and Pacheco's voices seemed to accelerate in pace as they talked – that's what a real, well-matched boxing contest can do. 'I make no bones about it, a really good, even match, which way is it going to go, it makes the hair on your neck stand on end,' said Jim Rosenthal, the veteran TV presenter.

Watson, wearing red shorts, walked to the centre of the ring at the sound of that first bell and actually threw the first punches, a trio of left hooks which Benn, who had abandoned his now trademark black shorts in favour of white, blocked. After maybe ten seconds, 'the Dark Destroyer' unleashed his opening salvo, a fusillade of hooks with either hand, power punches with the intent to knock out his opponent. Watson, with hands up, gloves cupped around his head, elbows tucked in by his ribcage, defended stoutly and without too much discomfort, although the sheer power coming from the man in white forced him from one side of the ring to the other. 'Can Watson survive the dangerous early rounds, it seems the only concern in his mind,' said Gutteridge, choosing his words carefully, fearful that anything could happen at any moment. If there were psychological blows to be landed, they were being delivered by Watson, who pushed Benn away, reminding the champion of his own undoubted strength, and also establishing his jab, a punch that kept Benn at distance. Even so, the punches continued from the pursuer, left hooks and right hands, aimed at body and head.

'The crowd are absolutely baying for Benn, aren't they, Jim?' said Gutteridge, as Watson retreated to the ropes.

'Well, I thought Watson may have been a bit negative in the opening rounds, especially the opening minute, but he hasn't. He's been on the defensive, he's been on the retreat, but he hasn't been negative. He's thrown good punches, he's looking at Benn all the way through and keeping his own defences tight,' answered Watt.

And so the pattern continued for the next two minutes, with Benn going forward, following Watson in a circle, throwing punches to all parts of the body and head but not connecting cleanly. He never hit air, but the damage he was used to inflicting wasn't apparent. Watson hadn't winced, wasn't cut and was still thinking clearly, making sure to throw a jab or hook at Benn's head when the opportunity arose. His tactic of moving to his left, away from the power of Benn's favourite punch, the left hook, meant he was largely untroubled for the majority of the opening round. At the bell, with Benn a yard from his corner, the pair exchanged a glance – Benn's seemed to say, 'I'll get you soon', while Watson smirked, as if to say, 'I'm still here'. In America, Pacheco had told viewers that it was the first time Benn had faced a man 'this big. Solid legs, solid middleweight and that may pose a problem.' He also noted that every one of Benn's punches was as hard as it could have been.

The second round began as the first had: Watson out in the middle of the ring, throwing the first punches, showing that he could stand toe to toe with Benn. Watson threw the first blows, a combination of jabs and left hooks, controlling the first ninety seconds of the action and blocking what came back. What he was unable to do was force Benn back. The circle continued, Watson moving to his left, stalked by the champion. 'Smart countering and covering by Watson,' remarked Gutteridge. During the final thirty seconds, Benn pinned Watson in a corner of the ring and landed a right hand. 'Benn got through with that one, Reg,' said Watt. A left hook and other hard punches followed but Watson took them all and continued to throw punches back. 'Can Benn keep this up for twelve rounds? He's using a lot of nervous energy!' said Pacheco. 'He's banking everything he's got on these hard shots.' Slow-motion replays showed that Benn had connected cleanly with a left hook and right hand, but Watson took the combination better than any of Benn's previous opponents. 'Watson is braced to take punches at all times,' added Watt during a second round which was even more punishing than the first, with both men walking back to their corners a little more gingerly than they had at the end of the first.

Both seemed to have recovered their energy for the start of the third round, with Benn once again unloading with power punches. 'Benn is standing off a few inches, and normally when he does that, he's looking to land the really big stuff,' said Watt, perhaps momentarily forgetful of the fact that all he had done for the previous two rounds was exactly that. By the end of the round, Benn's punch output was down considerably from the previous two and he was happy to engage in clinches with Watson, the first sign that his energy levels were going down. All the while, Watson was controlling the tempo of the action with his concise movement around the ring and the use of a stiff jab. 'Benn is wide open,' noted Pacheco, who also observed that he hadn't learned much from his brawl with Logan. The majority of the crowd seemed oblivious to the shifting nature of the fight, the chant of 'Nigel, Nigel, Nigel!' prominent throughout.

The fourth round began with the first, unquestionable change in the momentum of the bout. Watson lured Benn into a corner and, after the champion had missed with a power punch, Watson took advantage and threw a handful of shots at Benn, who, for whatever reason, decided to drop his hands and invite more punishment. 'That was a stupid thing to do,' said Watt, as Benn finally returned fire. 'Watson knows he can shake Benn, can drive him back,' added Watt. 'I can see in his movements that those punches have hurt him.' As the Scot was uttering those words, Watson hurt Benn again, marching him back down the ring, throwing and connecting with jabs and right hands. Again, Benn returned with those big hooks and roundhouse rights. 'His power is so natural to him, even on his way down, I think Nigel Benn could still knock somebody down,' said Watt. But, by now, Watson knew that if he had to take the odd lick to land a dozen, it was worth the sacrifice. In America, Pacheco and his colleague Marv Albert believed that Benn was trying to lure in Watson, that he was 'playing possum'. Perhaps more pertinently, he had now run out of ideas. All the while, Watson was growing in his role as matador: 'look at that rope-a-dope, look at peekaboo!' exhorted Pacheco, as the challenger rode a succession of Benn blows before returning fire towards the end of the fourth. As the bell sounded, Benn gave his opponent a respectful tap on the back. It was probably the last clean blow he'd land.

An anecdote that Benn related about the fight for years revolves around instructions given to him by trainer Brian Lynch before the start of the fifth round.

'Just go out there and steam him, Nigel,' Lynch is reported to have said.

'I'm looking at the boxing manual and I can't find that phrase! I know I'm in trouble. All he had to say was cover up and take your time and land your shots,' says Benn. At the same time, Watson saw his opponent's father and winked at him. The gesture's significance was obvious – Watson was telling Dickson Benn that he 'had his boy'.

The fifth round was the most savage of the fight – both men dug in and landed brutal, vicious punches. But the sight of Benn retreating on two occasions signified that his fire was starting to burn out. Dispirited and now swollen around his eyes – some blamed the haircut for the swelling, but not Benn – he looked more the destroyed than destroyer as the bell sounded to end the round. Neither man could continue for twelve rounds at this pace, but Watson looked better equipped for the immediate future. The statistics, which had always favoured him, were now being quoted by ringside sages – Watson averaged over five rounds of action per fight, while Benn was programmed to brawl for two. 'Watson's fighting a very intelligent fight,' added Pacheco as the fifth round came to an end. 'There are no lumps or marks on his face.'

In his corner Watson could feel the fight had swung his way. Benn's punches, 'the hardest I ever felt', were no longer as painful as they had been during the first four rounds. He had, after all, told his inner circle that the sixth round would be his moment of glory. With Benn being instructed by Lynch to 'box him, box him', Watson opened up with a flurry of punches, culminating in a straight right hand. Benn backed away, holding a glove to his eye. 'He got thumbed, he got thumbed,' shouted Pacheco. A thumb in the eye is an old professional's trick, designed to close the opponent's eye. Benn would suffer such a trick at the hands of another British fighter later in his career, but at this moment he had just been discouraged. 'A perfect punch, Reg. There was nothing wrong with that punch,' exclaimed Watt. Referee Coyle urged Benn to continue, which he did. But by now, the end was in sight.

'I was just exhausted,' says Benn. 'I was hitting him hard, and he just rolled, rolled. He always knew what was coming. All week, Michael had heard the talk that I was going to come out like an express train and all he had to do was cover up and I'd burn myself out. He never hurt me.'

Benn had one last burst of energy, tempting Watson on to him and throwing a handful of blows, all of which were blocked. His balance now gone, the champion was finally floored by a straight jab. 'Oh, he's gone!' shouted Gutteridge, 'so the big hitter has been hit.' 'Down goes Benn!' said Marv Albert on the other side of the Atlantic. 'A pinpoint left hand.' Benn, for what seemed like an eternity had been in midair, until he landed flat on his back. It almost felt as if, as his body landed, the crowd didn't know what to think. For the briefest of moments there was silence. And then a roar, from Watson's supporters, who, like their man, had waited patiently before really letting themselves go. Benn, oblivious to the noise, rolled slowly to his right, got himself on to one knee and cut a dispirited, pathetic figure. The referee counted to ten, all the while looking at the timekeeper, ignoring the fact that Benn had got up at nine. As he turned to Benn, Coyle automatically waved the fight off, perhaps indicating that he had already decided to end the bout after the knockdown. There were no protests from the beaten man, who immediately sought out an exuberant and elated Watson for a congratulatory hug. Benn was being spoken to by Duff. All the while, Watson was being feted by friends and his cornermen, very few of whom had genuinely believed he could pull off what was already being described as an upset. In the end, he was brought to a neutral corner for an interview with ITV's Jim Rosenthal.

'The main object was to keep my composure. I knew if I used my left hand, everything would flow from there. I was catching him with some good shots . . . I was punching with bad intentions,' Watson told Rosenthal. 'I must give credit to Nigel Benn. He promoted this fight very well. He gave me one of my hardest fights so far – he was very strong. He throws some solid shots.'

Benn had by now fled the ring, chased by Frank Bruno. The pair were friends, who would eventually spend time training together in Tenerife and could often be seen ringside cheering on the other. When Bruno found Benn on this evening, his friend was in his changing room, crying. By now, manager Mendy had been alerted to the fact that his fighter had left the ring and joined the inquest. 'It's all gone, the gold, the girls, the houses, it's all gone! I've fucked up,' said Benn. Boxer and manager had a frank exchange of views, before Benn was encouraged to go back into the ring, as he had done at the start of the night, flanked by his former Fusilier comrades. The beaten man grabbed the ringside microphone and told the audience how great a champion Watson was. When asked by NBC television what had happened, he replied simply: 'I got my arse kicked! But make no mistake, I'll be back.' Operation Save Face had begun.

The evening had started as Nigel Benn's coming-out party. Twenty-two wins over opponents that few had heard of had made him a television fixture because of the way he knocked them out. But he hadn't been tested. His supporters believed he would win but expected some resistance from the opposition. As Watson had covered up and fired back in the early rounds, it had looked as if it might be a tricky night for Benn. But by the time the end came, as sudden and dramatic as it was, it wasn't a surprise. Out of ideas and stamina, with his eyes swollen, he had the look of a beaten man. Even so, seeing someone so feared on his backside, a man who many felt was unbeatable, was an unforgettable image. If you were old enough to remember Foreman's cloak of invincibility being removed by Ali, the sight of a ring bully being dismantled wasn't a new experience. But for those who were new to the sport, who had climbed on to the Benn bandwagon because of the violence and the glitz, the sight of their man on the floor, devoid of fight, was shocking. In the battle of the two most promising middleweights in the country, a definitive answer to the question of who was the best had been given. They'd expected one punch to end the fight and it had. But it had not come from the fighter they believed in.

For Watson it would be the biggest win of his career and would earn him a fight with the WBA middleweight champion Mike McCallum, the talented Jamaican who had recently beaten Herol Graham. In theory, the world was his oyster. But boxing never works as smoothly as fighters hope. Nevertheless, Watson would watch his Arsenal team win the league title five days later and then see his mate McDonnell beat Barry McGuigan as their bet came in. The questions about his talent had been answered – he might never be box office, but here was proof that old-fashioned values of dedication and hard work could prosper. He'd watched the vast majority of the country get carried away by Benn's ferocious demeanour, which he knew was part real but also part of the business. He knew he was a more complete fighter but he also wasn't prepared to say or do the things that Benn would to remain in the spotlight. There was always a bit of theatre about Benn, an aura and also an expectation that he'd say and do things that made people notice. He represented so much of a period in which people got rich quickly and then found that their wealth had been built on uncertain foundations. Watson offered a stark contrast to Benn's approach – there were no short cuts on his road to the top. He'd learned his trade, how to box, fight and defend. His journey to the top had been longer and more demanding but the proof of whether it was worth it would be examined again when he fought McCallum.

The harder questions would be directed at Benn. Could a man with the desire to be a world champion really devote so much time to his hair? Why was he spent after four rounds? And in a sport in which courage is measured in how much blood a man sheds on his way to the top, should a single jab have been enough to put him on the canvas and keep him there? More than a few boxing writers were of the opinion that he had 'swallowed it'– in other words, had he quit? Was Benn yet another ogre who knew only how to bully and was redundant as soon as the man in the other corner blocked and punched back? Benn would cry many private tears before answering any of those questions.

Act II

Scene I

Michael Watson's reward for beating Nigel Benn was a fight with the WBA middleweight champion Mike McCallum. Hardly a reward, but, post-Marvin Hagler, McCallum was as good as it got in the middleweight division. The Jamaican, now in his mid-thirties, had been fighting at world title level for five years and had beaten high-calibre boxers like Don Curry, Milton McCrory and Herol Graham. He had earned a reputation for being a particularly dangerous body puncher but there was also evidence that he was on the slide. He had been 'outspeeded' by Sumbu Kalambay and many felt he had been lucky to get the decision against Graham. No one felt that Watson was in for an easy night, but he would probably start marginal favourite.

Watson was now the mandatory challenger for McCallum's belt and promoters were invited to bid to stage the fight.

Mickey Duff had put on McCallum's fight with Graham and it seemed obvious that he would win the right to promote a bout between the champion and his man Watson. What upset the applecart was the emergence of another promoter who was keen to get a piece of the action. Relatively new to the sport, Barry Hearn had spread his wings from snooker, where he had enjoyed great success with the likes of Steve Davis, to boxing. Hearn, who began life as an accountant, had promoted Frank Bruno's win over Joe Bugner at Tottenham's White Hart Lane in 1987 and, by the end of the 1980s, he was becoming a serious player in the sport, even though he lacked a world champion. Hearn's offer to stage the bout was more lucrative than Duff's. In winning the purse bid, Hearn established himself as part of the Watson camp and also increased the divisions between the fighter and his current promoter.

Watson had become convinced that Duff didn't believe in him, especially for the Benn fight. In his book *Twenty & Out*, Duff denies this and says he made money out of betting on his man to beat Benn. Whether he believed in Watson's talent as much as the fighter himself is another matter. Duff came from a different time and his grounding in the sport came during the 1950s and 1960s, where fighters would often have forty or fifty bouts before their first world title challenge. As far as he was concerned, he couldn't see the need to rush. Watson, was only twenty-four and had time on his side. Duff also didn't want Watson to fight McCallum. He could see the problems for Watson against such a cagey fighter, who knew as much about boxing as Watson and had been a practitioner for so much longer. Duff didn't think Watson would lose, but he would have been happier pursuing other, safer options. For Watson, Duff losing the purse bids for the fight was to prove a liberating experience.

If there had been joy for Watson in beating Benn, it was tempered by what followed immediately in the aftermath of the fight. The day after the win, his post-fight victory press conference was interrupted by Benn, who offered genuine praise to his conqueror before reminding those present that he would be back. If that irked Watson, it was nothing compared to seeing the former champion on television later that day admitting he had underestimated the challenger, had spent too much time on his hair but was now going to America to transform himself into the genuine article. He even had the nerve to say that, when he returned to England with a world title, he'd happily have a rematch. Watson's moment was gone – a winner he may have been in the ring, but the PR battle was a no-contest. The papers wrote as much about the loser as they did the victor. The softly spoken man from north London was seething. How could his career still look tame in comparison with that of the man he had so comprehensively dismantled?

Whether or not Hearn knew of Watson's dissatisfaction, he spoke the language the champion wanted to hear. Hearn spoke of future fights, which would include maybe another battle against Benn and also a bout with one of his stable. He had recently taken on another British middleweight who had been based in America before returning for home comfort. His name was Chris Eubank. At the time, mention of his name had little effect on Watson, who was focused purely on the world title challenge against McCallum. What Watson did notice was the way Hearn went about his business; while Duff was keen for his fighters to learn the business and pay their dues, Hearn saw boxing as business, where fights were made if people wanted to see them. 'It's a horrible, dirty, money-grabbing business . . . the one factor that binds it all together is money,' Hearn told me. 'We have fighters now that, as much as we love them, I will put them in against the devil himself with a bazooka gun, if the money is right. And they know that. And it's better to be honest with them. I'll say to them "Why did you start fighting? Did you start fighting because you wanted a belt on your mantelpiece in your council house or did you start fighting because you wanted the house on the hill? You started fighting because you wanted to change your life."'

As the eighties drew to a close, with another recession about to hit and the threat of the poll tax looming, money was an increasingly important factor for men in such uncertain pursuits such as professional boxing. The best way for Watson to make that money, to provide for his two daughters, was to win a world title. Watson would not be the first or last boxer to enter Hearn's offices in Essex and seek better recompense for his labours. While so many people seemed to be struggling to find the money to pay bills, Hearn, who had made a fortune through snooker, had the cash and connections to lure boxers into his stable. The bout would be in November 1989 at Alexandra Palace. Meanwhile, in America, Watson's old adversary Benn was busy.

Benn had gone to Miami, where he would be trained by Englishman Vic Andretti, a former British light welterweight champion. Jettisoned was Brian Lynch, his apparent failure to come up with an alternative game plan against Watson making him an appropriate and easy scapegoat. It wouldn't be the last time that Benn changed trainers. For now, he was immersed in boxing history – the 5th Street Gym, where he trained, had seen many of the greats go through their paces, Muhammad Ali and Sugar Ray Leonard to name but two. Those two may have been famous for their ability to dance in the ring, but Benn's initiation was more brutal. Whatever the truth about his dislike of sparring, in Miami he sparred and took his lessons the hard way. The 'crash-bang-wallop' style was replaced by a more patient approach, with the jab becoming a new and permanent feature. Andretti preached calm and Benn listened. Defeat had left him embarrassed to walk around London, where he feared those on the street might have thrown a few choice words in his direction. In Florida, he was no one. His children and partner, Sharron, remained in England, the theory being that distractions were harder to find in Miami. It had often been said in boxing circles that Benn's style was better suited to American audiences, where aggression was prized above defensive genius. If Benn was to achieve as much as possible with his natural talent, the States was a suitable forum on a number of levels. He wouldn't be reminded of what happened to him in Finsbury Park. He'd learn about his chosen sport from more experienced men and he could also, in theory, escape some of the distractions that life in London offered. However, life in Miami wasn't exactly a case of solitary confinement.

He had friends with him, like hellraiser pal Ray Sullivan, or 'Rolex Ray', as he became known, and Mendy was never far from the action. The manager divided his time between the two sides of the Atlantic, doing deals to keep Benn's profile high. On one occasion he returned to the States after reading in one of the national newspapers about a night of passion involving Benn and a local woman. The newspaper had, in graphic and intimate detail, told of how Benn had eaten strawberries off her naked body. When confronted about it by Mendy, who was trying to placate his fighter's partner, Benn not only admitted to the infidelity but also confirmed he had encouraged the girl to sell her story and make some money!

Benn's extra-curricular activities might have hurt those back at home and been a hassle for those in charge of his career, but they never seemed to affect the fighter's energy levels. He trained, as he had done in England, with a zeal and energy that bordered on the maniacal. Throughout his career, Benn would have disagreements with his trainers about the amount of sparring he'd need, but no cornerman ever had cause to reproach him for a lack of effort when preparing for a bout. In America, whether or not he'd been out the night before, Benn would always make his 6 a.m. run, which would range from six to twelve miles. In the 1990s, such burning of the candle at both ends wasn't uncommon for top athletes – the Manchester United and England captain Bryan Robson was known as both a prodigious drinker and ferocious trainer. But Robson paid a price – he was injury-prone, failing to complete two World Cups while still in his prime. Benn would find years later that his hectic private life denied him a longer career.

Despite his first defeat, Benn wasn't considered dead wood by some of the big players in American boxing. Bob Arum, whose organisation Top Rank had promoted several of Marvin Hagler's bouts, liked the Englishman's style and offered him a two-fight deal. 'He was a charming guy,' says Bruce Trampler, the firm's matchmaker, who put Benn in with the tough Dominican Republic middleweight Jorge

Amparo for the first of those bouts. The thirty-six-year-old didn't punch hard enough to pose a threat, but he wasn't the kind of opponent likely to fall after absorbing one punch. The fight, staged in Atlantic City, New Jersey, on 20 October, ended with Benn victorious after ten rounds. For the first time since he had turned professional, Benn had been forced to go the distance. While he proved that he possessed the stamina required and that maybe the exhaustion against Watson was an aberration, critics also wondered whether this proved Benn lacked the power at the highest level.

Five days later, his old amateur rival Rod Douglas had the biggest bout of his career. After thirteen consecutive victories, he was matched against Herol Graham, who went back to defending his British middleweight title after that loss to McCallum. Douglas was outclassed and then stopped after nine one-sided rounds. Shortly after the fight ended, Douglas suffered a blood clot and, although he would recover, the nature of his injuries meant he would never fight again. The doctor who cared for him was consultant neurologist Peter Hamlyn. It would not be the last time he'd treat a stricken boxer.

As Watson approached his first world title challenge, it seemed nothing could go wrong. He had not just reached the levels of fitness and conditioning which had proved Benn's undoing, he had surpassed them. His chief sparring partner had been an old friend named Ray Webb, whose lanky frame made him ideal for the challenge posed by McCallum. Sparring is usually done until the week before the fight, in order to avoid injuries, but with eight days to go until the bout Watson sustained a broken nose, which forced an immediate cancellation. All the momentum that

Watson had built after the Benn victory was lost. He had become, by virtue of that victory, the man to watch in the congested British middleweight scene. The setbacks he'd suffered before beating Benn had been put to one side and, with that, those feelings of envy and disillusionment also faded. But that training mishap made him question why things couldn't always go his way. Watson knew that an extra five or six months to prepare for McCallum would be of little use. All the while, he'd know that the man he'd beaten so emphatically in his last fight had picked himself up and was causing a stir in America. This should be my time, thought Watson. But fate was conspiring against him.

Barry Hearn rescheduled the contest for April 1990. If Watson didn't fight until then, he'd have spent nearly a year on the sidelines. Older fighters benefit from such a rest, their bodies needing time to heal, but Watson, who had had a relatively meagre twenty-three bouts in five years, needed the activity. He pleaded with both Hearn and Duff to get him a warm-up in the interim, but nothing could be arranged. This time, training was more of a slog, the sharpness that he had felt in 1989 replaced now by a feeling that he was treading water. To add further to his sense of disenchantment, Watson watched McCallum go twelve hard rounds with a young Irish fighter based in America called Steve Collins. That bout, which the champion won on points, took place two months before the rescheduled Watson fight. It was a double psychological blow for the Jamaican – it shook off the cobwebs and also sowed further seeds of doubt in the British boxer's mind. 'He should have had a couple of warm-ups,' says Leonard Ballack, Watson's longtime friend who could usually be seen at ringside.

Come 14 April at the Royal Albert Hall, Watson entered the ring not quite at the physical level he'd attained for much of the previous year. Even if the fight had taken place on the original date, he would have had his hands full against McCallum, but now, with a year of inactivity hampering his sharpness, it was a hard night for the challenger. Consistently beaten to the punch and outworked, Watson lost most of the first six to seven rounds. At that point, he put in one last effort, stepping in with harder punches. McCallum took them and marched on – in fifty-five fights, against some of the hardest punchers, 'the Body Snatcher' had never been knocked out – before reasserting his dominance, finally stopping an exhausted and discouraged Watson in the eleventh round. It was a beating that worried many who saw it – even Duff, who was being gently moved away from the apex of the Watson camp, implored his fighter to leave the middleweight division, so concerned was he at the scale of sacrifice being made. He'd watch Watson fail to draw a sweat after ten minutes of warming up before the bout and worried that his fluid intake after the weigh-in had been inexpert, leading to a dramatic loss of power and strength on the night. You can have all the perceived weapons you like in a boxing ring, but if the powder is damp before you've pulled the trigger it doesn't matter what ammunition you've packed.

There was no disgrace in losing to McCallum, who would go down in history as one of the best of his era, but Watson was now back to where he had been before the Benn fight. To add further pressure, his relationships with key people, such as Zara, the mother of his two daughters, and Duff, were deteriorating. The scale of his defeat meant a return to domestic matters was the only way forward. Watson hadn't done enough to deserve a rematch – McCallum had been tested more stringently by Collins. A victory for Watson would have been life-changing – a rematch with Benn would be worth at least three times as much with a world title at stake and there would surely have been more endorsements for becoming the country's first middleweight world champion since Alan Minter in 1980. Watson dreamed of earning enough money to secure the future of his daughters and also the respect of the boxing world, and the journey to those goals was far from complete. As he convalesced, he knew, not for the first time in his career, that bigger challenges awaited.

In America, the Nigel Benn experiment was enjoying some success. Six weeks after going the distance with Amparo, 'the Dark Destroyer' – a nickname that was fully embraced in the States – stopped Puerto Rican Jose Quinones in one round in Las Vegas. The performance was a perfect combination of the old and new Benn. Hard punches, thrown correctly and sparingly, producing the knockout. Benn left the ring with reporters being told by Bob Arum they'd just seen the 'English Marvin Hagler'. In truth, the man Benn most aspired to be like was Mike Tyson, at that time the undefeated and undisputed heavyweight champion of the world. The pair had met and Benn couldn't help but admire Tyson. The money, the female attention and the power of his celebrity had an effect.

Back in England, the night before Benn beat Quinones, his former manager and promoter Frank Warren was shot in the chest, the target of an apparent assassination attempt by a masked man. Warren would make a full recovery and return to the sport he loved. Police charged Terry Marsh, a friend of Benn, and Warren's first world champion, with the attempted murder, but the retired boxer would eventually be acquitted. During Warren's absence from the business, promoters like Hearn flourished. Young, promising fighters saw that Hearn had money to spend and signed with him, knowing they could expect better exposure as well as remuneration. But of more importance to Benn was the absence from his camp of Marsh, who had become invaluable as a source of mirth and encouragement. Despite his love of nightlife, Benn was naturally more comfortable in the company of friends and family.

Eight days before his twenty-sixth birthday, Benn would go the distance again, this time against American journeyman Sanderline Williams, who was a late substitute for compatriot Michael Olajide. The purpose of a proposed fight with Olajide – once again in Las Vegas – was to put Benn in a position to fight the legendary Roberto Durán for the WBC middleweight title. Neither fight transpired and, although Benn failed to shine against Williams, a slippery boxer who'd fight half a dozen world champions and never be stopped, fate was on his side. Bob Arum's Top Rank signed him to a new five-fight deal worth a basic £250,000 per bout and then positioned him to take on the WBO middleweight champion Doug DeWitt. The WBO were not recognised as an official sanctioning body in the United Kingdom and therefore the challenger was happy once again to fight in someone else's backyard. DeWitt looked to be all wrong for Benn. He had earned a reputation for toughness dating back to his days as Marvin Hagler's sparring partner. He'd mixed in good company for most of his career and had won the title the previous year against Robbie Sims, Hagler's half-brother. His experience and the fact that he'd fought better opponents for the majority of his career made him a strong favourite when the pair met on 29 April. Colin Hart of the *Sun*, who had tipped against Benn for the Watson fight, predicted another loss for the Englishman. Even Jim Rosenthal, who presented the coverage for ITV from New Jersey, says 'we all thought he'd get battered'.

Benn's American foray had taken him away from the distractions Britain had to offer as well as some of the pressures. Back at home, the country expected a string of explosive knockouts, bodies on the floor, followed by the inevitable question: 'who's next?' Such a strategy had led him to Watson and, after six rounds, he had been exposed as a bully, a fighter who knew only one way to win. While some had watched his bouts in America and wondered whether the old 'Dark Destroyer' had disappeared, the bigger picture was that Benn was evolving into a puncher who could also box. It might not have been enough to win a rematch with Watson, but it certainly gave him a better chance. Regardless of the fact that he had shown another dimension to his boxing ability, a win over DeWitt would be an upset.

Observers were reminded of the potential for the unexpected two months earlier when Mike Tyson surrendered his undefeated record and world heavyweight titles to fellow American James 'Buster' Douglas in Tokyo. You could have got odds of up to 40-1 on Douglas before the fight, so unremarkable had his career been up to that point. But he'd dared to dream the impossible. Now Benn was invited to do the same.

The setting was Atlantic City and it may well have produced the best performance of Benn's career. DeWitt says now that he might have been on the slide but his retirement from the sport two years later was no doubt hastened by the chastening experience of that evening. After flooring Benn with a left hook in the second round, he barely won a portion of any round thereafter. In total, he was floored four times by 'the Dark Destroyer', absorbing virtually every one of the soon-to-be new champion's power punches. In the end, the bout was mercifully called to a halt in the eighth, with DeWitt on the floor courtesy of a left hook and Benn also on the canvas, but this time crying tears of joy and pride. The late Emanuel Steward said that Benn that night would have beaten any middleweight that ever lived. 'Beating Doug DeWitt showed he still had bottle for the game. That was a great performance,' says Glyn Leach. It was also one beamed into households in both America and Great Britain, with ITV, which had shown all of Benn's bouts in the States, providing delayed coverage of the victory. If anyone thought the honest graft that had led to Benn's redemption would affect his approach to life, they were quickly dissuaded when the new champion flew home by Concorde.

Not everyone was bowled over by the performance. Michael Watson, still nursing his bruises from the defeat by McCallum, admits that watching Benn pick up a world title eleven months after their meeting left him feeling a little more pain. Even the knowledge that his beating had propelled Benn to the course of action which led to a world title was no consolation. How did this happen, Watson thought? He'd admired Benn's courage in learning how to box and expected that a rematch, if there was going to be one, would be for the world title he expected to take from McCallum. Instead, as Benn hogged the headlines, Watson would once again have to go back to being the quiet man in the background. Watson's anger didn't extend to his rival so much as those around him, who he felt hadn't done enough to make him headline news.

Speed was now becoming a major issue for Watson – there wasn't enough of it in the progression of his career. Not enough big fights at the right time and too much time spent away from the ring, while others, like Benn, staked their claim, seizing the opportunity for fame and fortune. His humble, low-key approach to the sport meant that, for all the admiration he enjoyed from those in the sport, he remained low key. 'Looking back at old tapes of me, even I'm surprised how quiet I was!' says Watson now. That quietness extended to his relationship with manager and promoter Duff. Rather than question what he was being asked to do and the amount of money he was being paid per fight, Watson would leave Duff in his office and then walk away, seething but having avoided a confrontation. Duff had no reason to question his ability to create a world champion – he would finish his career having worked with twenty. Whether he believed Watson could have been number twenty-one is a matter of conjecture and a question that Duff is no longer able to answer. But what is undeniable is that he did not realise the extent of Watson's unhappiness. As always seems to be the case in boxing, the catalyst for the break-up was money. Watson didn't think he had earned enough for his fight with McCallum and decided to break free from his contract with Duff. Following advice from Ambrose Mendy and sports law specialist Henri Brandman, Watson took Duff to court, on the basis that he should not be allowed to act as both manager and promoter for the fighter, as he would essentially be negotiating with himself.

Duff fought the action because he felt he deserved better from the contract he had with Watson, given the investment he had made in the fighter. Mr Justice Scott ruled in favour of Watson, exonerating Duff of any blame but deciding the existing contracts, issued by the British Boxing Board of Control, were not fair on the boxer as he had no bargaining power. A new clause would be inserted, allowing boxers to make deals; it would, in years to come, allow Joe Calzaghe to break free of Duff, before embarking on an amazing career of his own. The Welshman would retire undefeated, having beaten virtually every top super middleweight of his generation, including Americans Roy Jones Junior and Bernard Hopkins. All that had seemed a distant dream for Calzaghe, when he spent the early part of his career on the undercards of Duff promotions, despite having turned professional as a highly sought-after commodity, courtesy of a stellar amateur career.

Free now of obligations to Duff or any manager, Watson decided to retain his independence, essentially managing himself. He employed a man named Ross Hemsworth as his adviser but, in the main, he would seek and make his own deals. It was maybe the realisation that, after a career which had so far failed to achieve as much as it should have, now was the time for him to take charge of his own destiny, rather than blame others for failing to anticipate his desire to do things differently. He'd watched Benn rebound from a devastating defeat and within a year become even more successful. All the while, he'd see Mendy by his rival's side, making boasts about the boxer's progress and the future. Watson had not had a relationship like that with Duff. It might not have been an issue when he was winning, but it certainly was brought into focus after the McCallum loss. He was convinced he had more to offer to boxing than Benn, had proved it by beating him and yet, in his mind, because of the lacklustre way he was promoted and managed, had no tangible rewards. Watson ached for the glory and respect that comes from being a world champion. Financial reward would follow. Having lost at his first attempt to become a world champion, he decided the time was right for a change. He contacted Barry Hearn, who remains his friend to this day – 'my main man,' says Watson – and struck a deal to appear on a card in Birmingham in November, with his opponent Errol Christie, the former golden boy of British boxing. Christie had turned professional to extraordinary fanfare, because of an almost peerless amateur career. His signature had been coveted by all the top promoters in the country, none of them aware of his major failing – the ability to take a punch. He'd been a pro for seven years but had failed to win a major title. Nevertheless, a fight with Watson had value – did either fighter still have enough left to compete at the highest level? Watson needed an impressive victory to reignite his career and position him as one of the leading middleweights in the country.

Such had been the impact of Benn in his world title victory that his next fight would also be against a big name, in the form of New Yorker Iran 'the Blade' Barkley. Nicknames are sometimes totally inappropriate in boxing, but this wasn't the case with Barkley. He was one of the genuinely hard men of the sport, having traded life on the streets as part of the 'Black Spades' gang in the South Bronx for a life in the ring, most famous for absorbing heavy punishment for two rounds from Thomas Hearns, before knocking out the famous Detroit star. His last two fights had been defeats, though, against another legend, Roberto Durán, and then fellow American Michael Nunn. It wasn't that Barkley couldn't see the signs of his fading from the scene, so much as he couldn't see, period. A detached retina in one of his eyes was diagnosed after the Nunn bout, causing him to miss a year of action. When he began training, he was 60 lb heavier than he had been for his last fight. But Barkley was a name who could bring Hollywood stars like Ryan O'Neal and Tom Selleck to ringside, and that was always an attraction to promoters.

The marketing of Benn remained as important as what he was doing in the ring. Flyers, postcards and t-shirts adorned with his face and ring attire could be found on chairs at the smaller halls of Atlantic City, where Benn had many of his bouts. With Mike Tyson now humbled and the established pay-per-view stars such as Sugar Ray Leonard, Hearns and Durán now nearing the ends of their careers, there was a void that could be filled. Benn, with his aggressive style, was ideally suited to the American market, which had always frowned on the traditional, hands- and head-high approach of European boxers. He might not have been the biggest star in boxing, but there were more than a few people in America who would describe Benn as the sport's most exciting fighter. With that opinion gaining credibility with every thrilling victory, Benn and Mendy knew that another stunning victory could open the doors to big paydays, against the likes of Leonard and Durán. What had started as a mission to get away from it all was snowballing into something much more tangible. As long as Benn wanted to stay in America.

Critics had laughed at Bob Arum when he called his

newest recruit 'the English Hagler'. After beating DeWitt, the sniggering stopped. If DeWitt had been a step up for Benn, then Barkley, albeit after a significant layoff, was a triple jump. The New Yorker had the power to end the Englishman's American adventure. When faced with that kind of danger, Benn's nerves would precipitate a fury that seemed almost out of body. On that night in Las Vegas on 18 August 1990, the champion all but ran from his corner when the first bell rang, his purpose as obvious to the man at the back of the arena as to anyone ringside – to throw an overhand right. If that was amazing, more shocking was Barkley's inability to defend it. It seemed obvious that the left eye which had been injured had not fully healed. With less than thirty seconds gone, Barkley was on the canvas, having taken virtually every one of his opponent's punches flush on the chin. While trying to regain his senses on the canvas, Barkley took more, this time illegal, punishment from Benn. Although Barkley would also fire back later in the round, his inability to block any punches meant it was always a case of when and not if he would lose. Benn would knock him down twice more in the last minute of the first round, enforcing the rule which terminates a fight if one boxer has been floored three times in a round. On all three occasions, Benn appeared either to aim or land a punch at the fallen Barkley, something which can lead to instant disqualification. Veteran referee Carlos Padilla, whose impressive CV ran to officiating 'the Thrilla in Manila', the third fight between Muhammad Ali and Joe Frazier, warned the Englishman, but took no further action. A month later, when asked by *The Ring* magazine why he had hit his opponent when on the floor, Benn answered simply 'Because he was trying to get up'.

Victory secured, Benn then took on the British Boxing Board of Control in a post-fight interview, which lasted longer than expected, because ITV, who had shown the fight live, hadn't bargained on such a short bout. Annoyed at the BBBofC's refusal to recognise the WBO as a sanctioning body for world title fights, Benn looked into the camera and ripped up his licence. Or so it seemed. The licence was in fact part of a box of cereal; on returning home to England he'd sit down with administrators at the BBBofC and present his licence as proof that the act of ripping up a fake had merely been a piece of theatre. All the while, Benn savoured the support of the many vociferous fans who'd crossed the Atlantic. English sport was very much on the up, after England had reached the semi-finals of the football World Cup in Italy, with Paul Gascoigne's tears an indelible image of the year. Now Benn was redefining the stereotype of a British boxer – now he was the man to send to America to do a job, where so many had previously fallen, and hard.

There were two things he now had to confront: who he would fight next and his relationship with Ambrose Mendy. The pair had drifted apart during the period after the Watson defeat, with Benn in America, mostly on his own, while Mendy continued to scheme and sell in Britain. But, as with Watson, the issue that almost always alienates a boxer and his manager is money. Benn had been paid $400,000 for the Barkley win, not a small sum by any means, but after tax and other deductions, namely training costs, the eventual figure would be significantly less. If, as his promoter Bob Arum claimed, he was the most exciting fighter in the world, he wasn't being paid like one. Later that year, the new world heavyweight champion James

Douglas earned just under $25 million when he turned up 20 lb over his best fighting weight and lost his titles to Evander Holyfield. These were sums Benn could only dream of. On the flight back to London after the Barkley victory, he cornered an ITV executive and asked how much their contract had been worth to him and Mendy, who was asleep and unaware of the conversation. The executive told the champion that he'd have to ask Mendy for the full details, such was the confidential nature of the contract. A disgruntled Benn returned to his seat, in his mind the thoughts of why it was he who was doing all the 'fighting and training' but Mendy who had the big house and swimming pool continuing to manifest and increase. Mendy himself says that the relationship began to deteriorate because of his belief that the fighter was using recreational drugs.

They were still together when deciding what to do next. There were options in America, with fading legends Sugar Ray Leonard and Roberto Durán mentioned, along with a potential payday of $5 million. The American experiment had been a success: five fights and five wins in ten months against opposition that was generally of a better standard than he'd faced in England. He'd become a more rounded fighter, learning to be patient when the knockouts didn't come. Such had been the directions in which his and Watson's careers had moved that very few were now calling for a rematch. Positioning himself as one of the sport's most exciting performers, Benn had the world at his feet. However, not everyone was convinced he'd have lasted the distance in the States. Bruce Trampler, Bob Arum's matchmaker, believes Benn would have been swallowed up by the demands of being a world champion in a foreign country. That assertion was based on Benn's emotional make-up – he could be controlled, using his aggression in the right way, but, as he proved against Barkley, when he should have been disqualified, he could still go too far. Despite all his success, the bout against Barkley would be his last in America.

Scene II

The glamour of the States could satisfy most, but the street animal inside Benn responded to a more primeval emotion – he was being called out by Chris Eubank. In Benn's mind, Eubank didn't belong in the same boxing universe as him, so there was no harm in paying a visit back to Britain to sort out a little domestic trouble against a fighter, who, while unbeaten, had not faced the calibre of opposition that he had. This was going to be easy.

Like Nigel Benn and Michael Watson, Christopher Livingstone Eubanks (he dropped the 's' from his surname before he began boxing) was born in London. One of five children, with three older brothers and a sister, Eubank the younger came into the world on 8 August 1966, just days after the greatest moment in English sporting history, the winning of football's World Cup. Although he was born in Dulwich, south London, Eubank would spend the first six years of his life in Jamaica with his maternal grandmother, as his mother and father remained in England saving to buy a house. On returning to the United Kingdom, Eubank would live in various parts of London and showed early signs of being a talented thief. He remembers being given a fearful slap for stealing crisps from a local newsagent while shopping with his mother. Very much a mummy's boy, Eubank's life would take a significant turn for the worse when that maternal influence was removed while he was still young, his mother moving to New York, apparently tired of his father's constant womanising.

The immediate impact of that was Eubank being raised, during his formative years, by his father, a man he described as a 'colourful character'. Despite repeated rebukes from his dad, Eubank was trouble. He was suspended eighteen times in one year from the Thomas Calton Secondary School in Peckham, south London, before being expelled. Reports differ as to why he was always in so much strife – he says that he would normally be drawn into fights with bullies but others suggest that he was also one to initiate brawls because he had developed a love of fighting, born out of having to defend himself at home against three older brothers. Needing to establish himself in the eyes of his siblings, the young Eubank now graduated from stealing sweets and crisps to designer clothes. He would be taken into care by the time he was thirteen, a journey that would take him to Wales and then back to London. The homes didn't work – instead of learning how hard life could be, Eubank used the experience to eat well and chase the girls who were also in care.

After returning from care hardly at all changed, Eubank lived on the streets, having alienated his father. It was around this time that he began running with a gang that specialised in stealing expensive designer clothing, some of which he'd sell, some of which he'd keep and wear. His daily income, he remembers, was generally in excess of

£100, quite a lot of money for the early 1980s. He would eventually get caught attempting to steal six suits but then, having avoided a custodial sentence, Eubank, ever the opportunist, escaped to New York, with his mother wondering what she could do to tame this most unruly of children. The hope was that now, away from his street friends, the impressionable Eubank would find something to channel his energies into. No one could have guessed what that would be; this was a sixteen-year-old who had only so far indicated a fondness for a lifestyle that he had shown no inclination to work for.

Boxing was in the family. Peter Eubanks was a talented featherweight who would inflict the first defeat of Barry McGuigan's career on the Irishman. Young brother Chris says his motivation to enter a gym was to get fit but, almost certainly, the chip on the shoulder that developed after frequently having to fight his corner as the youngest sibling added to Eubank needing to find a way to prove he was the equal of his brothers. Just being a boxer wasn't enough – he had to be one who stood out. As he admits, he lacked the natural ability of a great fighter so therefore focused on becoming a showman.

He stood out in a New York gym because of his accent. By now, the voice that would become as well known as any other aspect of him had changed. Honed by hours of listening to the BBC's World Service, he had manufactured an accent and delivery at odds with anything you'd hear in one of boxing's toughest gyms. Such was the impression he left that British journalists who visit his part of New York are still asked to this day whether they know the man who strutted around their gym thirty years ago.

Dennis Cruz was a super featherweight boxer who would eventually retire after a thirty-one-fight career which saw him fight a handful of world-class opponents. Although a southpaw, it was his style that Eubank attempted to imitate. Cruz was a legend of that New York gym, even if his career became a case of what if. According to Eubank, Cruz had more poise than any fighter he had ever seen but lacked the discipline, something the British man learned from. All the while, Eubank was sparring hard in the gym – legend has it that quite a lot of the best fights in New York take place in those tear-ups when the cameras aren't on and the only spectators are gym rats. Having taken blows from his big brothers all his life, Eubank's innate toughness would earn him respect then, as it did throughout his career.

Even so, Eubank would be stopped by a body punch in his first amateur fight. After that, there would be twenty-five more unpaid contests, six of which he'd lose, the other nineteen victories, culminating in his winning the light middleweight Spanish Golden Gloves title. There is a glory associated with accomplishment in amateur boxing which can rarely be replaced – in general, the endeavours of those involved in amateur boxing are more honest and linked to a love of 'the sweet science'. But in the 1980s it offered no financial reward. Having already established a taste for the finer things in life, Eubank knew a successful professional career was the only way forward. Atlantic City was the venue on 3 October 1985, not long after Eubank had turned nineteen. American Tim Brown was the opponent and Eubank would win a decision after four rounds. He was paid $350 for the fight against an opponent who would fight only one more time. There would be four more bouts in

Atlantic City – Eubank would go the distance in all of them, with the best victory over Eric Holland, a stocky Washington middleweight who would lose thirty-three of his fifty-nine contests but always guaranteed the paying public they would see a decent fight. It was Holland's debut and he was knocked down for the first and only time of his career.

Eubank already had his unique selling point – he'd jump from the ring apron over the ropes, something he'd do for all but his last fight. As Steve Farhood remembers, 'Eubank had presence, even then.' If that remained a constant throughout his career, so did something else. 'He was occasionally in non-action fights,' added Farhood, who commentated on some of those early fights, broadcast on SportsChannel America. Eubank's style was primarily that of a counter puncher – he'd rarely make the first move in any contest, preferring instead to respond to what his opponent would do. During those early years in America, he'd work with a number of trainers, picking up knowledge from all of them. But his primary influence came from his interest in the martial arts. He'd watched and learned from tapes of the great martial artists the ability to keep his distance from an opponent and how to get out of trouble, something he'd need both in the ring and on the rough streets of New York, where he frequently found himself in life-threatening situations. It is a style that is impossible to copy – and not many have tried to. Some, like future featherweight world champion Prince Naseem Hamed, have tried to claim credit for influencing a man eight years his senior. In fact, television footage from one of Eubank's later fights in London show a young Naseem, at ringside, watching in awe the man in the ring holding himself in a way which was like nothing ever seen in a British ring. Those early bouts in America and his initiation in the gyms, where sparring was tougher than one might find in Britain, did much to build the toughness in Eubank, just as it had done in Benn. Surprisingly, Watson, the one fighter of the three whose style most resembled an American boxer, never based himself in the States for any period of time.

The problem with Eubank's particular style was that it had technical flaws. Despite his insistence that he trained as hard as anyone, Eubank was essentially stubborn and hard to change. A case in point is footage of him working out with former undisputed world heavyweight champion Lennox Lewis after both had retired. In the video, Lewis looks stunned at the way Eubank jabs, from distance and leaning in with his body. When Lewis points out that he can jab from closer in, Eubank tells him that he 'can't pivot'. Within seconds, Lewis teaches Eubank how to do just that. The advice, coming from someone who achieved more than any British heavyweight boxer, carries enough weight for Eubank to be persuaded to listen, even if he would never put it to use in the ring. But finding anyone he thought worthy of listening to and learning from during his career was close to impossible.

Eubank's five fights in America had taken him over fifteen months. He'd been combining fighting with studying but also admitted to missing his London family, specifically his brothers. On returning to England, Eubank slipped into the old habits – the shoplifting returned. The knowledge that there was no way for him to escape his past unless he returned to boxing meant he based himself in Brighton, where brothers Simon and Peter trained. It was there that he developed a friendship with Ronnie Davies, a former Southern Area lightweight champion who had become a trainer. Such was Eubank's self-belief that he saw Davies as the man to protect him from the nasty side of the boxing business rather than the person who could transform him from fringe contender to champion. What worked so well about the relationship was that Davies knew his man was so strong-minded that interfering was not part of his agenda. 'When you've got someone with that talent, you've got to step back.'

Eubank would hook up with a local promoter called Keith Miles and convince him to pay him a weekly wage so that he could give up the two jobs he had on the side, working at a fast-food restaurant and a department store. As a newcomer to the British scene, Eubank was not in a position to go to a promoter and earn a contract which paid him enough to concentrate purely on boxing. Like many aspiring pugilists, he had to take other employment to make ends meet.

After nearly a year out of the ring, he returned with a one-round knockout over Darren Parker in Copthorne in Sussex. The following month, he'd beat perennial loser Winston Burnett over six rounds in the same county. More notable was the presence in the crowd of Karron Stephen-Martin, the woman Eubank would fall in love with a few months later.

Eubank retained his unbeaten record over the course of the next twelve months, fighting frequently, most notably against former Benn foe Anthony Logan. While Benn had gone two life or death rounds with the Jamaican, Eubank, apart from a nervous moment in the opening stages, controlled the action and drew notable praise from boxing writers in England, who were starting to talk up the Brighton-based upstart. Eubank now had Benn on the brain. He understood the way self-promotion worked and calling Benn out was one way of getting people to notice him. At the time, Benn was the Commonwealth champion, awaiting a bout with Watson, and no one seriously believed Eubank was ready for such a fight or that he had the right connections for the bout to be made. What they and Eubank didn't know was that the man who would soon become the most powerful player in the sport was on the prowl, looking for someone with the talent to spearhead his empire.

Barry Hearn, the qualified accountant, also had an eye for opportunity. In the 1970s, the east Londoner bought a snooker hall, just as the sport was starting to enjoy an unprecedented boom. Hearn began to manage players, most notably a painfully thin ginger-haired teenager, also from east London, called Steve Davis. It took Hearn five years to help Davis reach the summit of professional snooker, becoming world champion in 1981 for the first time. Davis would win another five championships. Plenty of other players followed into Hearn's stable, impressed by how quickly Davis had become a celebrity. The likes of Ronnie O'Sullivan, Jimmy White and Dennis Taylor have all been managed by Hearn at one time or another.

Snooker wasn't the limit of his ambitions: billing himself as a sports promoter, he'd also been involved in darts, football and boxing. His first foray was putting on Frank Bruno v Joe Bugner at White Hart Lane in 1987. That seized the attention of the establishment, but what was missing from his stable was a Davis, someone who you could gamble on, with the endgame being that person becoming world champion.

Then he laid eyes on Eubank. Hearn was interested in the boxer, who was looking for representation.

'I'd been watching him and saw his fight with Logan and was quite impressed. It was a tough fight to take. At the same time, I got a phone call from Len Ganley, the snooker referee, who told me there was a boxer who wanted to have a meeting with me,' Hearn told me. 'We arranged to meet at the Grosvenor House hotel in Sheffield during the world snooker championships. He swanned in, looking immaculate, as always. Beautiful tracksuit, swagger and his opening words to me were "Before we start, I have to tell you that I'm an athlete and I know my value", so I thought, I like this. I've always liked characters in sport, I think they're almost as important as ability, in terms of marketability. I was impressed with him and we did a deal.' Eubank would be paid £1,200 a month for training expenses under the terms of the contract, which would only be renegotiated if he won a British, European or World title.

There are some relationships in boxing that just seem to work, even if the individuals involved seem slightly mismatched. Despite Muhammad Ali spending the vast majority of his career being represented by a radical black Muslim group, he retained a small white Italian American in the form of Angelo Dundee as his trainer, while Howard Bingham remains Ali's personal photographer. Hearn's East End patter seemed on the face of it to be diametrically opposed to the image of the Renaissance man cultivated by Eubank. But as brave as both might come across, either in the ring or in the negotiating room, both feared failure. Eubank had met most of the players in boxing by the time he sat down with Hearn. 'He probably scared the likes of

Maloney and Warren. They were pure boxing promoters, whereas I've always been a sports promoter. Boxing is a passion but I take a different view, in terms of my tolerance levels, which are a lot higher. I understand that geniuses are different people and we can't expect them to be the same as us,' says Hearn. Or, as one insider told me, Eubank was good for Hearn and Hearn was good for Eubank. Both saw the sport as a place where money could be made. Hearn's involvement in snooker had shown him that for every player who won titles by being professional without being flash, like Steve Davis, for example, there was a need for the showman, like Jimmy White. In Eubank, Hearn thought he had another White, whose act was so unique it would draw in people who were perhaps ambivalent to the allure of the sport.

There would be disagreements between the pair as time passed but, mostly, they saw life in similar terms. One of the few during those early days was the terms of the contract. Eubank was after a retainer which would allow him to train without having to take a second job. He picked up £300 a week, which would help meet the cost of the child he and Karron would welcome into the world in September 1989 (Christopher Junior is now a ranked boxer), but there was another part of the contract with which Eubank wasn't happy. Hearn insisted that the contract be voided if Eubank lost two fights. The boxer wanted that to be reduced to one, such was his belief that nothing could derail his career.

While Eubank would occasionally appear on ITV, the majority of his bouts were broadcast live on a fledgling satellite channel called Screensport, which showed boxing and golf. Hearn was happy to put most of his fights on that channel, even though he wasn't earning huge sums of money from them. 'Although I lost millions, and millions of pounds [in boxing], it set the business up,' said Hearn. The immediate problem for Hearn was how to make that move from small shows to world title shows. During 1989 and then in 1990, there was little to suggest in the quality of opposition that Eubank faced that he was ready to fight someone of Benn's calibre. Names like Hugo Corti, Frankie Moro and Jose Da Silva were unknown even to hardcore boxing fans, but at one of those bouts, against Kid Milo of the Midlands, Hearn brought along Trevor East, a producer and executive at ITV Sport. Hearn had given East the big sell about Eubank and, although there was not much in the way of action, East could see a personality, a presence, something a little different that could keep bums on seats when the TV came on.

Gym talk can fly around the world and can affect a boxer's mindset – in 1989, even though Eubank was toiling at the intermediate level of the sport, he was telling everyone and anyone who would listen that he could beat Benn. By the time Benn had become world champion and Eubank was the holder of the spurious WBC International title, courtesy of his win over Corti, it was looking like a very outlandish claim. But it was having an effect. He'd told *Boxing News* in December 1988 that Benn was a 'coward and a fraud', words he would use to goad Benn for as long as it took to get him in the ring.

What helped him even more was the comment that has flown with Eubank everywhere he has gone. 'Boxing is a mug's game,' he said in a magazine interview in 1990. Or that was how the quote was reported. In full, it read: 'Boxing at a very low level/journeyman level is a mug's game. Taking shots around the head for a pittance is without doubt a thankless task and a mug's game.' The majority in the sport heard or read the abbreviated version and took it as an insult. They had struggled to understand Eubank – 'a boxer with an opinion,' says Hearn – and this quote made up their minds for them. Here was a man biting the hand that fed him. He had also, in the minds of many, insulted the thousands of people who made their living from the sport, along with those who believed in boxing's ability to turn young tearaways into men by installing a sense of discipline into their lives as well as teaching them how to act like men away from the gym. To this day, there are many who have still not forgiven Eubank for his comment. In the early 1990s, boxing in Britain wasn't a sport you could casually be involved with. Generations of families were employed in the business, committed to the communities they worked in as much as they were to making a decent living from it. Only a select few made fortunes from it. They were the ones who felt hurt by Eubank's comment, who could never forgive him for an apparent sound bite that belittled their endeavours. There were also boxers who had slugged away for years, taking and landing punches, accepting fights at a day's notice and not getting paid what they hoped or expected, who could relate to Eubank.

What was immediately clear was that Eubank's comment enhanced his reputation as a dilettante, someone so completely removed from the rest of the industry that he was now essential viewing. In the image-conscious twenty-first century, it is easy to believe that any self-respecting PR company would have apoplexy trying to limit the damage to their client's reputation. Equally, many would have identified with Eubank's position. How was it that so many boxers seemed to do all the work and yet ended up slurring their words and living off benefits, while their promoters sported none of those bruises and seemed to have endless amounts of cash? Eubank never spoke without thought, his utterances calculated to give the appearance of someone different from the crowd. He was convinced that people would pay to see him, whether because of his show or to see him lose. He'd preferred to be loved, but what he desired the most was respect.

On 25 April 1990, Eubank defended his WBC International middleweight title against Eduardo Contreras in Brighton in the kind of fight with which he would become synonymous – there was little in the way of action. It was on that evening that he first became acquainted with the ITV reporter Gary Newbon. The pair would develop a relationship which, over the years, would deliver televised exchanges more interesting than some of the fights under discussion. 'You'll never be world champion if you fight like that,' Newbon told Eubank. 'If that's what your view is, you know nothing about boxing,' the boxer replied. He had won a unanimous decision that convinced no one he could be a future world champion. The only people who still had belief were Eubank, and Hearn. That lack of credibility would suit the pair when it came to negotiating the big fight that they'd face at the end of the year – a challenge for the WBO middleweight title, now held by Nigel Benn. The returning hero might have been in America for most of the last eighteen months, but he knew all about Eubank and his mouth. Because the only fight Eubank wanted was Benn. Ever since he had beaten Logan, Eubank had been nagging away at Benn for a fight. Now that Benn had a world title, the goading became more intense. There were many things that set Eubank apart from other fighters and one of those was his certainty about who he could or could not beat. In 1989, he served as one of Herol Graham's sparring partners as the Sheffield man prepared to fight Mike McCallum for the world middleweight title. Eubank contends that he spent a week chasing Graham round the ring, before finally landing a punch which floored 'Bomber'. Graham says the first punch that Eubank threw put him on the canvas, after which the sparring sessions became so one-sided that Eubank left after a week, chastened by the knowledge that he had found someone more talented and complete than himself. 'He was sick of me. We sparred for a week and at the weekend he went home. He needed a break because he couldn't work me out. He didn't know what I was doing or how I was doing it. He promised never ever to box me for a championship. And he was good to his word,' says Graham.

Eubank did not feel that way about Benn; he'd seen vulnerability in 'the Dark Destroyer' from the moment he first met him. And with every Benn success, he had let it be known that he could beat him. He understood Benn's psyche to the point that he knew a few choice words, be they in print or into a camera, would bring the world champion to the table.

Scene III

September 1990, at a studio in London. Present are Nigel Benn, the WBO middleweight champion, Chris Eubank, challenger for Benn's title on 18 November, Ambrose Mendy,

Barry Hearn, Eubank's promoter, and Nick Owen, presenter of ITV's *Midweek Sports Special.*

A short video of both fighters ends with Eubank knocking out a Brazilian called Renaldo dos Santos and then speaking into the camera.

'*This is why I shall I take you on the night of 18 November. You are mine, you belong to me. I am the man,*' says Eubank.

Back in the studio.

Nick Owen: Nigel Benn, he's talking to you.

Nigel Benn [dressed in a suit, shirt and tie]: Tell him to face me. The thing about him is, he's all hype, he's all hype. I can't wait till 18 November and give him a good, good hiding. You know, he went out there and did a job on the guy. Who is he? Another Sanchez, Gomez, Lopez. Who is he . . . another road sweeper? Hey, I've done that before. Now I'm with the big boys. I'm there, I'm there already. He's got to prove himself, not me.

Nick Owen: Will you prove yourself, Chris?

Chris Eubank [sitting to Benn's right, in a check suit, shirt and tie]: On the particular night in question I will show I have what it takes. This man is nothing but err . . . he's just, err, he's the real hype. I came up the hard way.

Nigel Benn: I proved myself, boy.

Chris Eubank: You've had your time, let's have some parliamentary procedure here, all right? [Benn sighs] I didn't come up the easy way. I came up hard. I didn't have Frank Warren, I didn't have Ambrose Mendy. I came to Barry when I was fourteen and zero.

Nick Owen: What makes you think you can beat Nigel Benn?

Chris Eubank: Because he's just a puncher. He's only got

a puncher's chance. I'm a skillster, I'm a fighter, I can punch as hard as he can. I can box, I can slug. Everything is loaded in my favour for this fight, because in my opinion, although he's a great puncher, he has nothing else apart from that.

Nick Owen: Do you agree with that, Ambrose Mendy?

[Benn mutters, but Mendy answers]

Ambrose Mendy [sitting at the end of the table, to Benn's left]: Not at all. Nigel Benn came up the hard way. We'll find out on the night who's fooling who. In my opinion, Chris Eubank tries to talk as if he came out of some silver spoon society. He's a kid off the street, same as us, and we're going to find out on the night just who's fooling who. In regards to Chris saying boxing is a mug's game, we've got something to show you. It's a piece of our own artwork. Perhaps you'd like to home in on that. [Mendy holds up a poster of a mug with Eubank's face on it. In the studio, Eubank doesn't turn to look at the poster] And I'll say this, a Shakespearean quote for you, young man, to learn. 'How much sharper than a serpent's tooth it is to have a thankless child.' That's from all the professional boxers in the country.

Nick Owen: Barry Hearn, why is this man the boxer they all love to hate?

Barry Hearn [sitting to Eubank's right]: Well, I don't think they do. I think that's a reputation that's been afforded to him by some of the Fleet Street journalists. It takes a bit of time to appreciate Chris Eubank. But having said, I'm not detracting from either fighter, but we have a situation where Nigel Benn fought Michael Watson and Nigel Benn was the unbeaten fighter going in. Chris Eubank now is the undefeated fighter, he's there on merit. He is the man until he's beaten. And, it's going to be a very highly competitive fight between two great athletes. One other point I have to make is Ronaldo dos Santos is not a Gomez, Sanchez or Pedro or whatever. That man had never been knocked out before. In fact, in his professional career of some twenty fights, he'd never visited the canvas.

Nick Owen: Chris, how important is it to you to lay Nigel Benn out on the canvas?

Chris Eubank: That's not important. I've just got to be the man. It doesn't matter whether I knock him out or take him twelve rounds and give him a boxing lesson.

Nick Owen: But why is it so important to beat this particular man?

Chris Eubank: This is the business. This is the business. And I will do what is required on the night. Not only that, if he doesn't extend me, which I'm sure he will, I shall not do anything more than I have to do.

Nick Owen: Why won't you face him tonight?

Chris Eubank: I'll face him in the ring.

Nigel Benn: Any time, any time.

Chris Eubank: You're asking me questions and I'm being polite, I'm looking at your face and answering you. I have nothing to say to Nigel. I find the man intolerable, in fact he's so wild. I have no time for such people, he has no class as far as I see it. About Nigel Benn, I will say this. He's a powerful puncher, a very powerful puncher. Before this, I would like his autograph, because after I've finished with him, he won't be anybody.

Nick Owen: Nigel Benn, will you be anybody after the fight?

Nigel Benn: Ah, yes. The thing about this is, I've seen both sides of the coin. Like I was saying before, after Watson kicked my butt, hey, I got up, brushed myself down, went and fought Quinones, Jorge Amparo, Doug DeWitt, Iran Barkley . . .

Nick Owen: It seems this one is working you up more than any other fight.

Nigel Benn: More than anyone else. I think the public is demanding this. I walk down the street and people say, 'Hey, give this boy a hiding.' I am determined to go out there, firing on all cylinders.

Nick Owen: Well, let's make sure the fight takes place by signing the contract right now. I have to say there seems an element of genuine hate between the two men, Ambrose.

Ambrose Mendy: For sure.

Chris Eubank [Talking while signing the contract]: I don't hate the man, I just want his WBO middleweight title. I pray that I have enough dignity not to hate the man. Hate doesn't come into it for me. Hate destroys the game and makes it look brutal and that's why a lot of people don't take to it. I don't hate the man, I want to take the man's title. I intend to prove I am a better fighter than the man, which I am.

Nigel Benn: I personally do hate him. I personally do hate him.

Nick Owen: So is there any point in asking you two to shake hands?

Nigel Benn: No, no, no.

Nick Owen: Thanks for joining us tonight.

Scene IV

'**H**e insisted that he wanted to fight Eubank,' says Ambrose Mendy about Nigel Benn. Barry Hearn knew there was no need for Benn to entertain Eubank, who did not have an especially high ranking with the WBO. At the time, the number one ranked contender for Benn was an American fighter called Gerald McClellan. In years to come, McClellan would become a household name on both sides of the Atlantic for tragic reasons, but for now he had neither the profile nor the connections to force a bout with Benn. There was no insistence from the governing body that the Englishman had to defend his title against the American. 'They didn't have to take the fight,' says Hearn. What amazed him even more was that the contract that was signed that night on *Midweek Sports Special* contained no provisions for a rematch or any options that would keep Benn in the loop if he lost. 'I was waiting for a phone call from a smart operator like Bob Arum for options, but it never came,' added Hearn. 'But Arum listened to Ambrose too much.'

That televised contract signing added more publicity to the fight. Nick Owen, who was the presenter for the segment that was pre-recorded, says that even though both boxers were cordial before the cameras were switched on, once they were sitting next to each other the atmosphere changed. 'There was genuine menace in the air. I felt it, the cameramen felt it, so did the producers and the floor managers,' says Owen, who, even as an experienced presenter, remembers sweating quite a lot as the hostility grew. 'Eubank never looked at Nigel during the ten minutes – that arrogance wound Benn up even more.' Benn agrees. 'He didn't look at me – as if I was beneath him. That just switched something on in me. I just wanted to jump on him and fight him right there and then! We both disliked each other with a passion.'

'He just came from nowhere and all of a sudden he's challenging me!' says Benn. 'I wasn't thinking about him and then he's shouting his mouth off. Maybe Barry Hearn had something to do with that. The next minute, I'm fighting a guy with a cane, who wears a monocle, driving a juggernaut! He was a dapper dresser, I'll give him that. He'd wear a suit and it would fit him like a glove. But he [came across] as a man who felt like the Queen should live in Hove and he should be in Buckingham Palace. He didn't like the way I conducted myself and I didn't like the way he conducted himself. He called me a "ragamuffin" and looked down on me.' Benn would also admit that it was one of the few times in his life that he fought someone he genuinely hated. With a passion.

A wound-up Benn was what Eubank wanted. He believed he could beat the champion, who was being encouraged by most of the general public to silence the challenger. There were other things that Eubank said about him that went beyond the normal pre-fight braggadocio. He labelled Benn a 'fraud' and accused him of not being genuine. Eubank didn't know Benn well enough to elaborate on why he labelled him as such. It was all part of the hype, a game that, despite his protestations about the sport and the nasty side of it, which he abhorred, Eubank was happy to play. The majority of pre-fight insults are usually about the opposition's ability; when the taunts become personal, bad things can happen. In 1971, Joe Frazier, the then world heavyweight champion, fought Muhammad Ali in what is generally considered the greatest fight in boxing history. The occasion would have been big enough, given that these were two unbeaten fighters and Ali was a former champion who lost his titles and his freedom because he had refused to enlist in the US Army, then engaged in the Vietnam War. Spice was added by Ali calling Frazier 'an uncle Tom'. Frazier could put up with the references to his looks, which weren't flattering, but being accused of betraying the black man was the ultimate insult.

Being called a fraud probably hurt Benn the most. To this day, he says of himself, 'What you see is what you get'. What also agitated him was the knowledge that both came from similar backgrounds. Both had several dominating elder siblings and both were in trouble a great deal in their teens. In order to reform themselves, both needed to flee the nest – Benn to the army, Eubank to New York – and both those moves came about after a degree of parental intervention. While Benn mixed with the rich and famous once he was in the limelight, he never sought it. Eubank, though, quickly became the darling of the chat shows, guaranteeing engaging television through his controversial views and his unique delivery. Being in the spotlight was what he wanted, although it was an effort for him. More than one television presenter told me that, before interviews, Eubank would ask what a certain word meant before he used it. And more than one fighter confirmed that the accent was manufactured, that Eubank could, in private, speak with just a hint of West Indian patois. Those in boxing knew that and more than a few felt that Eubank was the real fraud. The resentment grew further at seeing him placed in a world title fight – he may have been unbeaten after twenty-four fights, but he was where he was because he could talk a good game. Eubank believed that he had got the better of Benn during that TV exchange and that it was the first step towards victory, but Benn genuinely did not see what Eubank had that could hurt him. That one-punch knockout of dos Santos was highlight reel stuff but the opposition was of the calibre that Benn had been fighting two years before. You could make a case that Benn's previous two victories had been against fighters tailored to his style, but there was nothing resembling the quality of those fighters on Eubank's record. The promotion title for the fight may have been 'Who's Fooling Who?' but the questions being asked were aimed almost entirely at Eubank. How would he cope the first time he was hit? Did he have the stamina to go twelve hard rounds? And was he the master boxer he professed to be? If his aim was to reduce Benn to the whirling, fevered slugger who punched himself out against Watson, it was surely a miscalculation. And there were concerns about Eubank's own fitness. He spoke openly about his dedication to the trade he despised, but it was also common knowledge that he loathed roadwork, preferring hard sparring as a way to hone his body to the peak of fitness. The science of training a fighter may have changed, but the early morning runs remain an integral part of conditioning. By his own admission, Eubank felt he did not need a trainer, having learned all he wanted during those days in New York. So it was pointless on Ronnie Davies's part to try to change too much – the old 'pit bull', as he was lovingly nicknamed by Reg Gutteridge, might make a suggestion or two, but mostly he was good company for Eubank.

The contracts for the fight specified that Eubank would be paid £100,000. Benn would receive four times as much.

It was promoted by Hearn's Matchroom company and he admits now that he didn't make any money out of what was the first all-British world middleweight title fight. In 1981, he had staked a large amount of money on the development of Steve Davis and was rewarded when 'the Nugget' won the first of six world titles. By his calculation, he had also invested heavily in Eubank, to the tune of around a quarter of a million pounds. 'A lot of money in comparison to what my business was worth,' says Hearn. 'We were losing a lot of money . . . the Benn fight was the gamble of all the investment we had in boxing. There does come a time when if you're going to get your investment back or you're going to justify further investment that you have to show what you're got.'

What helped to convince Hearn to take the gamble was his view on what would happen when the two met. 'Eubank fancied the fight, I fancied the fight. Styles have always made fights. I was convinced he was going to win. Ambrose was equally convinced that Nigel would win. But Eubank is one of the best counter punchers that's ever lived and Nigel always came forward. He was made for Chris.'

The NEC Exhibition Centre in Birmingham, one of the favoured venues for boxing outside the capital, was chosen, with alternative locations in London unavailable. The arena was filled to its 12,000 capacity, something that some boxing purists struggled to understand or applaud. John Rodda wrote in the *Guardian* on the eve of the bout: 'Although Benn's World Boxing Organisation title is at stake, the WBO is not recognised by the British Boxing Board of Control and not regarded seriously by anyone other than fighters, managers, promoters and TV executives . . . The hyperbole has undoubtedly succeeded, for the arena, which has a 12,000 capacity, is almost sold out and ITV are paying to screen the fight live; a dozen countries are also taking the broadcast in some form or other. There can be no doubt that the protagonists and their agents have been highly successful in drawing attention to the event, but whether they can match expectations is doubtful.'

There was every chance that Eubank could find himself out of his depth and be overwhelmed in one round, just like Iran Barkley and others, given the dramatic rise in the quality of his opposition. But he didn't lack belief in his ability – he had already shown that by telling Arum he had the talent to beat another world champion, Mike McCallum. Talent-wise, McCallum was a cut above Benn, but lacked that concussive power that can end a fight in a blink. Rodda, and others, felt that if the challenger could avoid those punches for the first half of the bout, victory could be his by points or a late stoppage. The problem for Eubank, one which surfaced throughout his career, was making the weight. Like Benn, he stood no taller than 5 foot 10 inches, but his frame was naturally wider. When not in training, his normal weight was about 13 stone and the fact that his roadwork consisted of jogging, not running, meant that he shed weight a lot more slowly than most boxers. But it would not be his weight that would play a pivotal role in this fight.

Back in the 1990s, fighters weighed in on the morning of the bout, as opposed to the day before, which is how things are done now, in order to let the fighters hydrate. On the morning of his fight with Eubank, Benn woke up at around 6.30 a.m. to find he was over 6 lb heavier than the middleweight limit. He'd been locked away in a hotel in

Birmingham and to this day has no idea how he managed to put the weight on.

'I was just eating fruit and watching *On the Waterfront* with Marlon Brando and when I got on the scales, I was twelve stone dead!' he says now. Others have suggested to me that there may have been something else that distracted him from his training schedule. But it's hard to believe that, given his honesty about everything he did during that period of his life, Benn would not be truthful about anything in his life during that time. The problem for Benn and his advisers, then, was how to take the weight off without anyone knowing.

'Mendy had asked me if he could use a gym' says Gary Newbon, the ITV reporter for the fight who was also commentating on a live football match for the network. The gym was called Stocks and was located near Aston University. Mendy didn't tell Newbon what they needed the gym for and, with the reporter 100 miles away in Liverpool, the secret was safe. But there was a deadline for Benn to make the weight – he had until midday to shed over 6 lb or face the possibility of losing his title – in those days the belt was forfeited if the champion was unable to defend his title because of weight. So at Stocks he ran three furious miles on the treadmill, fully clothed, to lose two of the pounds, he shadow-boxed in a steam room, clothes still on, for forty-five minutes, to lose another two. By the time of the weigh-in, Benn was actually a quarter of a pound under the limit, but his team were concerned at how much work the champion had got through with less than ten hours to go till the fight. He was struggling to rehydrate and so began a concerted campaign to put the challenger off, using tactics that would be difficult to repeat in the modern era. Towels and ice were removed from Eubank's dressing room – standard provisions for a trainer and cutman before a fight. Mendy also managed to get himself into the Eubank dressing room before the fight and act as an unofficial WBO representative, watching the wrapping of tape on the challenger's hands and checking the height of the protectors worn under the boxer's shorts. The Benn camp still had a stroke to pull before the two fighters came face to face in the ring.

On the undercard, new met old as Michael Watson took on Errol Christie in his first fight since losing to McCallum in April. This wasn't the way it was supposed to be. Watson had expected to be the headline act by now, courtesy of that win at Finsbury Park, but in the eighteen months since, fate had contrived to put him back to where he had been before that victory. With his relationship with Mickey Duff coming to an end, Watson had sought assurances from other promoters. Barry Hearn outlined a strategy for him to fight for a world title; he visualised a victory for Eubank against Benn in the main event later that night with Watson becoming his main challenger the following year. That plan helped appease Watson who admitted that watching Benn rise from the ashes and reinvent himself had tested his faith. He knew that Benn had no need for a rematch with him and his resentment wasn't with his fellow fighter but with the nature of the sport. That, despite all he'd done on the way up, he felt like he had to start all over again. One of boxing's oldest and cruellest adages is that you're only as good as your last fight. In Watson's case, that meant he was a failed challenger who'd come up short at the highest level. Benn was, on current form, the most exciting fighter in Britain and Eubank the most enigmatic. Whether he liked it or not,

Watson needed a new sales pitch, a chance to re-establish himself as the best of the bunch. That journey would start in Birmingham that night.

Watson was only two years younger than Christie but his mind and body were at least ten years younger. Christie had once been the golden boy of British boxing, but five knockout defeats had left his confidence all but shattered, while trying to meet the expectations he'd set himself during an outstanding amateur career had taken its toll. By now, Christie had gone from prospect to opponent, being used as a sparring partner by, among others, Eubank. He was floored within the first minute by Watson, before being stopped in the third round. Given that he hadn't fought for over seven months, Watson looked very impressive. Job done, Watson took his place at ringside to watch the main event.

'Who did you want to win?' I asked him years later.

'Is that a difficult question?' he replied.

'Benn?'

'That's right.'

Eubank's preparation in his dressing room had been almost perfect. He had arrived at half six, surprisingly early for someone renowned for his tardiness. Promoters, trainers and reporters would get used to Eubank almost never being on time for any appointment for years to come. His routine involved massaging his feet and then insisting on trainer Ronnie Davies singing. After the referee came in to give him the fight rules – a legal obligation – Mendy would arrive to supervise the taping of the boxer's hands. Eubank brushed Mendy off, telling him that he could appreciate what he was doing for Benn but that it would be to no avail.

As befits tradition, the challenger Eubank entered the

arena first. It soon became apparent that the Benn camp had more up their sleeve. Since he had joined Hearn's Matchroom stable, Eubank had entered arenas to the sound of Tina Turner's 'Simply the Best' (an idea first suggested to him by Hearn's wife). That night was no exception, but for the fact that when Eubank got to within fifty yards of the ring the music stopped. Hearn, suspecting this was no accident, rushed to the studio where the music was coming from. 'I whacked someone upstairs – the only person who was calm was Eubank. I was foaming at the mouth!' says Hearn. Though always denied by Mendy, it has been claimed that at his insistence, the sound operator had been told to play half of Eubank's music before shredding the tape. Hearn was talked back into the ring by Eubank and the team headed for their date with destiny, the challenger still looking imperious. This was the moment he had waited for his whole adult life; rather than being daunted by it, he was soaking it up, putting himself in a position to seize the day. None of the stuff attempted by Mendy stopped Eubank, who was wearing a white poncho and matching shorts, from vaulting into the ring (more than one member of the press has told me that they secretly hoped he'd slip and fall on his behind) or stalking the canvas with his gloves by his side. What was also apparent was that, for all the talk about him being a divisive hate figure, Eubank wasn't booed much on his way in and many even cheered when he jumped the rope.

Seconds after entering the ring, the sound of drums could be heard, followed by the sight of members of Benn's former army regiment coming into view. Despite the energy he had expended earlier in the day, Benn jogged to the ring, clad in a black sequined jacket and shorts. Once in, he eyeballed

Eubank, looking desperate to get as close to the challenger as possible. As if the hype for the bout hadn't been rich enough, especially after the pair's contract signing, Benn had stoked things up even further the day before the fight by announcing he'd retire if he lost. Conversely, Eubank had let it be known that he had bet £1,000 at 40-1 to knock Benn out in the first round. After the introductions, both men were invited to the centre of the ring to be given the fight instructions by American referee Richard Steele. Benn, snarling, moved forward, but was made to wait by Eubank, who, hands by his side, finally strutted to Steele's right. When asked to touch gloves, Eubank left his right hand low, and it was smacked hard by the champion, whose facial expression had never softened.

As the timekeeper prepared to ring the first bell, Eubank once again reverted to pose – this time, both arms crossed, the right slightly above his waist. Again, Benn just glared. At ringside, a nervous Hearn turned to Benn's promoter Bob Arum and told him, 'You know you're fucked, don't you?' Arum asked why. 'Because you haven't got any options,' replied Hearn.

As convinced as he was that his man would win, so was Mendy. Something had to give.

Scene V

'Chris Eubank was the kind of man you'd want with you in the trenches, if things were going bad. Tough, tough man'

– former world super featherweight challenger
Jim McDonnell

'Let's just say Nigel Benn enjoyed his job'
             – TV presenter, commentator and interviewer
                                      Jim Rosenthal

Once the introductions were over, this was a fight that oozed tension. Noise from the crowd was occasional, and when it came, loud. But everyone there, and that includes fans, reporters, fighters and trainers, remembers it as a night full of tension. 'Television neutered the event. It cut out the atmosphere which enveloped the ring,' wrote Harry Mullan, editor of the trade paper *Boxing News*. The fans, the bulk of whom followed Benn, were nervous, as they always were before one of his bouts. 'The Dark Destroyer's' vulnerability, exposed against Logan, Watson and, in his last fight, against Barkley, meant he always seemed a punch away from defeat. That small band of supporters chanting Eubank's name had no real idea how good their man was – but they probably suspected that he had a chance. But Eubank hadn't demonstrated in his previous fights that he had the ability or stamina to take a fight by the scruff of the neck and control the tempo. As he had been on the street, as a pickpocket, Eubank was an opportunist, seizing the moment and maximising it. That's why his knockout of Renaldo dos Santos had become such a defining point of his career – winning in twenty seconds hadn't been as impressive as the pose he gave to the camera in the corner, with the stricken fighter also in shot. 'Most fighters are great actors, performers' says Nick Owen. Few enjoyed the theatre as much as Eubank because his mind was set up to take advantage of any time the camera was pointed in his direction. That clarity of thought was a massive advantage in the ring as well.

Future Olympic 100 metres champion Linford Christie and Frank Bruno were just a couple of the 150 or so sporting celebrities in attendance. The televised contract signing between Benn and Eubank, and the subsequent replays of the snarling and goading between the pair, had piqued the interest of the general public. So many fights seemed to involve one boxer playing the role of the straight man and the other the instigator. Here, both men seemed to take turns in trying to unsettle the other. 'We worked the crowd,' Benn would say years later, but in 1990 there was no collusion in order to hype up the fight. Their mutual dislike and antipathy had transferred into true box-office theatre. Benn, so full of hate, was obviously irked by his opponent, whose cold but articulate demeanour was superficially the very opposite of his. They were both men of the street, but while Benn had taken to them to try to rid himself of an inner fury, Eubank's personal circumstances had offered him very few options. At the time, little of this was common knowledge. What sold the fight was the placing of these two men against each other, the furious Benn, back from his American adventure to take care of some domestic trouble. But the trouble wasn't in the form of the honest and dedicated professional Watson, or even the dancing Herol Graham, but in the strutting and pontificating Eubank, who you sensed wound Benn up before he'd even said a word. The weight of public opinion was behind Benn – people generally didn't like Eubank and they wanted him silenced. They identified with Benn's anger.

These were unsettled times for the country, with rising unemployment and inflation and Benn, his scowling and snarling, whether he knew it or even liked it, had come to represent the maligned and frustrated who wanted their boxing to be violent and quick. They couldn't see past the fact that Benn actually had more in common with the Thatcher principle of 'go get yours'. Here was a man from a modest background who had managed to turn his life around by finding a sport which catered to his ability and then rebounded from his first setback to become even more successful. Those same people probably couldn't work out Eubank and the apparent hypocrisy of making a living out of something he so openly disdained. And yet there was another class of fan who enjoyed Eubank for what he offered – entertainment. He didn't fight with the energy and electricity of Benn, but at least he had an act. He dared to be different and in every generation there is a percentage of people who can identify with that desire to stand out, to make their own way, while paying scant regard to authority. At the start of the nineties, with the country in recession, with the message being sent out that things weren't necessarily going to get any better any time soon, Eubank offered a little escapism, some theatre that you didn't expect to find in a boxing ring. Those fans began as a minority, not nearly as vocal as the followers of Benn, but just as loyal. And when Eubank told them he was the superior boxer, they believed him, turning what seemed like a mismatch into a contest you had to watch either in person or on TV. Around twelve million, nearly a fifth of the population, would turn on for the fight, believing something special would take place that evening. And they had to pick a side. Both boxers had such strong personalities that they urged you to choose one. There could be no middle ground.

The fight began, as expected, with Benn following the

challenger around the ring, in a clockwise circle. That itself was a dangerous policy, with Eubank, in theory, travelling in the direction of Benn's venomous right hand. But the challenger was not in survival mode – he might have been in retreat for most of the opening round, but it was his counter punches, mainly with his own right hand, that scored the points. On a couple of occasions, it seemed that he might have stunned Benn, but the round ended with the challenger establishing his jab and also demonstrating his power. Screensport commentator Dave Brenner accurately summarised the round: 'Definitely the challenger's.'

Brenner got to know Eubank as well as most during the beginning and interim period of his career: 'He is a lovely guy, but could never be told.' Indeed, after the round ended, Eubank, rather than return to his corner, strolled around the ring, gloves cupped at his waist. At the urging of cornerman Davies, he finally sat down, but the posing did him little good. He spent the majority of the second round swallowing leather, including a right hand which nearly lifted him off the ground. Although he stunned Benn at the end of the stanza with a left hook, the cleaner and harder punches had come from the champion. Eubank would later admit that he feared the pace of the first two rounds such that, for the first time in his career, he considered he might have to take a count. Even when he had Benn in trouble, Eubank didn't really go in for the finish, wary that the champion had a reputation for exaggerating the danger he was in, before landing a potentially concussive blow.

The third round saw Benn concentrate his attack on Eubank's mid-section. 'I'm worried that Chris doesn't take a great body punch,' said TV analyst Barry McGuigan. In the majority of the exchanges, Benn's power seemed superior – but it was also obvious that Eubank could take the punishment. Both men talked to each other throughout, but for much of this period the challenger's words were more prolific than his punches. Even a late flurry, which included an uppercut that rocked Benn's head back, wasn't enough to swing the fight in Eubank's favour. But he had done something which, intentionally or not, would later prove pivotal.

By the end of the third round, Benn's left eye was swollen and seemed about to close. 'He got me with a thumb – and that hurt! It was like someone had pricked me with a needle. It was sending pain to my brain . . . it was killing me, killing me,' Benn told me. In the early twentieth century, an American middleweight called Harry Greb became as famous for his whirlwind punching style as he did for his ability to use the heel and lace on his gloves to wound his opponent. The tactic was so routinely employed in that era that Greb would partially lose the sight of both his eyes because of opponents out for some measure of revenge. The problem for Benn was that only partial vision in his left eye meant he could not see the Eubank right hand.

Benn could play the dirty tune as well – many of his body punches were only just about legal and some were clearly hurtling too close to Eubank's groin. But those punches weren't the ones that caused Eubank the most distress in the fourth round. 'We were in a clinch . . . and when you are in a clinch you actually put your head over your opponent's shoulder. When you do that and drop your head, your jawbone automatically opens. And when your jawbone opens, your tongue slips between your teeth,' Eubank remembers. At that stage, the challenger was weary, having absorbed numerous painful body punches. He was in the clinch, seeking rest. But Benn bobbed and rolled out of the clinch and landed a tremendous uppercut. 'And there was a half-inch gash in my tongue,' continues Eubank. It gave him a number of problems. The tongue was now a liability, causing him huge pain and also forcing him to swallow blood in steady amounts. He knew that if either his corner or the referee discovered his predicament, the fight would be stopped. It looked bad enough for him at the end of that fourth round, after absorbing nearly a dozen hooks to his abdomen which left him so disorientated that he nearly went to the wrong corner. It looked now, finally, as if one fighter had established dominance – but the champion's left eye was now closed and he was, because of the ridiculous weight fiasco less than twelve hours earlier, operating on less than a full tank of gas. McGuigan, who is rarely wrong about much in boxing, would say at the start of the fifth, 'This is all down to who is the fittest.'

Round five was the first that saw both men fight as if they had been in war – both were more circumspect and less willing to go to the trenches. This suited Eubank, whose superior boxing ability on the retreat meant he was able to hit and not get hit as Benn took a breather, his work rate conspicuously low. The eye looked worse and worse, so bad that today it could well have forced a stoppage. Benn's corner, including Vic Andretti and veteran cutman Percy Armstrong, were unable to do anything to prevent the swelling increasing and the fight was turning slowly in Eubank's favour.

It's at such moments that boxers have to find something within that defines them, not just for one evening, but for the rest of their careers. Labelled a quitter when floored by a jab from Michael Watson, Benn now had the chance to erase all questions about his mentality. Boxing is a natural haven for bullies and his attitude before and during fights fitted the profile of one. As Eubank would say many years later, the force of Benn's intimidation could beat 90 per cent of those who stepped into the ring with him. But now, nearly halfway through this contest, the scowl had been replaced by a squint. His face disfigured, could Benn find another way to victory?

In the other corner, Eubank himself was hardly fresh, but his countenance remained implacable. His gift for theatre was an advantage – he had absorbed numerous hard punches but had yet to give Benn an indication that one more punch was all that was required to finish matters. Benn thrived on fear and he had yet to find it in his opponent. Eubank's strategy since the fight was signed was to show as little weakness as possible. He'd refused to make eye contact when they were in a studio together and even now, with blood pouring from his split tongue down his throat, he made every effort to remain, at least on the outside, stoical and unbowed.

Round six was another going Eubank's way until Benn dug a body punch below the belt. Referee Steele gave the challenger a minute to catch his breath – and he would spend the remainder of the round being chased around the ring by an energised Benn, who, advised by Andretti, concentrated on the body attack. As the bell rang, it was still not obvious who held the destiny of victory or defeat in their fists. Benn's face looked worse, but the body language from Eubank wasn't great. He may have loathed the sport, but he knew the history of great champions digging deep, even in situations where they couldn't win. Muhammad Ali going twelve hard rounds against Ken Norton, at least half of them with a broken jaw, knowing he'd lose the decision, or Sugar Ray Leonard, with one eye closed, stopping Thomas Hearns in the fourteenth round of a contest which had seen the latter dominate for large portions. Although never in their class, Eubank was, like Ali and Leonard, at times regarded as a maverick, someone who danced to his own tune, rather than the one played at every gym, arena or small hall. What critics of Ali and Leonard would always agree on was the toughness of both men and their willingness to take their bodies over the edge in search of victory. Neither ever sought a way out when things were too tough.

The seventh would be another test, for both men. The first minute showcased Benn's murderous body attack. This wasn't mindless aggression, but a strategy calculated to expose Eubank's one real weakness. He could take punches to the head without too much inconvenience, but he'd attempt to evacuate the area when the blows connected further south. All the time, though, he was thinking about how to hit back. A right-left combination stunned Benn, who with eye closed, suddenly looked beaten. But the doubts about Benn's courage, based entirely on his performance against Watson, had been erased. Maybe it had been too easy to admit defeat to Watson, a man Benn liked and respected. As each round passed against Eubank, with Benn's face looking more and more contorted, you began to realise that quitting against this man was anathema to the champion. While Eubank needed the victory and title as a guarantee that his standard of living would improve, Benn saw victory here as proof of his reputation, most of which he had recovered after beating DeWitt and Barkley.

'People have been asking questions of Benn's chin but I think he's answered a few of them tonight,' said McDonnell in the commentary box at the end of the seventh, as replays showed just how hard he had been hit in the seventh by Eubank's left-right combination. The next round would be Benn's best – he boxed with Eubank, before chasing him round the ring and knocking him to the floor with an overhand right. The authenticity of the fall was instantly challenged by Eubank, who pleaded with referee Steele that he had slipped. That he was able to make such a coherent argument was proof that he probably had slipped. But the knockdown was also proof that, in choosing to train himself, his footwork had suffered and was naturally poor. When the punch hit the top of his head, his legs were as far apart as they could be without being in the splits position. Knockdowns are awarded when a punch's impact sends a man to the floor, and this was just such an occasion. At the end of the round, Benn decided to imitate Eubank's strut, which simply spurred the challenger on to do what only he could do. It drew a roar from the crowd, but others, around the world, were less impressed. 'A lousy fight – two guys posing,' were the words of American boxing magazine *KO*.

By the end of the eighth round, Benn led, by virtue of that knockdown, by a point on two of the judges' scorecards and trailed by a point on the other. With a quarter of the fight left, the challenger needed to stop his opponent, or win at least three of the four remaining rounds.

'This is the sort of fight that makes you an old man,' said McGuigan midway through the ninth round. Defence, which had been, for the most part, neglected throughout, was now dismissed entirely. That suited Eubank, who was a step quicker than the champion, landing jabs at will. Benn's eye was looking more vulnerable than ever and on more than one occasion the champion seemed uncertain of his balance, as if fatigue had finally set in. Eubank knew it – he set Benn up with a series of jabs, before landing a right hand that left the champion defenceless. On previous occasions, when Eubank had hurt Benn, he hadn't followed up with relentless attacks. This time he did. There were less than thirty seconds remaining of the round and Benn didn't even have the strength to hold Eubank in a clinch. With ten seconds to go, Eubank threw a straight right hand which not only hurt Benn, but also forced him into a neutral corner. With Steele looking on closely, Eubank threw a flurry of punches, which Benn absorbed, but for the first time that night didn't retaliate. In truth, both men were at the point of exhaustion, but having taken Benn's best and survived, and having had a plan to take the champion into the later rounds and then administer the final blows, Eubank was undeniably in control. What he needed now was for the referee to decide that Benn was no longer able to continue.

Richard Steele was regarded as the most high-profile and competent referee in the sport at the time, but his reputation had been called into question earlier that year when he refereed an amazing world junior welterweight unification title fight between Julio César Chávez and Meldrick Taylor. Taylor had dominated the feared Mexican and needed only to survive the last round to claim a points victory. With sixteen seconds remaining, Taylor was floored.

Like Benn, Taylor's face was a mess, even though he had had the better of much of the fight. After giving Taylor a mandatory eight count, Steele looked into the fighter's eyes and decided, with just five seconds remaining on the clock, to stop the fight. In the opinion of most, Chávez would not have had time to get across the ring and land another punch but Steele defended himself by saying his job was only to safeguard a boxer's future and enable him to fight another day. With Benn apparently defenceless against Eubank, Steele stopped this fight with just two seconds remaining of the ninth. Benn complained, but mostly out of despair. He knew his race was run that night.

Eubank turned away and sank to his knees, congratulated within seconds by Davies. In time, Eubank would say this was his greatest night as a professional fighter, but he had to pay a terrible price. His ribs were bruised, his left eye was also swollen. 'Nigel smashed him around . . . Chris urinated blood for days afterwards,' said Hearn. Even so, Eubank, as he had during the fight, still had his wits about him. He remembered he had promised himself that, having answered all the questions about his courage and fortitude, if he did win the title he would himself ask one question.

'Karron, can we get married now?' Eubank said into the camera as he was being interviewed by Gary Newbon. Hearn had encouraged the boxer to take the plunge. Eubank could not hear the word yes coming from his future wife, who wasn't at ringside. The new champion was fulsome in his praise of Benn, saying he'd extended him in ways he didn't think possible as well as lauding his ability to take a punch. Usually ebullient when faced with a Newbon interrogation, Eubank was short of words, admitting he was in too much pain. That would be softened by the knowledge that he had earned every penny of his £100,000 purse and could look forward to earning more.

'The show made no money,' said Hearn. 'But we walked away with a clean title and that's what the investment was all about. It was an amazing evening.' Others who had seen more top-quality action than Hearn were even more effusive in their praise. 'I don't think I've ever seen two men with a more intense will to win. How much should you pay a man to bare his soul? Because that is what Benn and Eubank did, in the most thrilling contest I have ever watched in a British ring,' said Harry Mullan.

More than twenty years on, there are still revisionist theories about the fight. On an edition of Sky Sports' excellent *Ringside* programme, Eubank stated that he beat Benn that night because the loser came in angry. I prefer Benn's rationale. 'It was his night. He was the better man.' Eubank had needed to be. As Hearn admits, it was the biggest and most important night for his boxing promotion. He had invested heavily in Eubank and, with no options for a rematch if his man lost, there was every chance that both of them would have been in the wilderness. In victory, Eubank claimed he had achieved 'exoneration'. Maybe, but he also now had the freedom to call the shots, to dictate to those who he felt made the sport 'a mug's game'. Promoters may be the most consistently powerful force in the sport, but fighters, especially ones with as forceful and unique a personality as Eubank, could also hold sway. As champion, Eubank could decide who he would fight and when. And on his list of future opponents was Watson, whose victory over Christie had been destructive enough to make him a viable contender. If Eubank and Watson were on the up, then Benn had to climb the mountain again. Some doubted whether he could. 'Today's hero is tomorrow's opponent,' said Harry Mullan, insinuating that Benn's world title aspirations were now at an end. Certainly, the task of rebuilding his reputation would be harder than it was after the loss to Watson. That defeat was put down to overconfidence; this latest defeat seemed to represent a truer reflection of Benn's abilities, in that when the opponents didn't go down after the first punch, he did not possess enough tools to find victory. Not yet, anyway.

Sifting through the millions of words said about the fight, most of them Eubank's, it became apparent that the Brighton man lived the fight, then and now, as some kind of theatrical experiment, oblivious to the stakes involved, probably because he won. He had not spent the whole of the fight looking like the winner. A tongue nearly sliced in half, a face bruised and swollen, with pain etched on his features every time Benn dug a punch into his stomach: he looked like a winner when, after wincing, he carried on. That was something that most of Benn's opponents did not do. A much more accurate reflection of Eubank's state of mind and of the warrior within came when he spoke to Jonathan Rendall afterwards about the moment he had first laid eyes on Benn, when the pair locked eyes during referee Steele's final instructions: 'In the ring I looked at him and saw a relentless savage. But I also saw a man with a slight doubt in his mind. I saw that when he looked into my eyes he needed reassurance. I thought: "It's too late for that, mate. You're mine."'

That's how fighters operate. They look for weakness, perceived or not. They smell it and then try and seize it on the night. Eubank was on the point of exhaustion for most of the night but that sign of weakness at the start was what kept him going, what made the pain seem worth it. And the brutality of what he did had not escaped him: 'In the ninth I hit him with a right hand to the side of the jaw and his legs went. He went back and I knew there was no power left. I measured him and whacked him. He came off the ropes but I'd broken his spirit. No more resilience left. Right hand, straight left, right uppercut, left hook . . . the referee steps in.'

It's why Eubank is loved and loathed in equal measure. Because he thinks like a fighter. But he'd like you to believe that he doesn't.

Chris Eubank had always wondered why there wasn't a photograph of him on the walls of the Matchroom offices in Brentwood. He was told it was because he wasn't a world champion. A few weeks after he beat Benn, Eubank walked back into that Essex office and found a suitable place to hang his picture.

Nigel Benn cried after he lost to Watson, but the defeat to Eubank evoked even more emotion. He immediately announced his retirement and apologised to his fans in the arena. The retirement wouldn't last long, but, even now, the hurt remains. 'He beat me fair and square,' he told me. 'But losing to someone like him was just awful . . . it was hard to swallow, to tell you the truth. Really, really hard.'

There was a moment while we talked about the fight when Benn misunderstood me. He felt that I insinuated he had been knocked down in the fight. (I didn't think I had, but arguing my point didn't seem wise.) 'Did I get knocked down? Did I get knocked down? I've got to make sure you get that right, because I know I didn't get knocked down! I remember that – I didn't go down. Change that!'

Yes, of course the hate was real then. It's real now. Benn would spend the next three years chasing a rematch that he felt would offer one more chance for redemption. He'd tell me that, years after they'd both retired, Eubank approached him about doing an exhibition, in order to make some easy money. 'Chris, I can't do exhibitions with you,' he had replied.

Nigel Benn's reign as world champion had lasted 203 days, but a much longer stay of office came to an end later that month when Margaret Thatcher resigned as prime minister after eleven years, the longest tenure of a British premier in the twentieth century. Both fighter and politician had reputations as bullies. And both, it seemed, were finally undone by words. While Eubank had prodded away at Benn with little digs about his manner and how he'd probably have been a bouncer with several illegitimate children but for boxing, so Margaret Thatcher was finally undermined by the words of one of her most loyal servants, Geoffrey Howe, who turned on her just days before her resignation. The argument between the pair had been about Europe and Britain's involvement, or lack of it, in the setting up of a European Council. Thatcher preferred to have no part of the European currency but it was her lack of conciliation, the 'my way or the highway' attitude that characterised so much of her premiership, which finally undid her. Howe himself was resigning from

Thatcher's cabinet and closed his speech by asking others 'to consider their own responses to the tragic conflict of loyalties with which I have myself wrestled for perhaps too long'.

Benn had a similar reputation – 'the Dark Destroyer' did not deal in shades of grey. Who knows if he could have beaten Eubank if he learned another way of fighting? He'd have to wait to find out. As the Conservative party moved to replace Thatcher with John Major, an altogether milder and more democratic figure, so boxing in Britain had a new star and perhaps a new direction. But like Major, whose first eighteen months in office would provide some of the most testing times for any prime minister, including sending troops to the Gulf War, so would Eubank find remaining at the head of his little kingdom more difficult than the ascent. There would be tragedy and self-doubt aplenty.

Act III

Scene I

'Chris lived the life that he thought a world champion should,' commentator Dave Brenner told me. He got to socialise with the new champ for as long as he commentated on his title fights (about three years on Screensport, until Eubank changed networks.) 'He was a lovely guy. He loved being Chris Eubank and it was enormous fun being in his company. Ninety-five per cent of his public persona was an act.'

What wasn't an act was his love of the good things in life. Although he fiercely contests one quote attributed to him, that the four best things in life are 'sex, champagne, chocolate and cocaine', he did enjoy spending the fruits of his labour. His image now featured three-piece suits, riding jodhpurs, a cane and a monocle, affecting the look of a refined country gent. As always, Eubank was doing things his way, creating his own style, or, to coin a very modern phrase, his own brand. The media ate it up as well, the look, the voice and the opinions all now carrying more weight as they came under the title of world champion. The excesses were treated as lovable eccentricities. 'My wife and I had gone for dinner with Chris and Karron and we'd gone back to his house for a late drink. And I was in his sitting room when I said Chris, "Why is there a Harley-Davidson motorbike in your lounge?"' remembers Brenner of that post-Benn victory era. Eubank would never concede what his faults were, but he would admit years later that he never quite understood the phrase 'less is more'. He spent lavishly on clothes and cars and the level of spending meant he could not afford to stop boxing. But it was all worth it for Eubank, because it enhanced his fame. In among the reasons he boxed – financial, respect from his brothers and also because he had a talent for it – perhaps the single most important was the love of the limelight.

Twice he was voted the country's best dressed man – while also coming third in a poll to find who was the nation's silliest celebrity. He added a Hummer to his collection of vehicles that already included an American Peterbilt truck. He appeared frequently on chat shows and breakfast television. And his fights were in demand. Gary Newbon, who had a dual role as television executive, remembers that ITV were desperate to show Eubank fights because of the ratings and revenue they would generate. And his promoter Barry Hearn knew that now was the time to milk Eubank's fame, rather than risk an immediate rematch with Benn. 'There was no rush,' said Hearn. Eubank was blunter, telling Benn that he would 'have to wait in a queue'.

If that public persona could exude arrogance, others knew a different side. John Wischhusen, the man in charge of boxing public relations at Matchroom, recalls Eubank happily talking to and engaging with the general public, who were eager to meet the most notorious man in British sport. 'He was very generous, very kind. Sometimes, after one of his fights, I'd meet my mates and he'd come over and talk to them, buy them a drink. All things he didn't need to do.' Newbon also confirms that gentle side to Eubank which quite often got lost behind the monocle and cane. 'He can be a pain in the arse and he can mess you about something rotten. But I've never seen him malicious or do anything nasty or be rude to people or show a lack of respect.'

Eubank was also not alone in trying to redefine how boxers could negotiate their way through the sport. Colin McMillan, a London-born featherweight, actually had the qualifications to back up his slightly detached view of the sport. 'Sweet C', as he was nicknamed, left school with three A levels and combined his boxing career with jobs with the government and British Telecom. He only committed to the sport full time when he received sponsorship and spent the majority of his career being advised by the journalist Jonathan Rendall. McMillan spoke clearly and concisely and boxed even more smartly, using his speed and reflexes to befuddle opponents and thrill even the most jaded of hacks at ringside. Rendall and McMillan navigated their way through the sport, striking deals with promoters when it suited them. Only an inherent weakness in his physical make-up – McMillan cut easily and also had problems with the muscles in his shoulders – prevented him from fulfilling his potential. But McMillan would walk away from the sport with his faculties and reputation intact. In 2000, he was employed by Olympic gold medallist Audley Harrison to advise on the start of the heavyweight's professional career. McMillan may have heard the odd boo when he aligned himself with Harrison, whose professional career was as unspectacular as his amateur one had been successful, but with the gloves on he heard only cheers.

Eubank heard cheers – but the boos were louder. His supporters liked his shtick, his unbelievable confidence and the fact that he had something to say. Before agents became so powerful, almost as big as their clients, sports stars could speak freely. In football, plenty admired the clean-cut Gary Lineker, but how the masses loved Paul Gascoigne, his teeth a mess, his speech often muddled because of his intimate relationship with the pub and his tackling as refined as dog fighting. He was different – and he couldn't possibly exist in the twenty-first century. Neither could Eubank – a PR company would have him locked away for an extended period, trying to repair the damage of his latest spontaneous remark to make the headlines. Witness his appearance on a Sky Sports boxing broadcast where he made several remarks about Desiree Washington, the woman Mike Tyson was convicted of raping. So strong were they that the show's presenter, Paul Dempsey, was forced to disassociate the company from Eubank's views. In the early 1990s, Eubank was often quoted by the mainstream press, even if he would only grant interviews to journalists who did not write about the sport from which he derived his income.

The new champion talked frequently about the integrity he brought to the sport, about how he was one of the few who dictated his terms to others, rather than be placed in situations against his will. But the word integrity would be called into question with his first defence of the WBO title. No one was entirely surprised that it was against a fairly nondescript opponent, Canadian Dan Sherry, who was the same age as the champion, also unbeaten but entirely untested. The bout took place at the Brighton Conference Centre and would end up creating yet more notoriety for the champion. He had seemed on course for a comfortable victory when he floored Sherry in the opening round. But, rather than shrink from sight, Sherry hung around and started to irritate the champ. He wouldn't be the last person to discover that Eubank could become annoyed if he was asked to make the running. Whereas Benn came forward relentlessly and demanded Eubank's attention, Sherry almost affected a will-o'-the-wisp presence, while also pausing long enough to have the odd chat. His words have never been revealed but the effect, along with the fact that he was not playing the game as Eubank would have hoped, meant the champion was ruffled. He'd claim afterwards that the words he heard had a racial context to them, an accusation that Sherry refuted, but that couldn't obscure the fact that Eubank was being outworked and frustrated. At one point in the eighth round, he did in fact stop fighting, holding his gloves to his belly and scowling as Sherry taunted him. 'He's not doing enough here,' said Barry McGuigan, in the commentary box, about the champion. 'Chris is frustrated, but he should be frustrated with himself.'

By the tenth, Eubank had started to put the pressure on and looked on course for a stoppage victory against a now exhausted challenger. The Canadian managed to smother one attack and the pair found themselves in a bizarre clinch, where Sherry was facing the back of Eubank's head. Not many people can claim to have been hurt in a ring by the back of a man's head, but Sherry was about to suggest just that, as Eubank threw his cranium in the direction of the challenger, in response to what he thought were kisses being planted on the back of his neck. Television evidence doesn't suggest that to be the case and neither does it support the force of the blow and the extent to which Sherry then danced around the ring, on seemingly unstable legs. The referee declared the fight over, with Sherry unable to continue. He also deducted two points from Eubank, with the fight now in the hands of the judges and their scorecards. Eubank was awarded a split decision, much to the relief of those in attendance. Others were more critical. 'He should have been disqualified,' said trainer Jimmy Tibbs, who was working as a cutman in Sherry's corner. The great Henry Cooper said Eubank was too serious and had 'an attitude'. The British Boxing Board of Control cut to the chase more quickly, fining Eubank heavily and accusing him of bringing the sport into disrepute. The champion did not disagree and made no attempt to contest the judgement, perhaps aware how fortunate he had been to escape the night with his title intact, if not his reputation.

The controversial nature of the victory only hardened the resolve of those of the general public who didn't like him and were looking for someone who could beat him. The next sacrificial lamb was Gary Stretch, an exceptionally handsome man who had excelled as an amateur and combined boxing with modelling. Years later, Runcorn middleweight Robin Reid would do the same and win a world title. The difference between the pair was that Stretch lacked the dedication to achieve the most from his talents in the ring. He was also a light middleweight at best when the bout was held. Although he allowed the quote 'I'd rather die than be beaten by him' on the fight posters, he lasted just six rounds, during which time he looked completely out of his depth. Stretch had prepared for life as a champion by getting his teeth fixed before the bout – and with the money he earned he could afford to get them done again.

It was a more impressive performance by Eubank, but few were convinced that his first two defences of the title were against opposition designed to test him. Although Sherry had been a tough contest, the object of that fight had been to give Eubank an easy night. The principle of that in boxing is understandable – the beating he took at the hands of Benn even in victory was severe enough to allow him to take a year off – but instead he was back in the saddle just over three months later. An ever-present theme in his career was activity – he fought regularly and was paid enough to fund his lavish lifestyle. The problem for him was twofold – he was following in the footsteps of Nigel Benn who had been much more popular, who also fought often and against a far higher calibre of opposition. And, secondly, he was fighting on terrestrial television, being watched by a discerning audience that had grown bored with heavily hyped contests delivering little in the way of action or competitiveness. The authenticity of those fights was questioned a great deal more in the 1990s than one would expect nowadays, sometimes by the networks actually showing them. ITV's ringside reporter Gary Newbon was often dismissive of fights he considered mismatches and that critique could sometimes be found in the questions he'd ask of fighters, promoters and managers, before and after the contests.

It all added up to a situation that demanded a better quality of opponent. A tentative offer of a rematch with Benn was made to the former champion, but was rejected because of the size of the purse (Benn wanted parity and more than the £250,000 on offer). But Barry Hearn's plan all along was to create another British challenger for Eubank. In the promoter's mind, Michael Watson still had plenty to offer, and another domestic showdown could sell handsomely. After all, Eubank was very much the man to beat and the man who many wanted to see beaten. A rematch with Benn could wait – in fact, the longer it was delayed, and as long as both men continued to win, the better the chance it would turn out to be bigger than the first one.

Michael Watson might have guessed that his impressive stoppage of Errol Christie would be overshadowed by the main event in Birmingham that night. He had other things to worry about – the court case with Duff in February 1991 (which he'd win) and a defence of the Commonwealth title against Craig Trotter a month before that in Essex. Watson was not officially a Matchroom fighter, even if this bout was taking place in Brentwood. Trotter was a light middleweight at best, but was durable. As commentator Jim Rosenthal said, 'Trotter has never met anyone of the class of Michael Watson.' The Australian was repeatedly hit and hurt until his corner threw in the towel at the start of the sixth round. Before his next fight, against Trinidadian Anthony Brown, Watson had his day in court against Duff. As soon as victory was secured, he sat down with Barry Hearn to outline the future. 'Watson, I'd known for years. I'd always liked him – too nice a person.

Watson always thought he'd been held back by Mickey Duff. And he had been held back in the profile sense,' said Hearn. When he had begun boxing, Watson was shy and, even now, as an adult, he remained outwardly humble. But that fooled some into thinking that he lacked belief in his own ability, whereas the opposite was true. He still believed that he was better than Mike McCallum, despite the one-sided nature of their bout. He knew and had proved he was better than Benn and he was also convinced he was superior to Eubank. While he had struck up a friendship with Benn after their fight, there was no warmth between him and Eubank. He didn't like the comments about boxing being 'a mug's game' and he didn't feel Eubank had done enough to merit the world title chance he received against Benn. In Watson's mind, Eubank represented what was wrong in boxing, in that he hadn't needed to work hard to get to the top. There was no Don Lee, Ricky Stackhouse or Reggie Miller on his record, just a series of cheaply imported South American opponents. And now he was world champion, courtesy of a victory over a man Watson had beaten more quickly and more easily. Eubank had what Watson had always dreamed of: a world title. Even now, seven years into his professional career, all Watson wanted was that belt around his waist. He always felt the other things he wanted – the money, the respect – would follow.

The plans were for Watson to be moved into position to fight Eubank. On 1 May 1991, he beat Brown in a round at the grand old venue of British boxing, York Hall, in the East End's Bethnal Green. Shortly after that, he signed a contract to fight Eubank on 22 June at Earl's Court, another venue associated with the sport for much of the twentieth century. Watson admitted that, while, for the first time in ages, his mind was clear, one issue troubled him: who should be in his corner?

For his entire professional career Watson had been trained by Eric Secombe and the fighter felt that he needed something extra. His schooling in the hardest gyms in the capital had seen him spar often with Mark Kaylor, one of the most popular boxers of the 1980s. Kaylor, always visible because of the claret and blue shorts he wore in honour of his beloved West Ham, was trained by another Hammer, Jimmy Tibbs. A useful light heavyweight and middleweight during the late sixties, Tibbs had lived a life as full and frightening as any in British boxing. He spent four years in jail during the early seventies, because of 'trouble', as he says. It's worth noting that Tibbs came from a family so strong and dangerous that even the Krays avoided them. A life spent in and around boxing meant Jimmy Tibbs once sparred with Muhammad Ali, met fighters like the legendary Willie Pep, who's defensive skills were so fundamentally sound that he once won a round without throwing a punch, and worked tirelessly with Terry Lawless, particularly during the period when the latter was bringing along a raw, muscle-bound heavyweight called Frank Bruno. He had experience of training at the highest level as well, having worked with Lloyd Honeyghan, Charlie Magri and Jim Watt.

By 1991, Tibbs's troubles outside the ring were a thing of the past – he'd become a born-again Christian and, given Watson's own intensely religious background, the pairing seemed a natural fit. Tibbs would share duties with Secombe on the night but it was the new man's voice that

Watson listened to. A nice guy Watson may have been, but he also knew there were things he needed correcting and was prepared to upset the man who had helped him come so far.

'By Public Demand' was the title of the promotion, although, in truth, what the public demanded was a fight with action, between two guys capable of beating each other. Watson guaranteed work rate and talent and the three wins he'd recorded since losing to Mike McCallum indicated he still had plenty left in the tank. Neither Eubank nor Barry Hearn had any great interest in matching themselves with the big names in America, the likes of Michael Nunn, James Toney or Roy Jones Junior. Fights with Watson and Benn could meet the demands of the television companies, while there was easier money to be made fighting some of the division's lesser lights. As charismatic as Eubank was, the public would not turn up or tune in if all he did was fight the Dan Sherrys or Gary Stretchs of the world. There had to be a Michael Watson or a Nigel Benn in there at some point.

When Watson first fought for a world title, against McCallum, he was rusty and dissatisfied with his promoter and manager, Mickey Duff. Now there was tranquillity in his life; he managed himself and knew that anything that went wrong was down to him and he also had, in his opinion, the right people around him. Which meant that, when he invited the press to watch him train eight days before the bout, they saw him spar against two amateurs and a novice professional. Even worse was the rumour that the one fighter hired on the basis of having a style similar to Eubank was ushered away after being informed that, if he wished to provide in-ring competition, his payment would only be sent after the fight. As someone who had striven for financial and professional independence, Watson must have known that the terms he was offering others weren't suitable.

Like Eubank, Nigel Benn would tie the knot after that epic fight in Birmingham. He'd been engaged to Sharron for two years and, despite the tempestuous nature of their relationship, they had children together. The wedding, in Las Vegas, would prove to be the beginning of the end for the couple. Some of his friends described Benn's marriage to Sharron as 'probationary' and that his inability to make it work hurt him immensely. But the womanising continued.

Boxing was still what Benn knew best and his first fight back was also at York Hall. The opponent was no 'gimme', though. Robbie Sims had a reputation for toughness, based as much on who he'd fought as who he was related to – he was Marvin Hagler's half-brother. Never as talented as the Marvelous one, Sims had nevertheless fought some quality opponents and had twice challenged for a world title. But he was now approaching his thirty-third birthday and was on the slide, having lost three of his last six fights. But he'd never been stopped and that was the test for Benn. If he was fully recovered, physically and mentally, ending Sims's enviable record would be within reach of his talents. For his part, Sims said that Benn was a dirty fighter, who led with his elbows. It was all part of the routine to hype a fight – Sims also brought along his half-brother, who'd been retired for four years after losing a controversial decision to Sugar Ray Leonard.

Commentator Jim Watt noted that Benn's timing was 'slightly off' during the opening stages. Sims had good fundamental skills and made sure he was never stationary long enough for one of Benn's bombs to explode off his jaw. When things weren't going Benn's way, he could look vulnerable, but just like Eubank that appearance could be exaggerated for effect. In the seventh round, Benn was being attacked on the ropes and appeared headed for the same fate as his last fight. He'd already admitted that another defeat would make it all but impossible to regenerate his career, but despite his reputation as an out and out brawler with scant regard for tactics, he always had streetsmarts. They say in football that a team is never more vulnerable than immediately after scoring a goal – in the same way, it's tempting to say that a fighter is never more at risk than after he's hurt Benn. Rolling and recoiling, just as he had done against Logan, Benn reached out for a left hook that connected surely and with devastating fashion on Sims's exposed chin. The punch appeared to place him in a state of suspended animation, a statue of a man now in the perfect position to absorb another left hook. Knocked down for the first time, Sims bravely rose, only to be punched into the other side of the ring, where referee John Coyle did the sensible thing and waved the fight off. It had not been easy and there were times when he had looked a little rusty, but Benn was back.

It would be the last time he was seen in the company of Ambrose Mendy. The flamboyant manager was in trouble with the law and the misgivings that Benn had about their relationship were amplified by the legal troubles (Mendy would serve time at Her Majesty's pleasure more than once during the next fifteen years). In his autobiography, Benn states that he lent money to Mendy, much of which was never paid back. There were no rows that either man would refer to twenty years later, but the parting of the ways was permanent. It also paved the way for Benn to join Barry Hearn's growing stable. Their relationship was altogether more volatile. 'He'd come in the office sometimes and say I want to kill you,' remembers Hearn. 'And other times he'd come in, sit in the chair opposite me and bawl his eyes out, saying, "No one likes me!"' Regardless, the pair never became close, mostly because Benn suspected, rightly, that Hearn's loyalties were with Eubank. That didn't stop him signing terms, because the only fight that really interested him was with the Brighton man.

He'd been offered a rematch quickly, but the purse offer of £250,000 was, as we have seen, in his opinion well short of what he thought he was worth. It was also less than Eubank would earn. Benn had yet to understand that, as the ex-champion, he could not expect to earn as much as Eubank. Whether or not he knew who was behind the negotiations or the proposals, Benn took them as proof of Eubank's arrogance, his desire to put him in his place. While Eubank also claimed he didn't hate Benn, he resented his ascent to the top, stewarded as it had been by some inventive marketing by Ambrose Mendy. As such, he was happy to keep Benn at bay for now and remind him that he was calling the shots. And that enraged Benn further. His first instinct after defeat to Eubank had been to retire. Now he wanted revenge. But for the first time in a while, he was on the outside of things, looking for a way back in.

Scene II

'I've never hated anyone,' Michael Watson answers when I ask him about Chris Eubank. There is a 'but' in there – this intensely religious man doesn't do misdirection or mistruth – but his answer is more poignant. 'He's lost. He doesn't know who he is.' That's what he thinks now and that's what he thought then, back in 1991, when the pair prepared to fight each other. But there was not an edge to that, no dislike. Watson knew he was better, an all-round boxer/fighter who could stalk, retreat, defend and attack. He saw in Eubank weaknesses he believed he could exploit. And he wanted Eubank's title. Regarded by so many in Britain as the best middleweight in the country, he had yet to taste the glory of being called a world champion.

Eubank didn't see the fight as being as difficult as the one he'd had with Benn. In training for 'the Dark Destroyer', he'd mentally awarded his opponent a score of ten out of ten. Watson was an eight – Eubank just didn't see the man from Islington as being particularly special. It might have explained a haphazard training camp which left him bruised from sparring and also massively overweight. Four days before the fight, he weighed close to 13 stone, meaning he'd have to lose more than a stone in order for the bout to go ahead. Eubank's weight making was something of an insider joke – everyone who worked in boxing knew he took liberties with it, waiting until the last minute before making the sacrifice, which seemed to observers to be beyond dangerous. Jim Rosenthal remembers: 'I saw him once when he lost weight in a similar fashion. I looked at him and his skin was totally dry. And I said, "You look awful", and he replied, "My eyeballs feel dry".' But it was a routine he would go through for most of his career, until he moved up to cruiserweight, which was his natural weight. And because he didn't do roadwork like others – 'He jogged!' one former pro told me – the excess with which all fighters began their training camp wasn't coming off. His method for taking off the weight was simple – starvation in the week or fortnight before the bout.

Regardless, he was favourite for the bout, to be held on 22 June. Writing in the *Observer*, Hugh McIlvanney said, 'Eubank's eccentric spirit could yet prove vulnerable under bombardment but in the three wins Watson has scored since suffering his cruellest night [against McCallum] there has been little to indicate that he is the one to give the fantasist a bitter dose of reality. The challenger is an admirable performer but his are solidly respectable rather than soaring talents. Habit and pride may incline him towards pursuit of Eubank and, regardless of his faith in his ability to outcounter the counter puncher, that will be a hazardous game.' McIlvanney was not alone in his assessment that the challenger was slightly too predictable to overcome the unorthodox.

By virtue of Eubank's unpopularity – 'I feel sure that many of you are tuning in to see him lose,' said Jim Rosenthal more than once before a Eubank bout – Watson had the country on his side. And, publicly, there had never been any sense of anything other than positivity about Watson and his image. As Benn admitted, it was impossible to hate him. In his autobiography, Eubank bemoans the negative vibes surrounding his tenure as champion back then, but those who knew him closely believe he was well aware of the hostility he provoked and used it to his benefit, knowing he was a one-off and that he was in the sport for one reason only – money. He never seemed to tire of telling people what his burden was. 'Boxing is not a noble art. It is brutal and I am merely using it to set myself free from the system that tries to hold me down. All I need to know is that it is dangerous. My mind is focused only on this truth which is why I will administer a fearful beating to Michael Watson and move another step beyond this terrible game.' Watson joined in the pre-fight hype by labelling the champion 'a phoney' who was tarnishing the name of the sport.

If there was any consolation for Eubank in terms of the weight making, it came in the fact that Watson, too, was struggling. A naturally big middleweight with broad shoulders, he would need to shed a pound on the day of the fight, having already had to lose three during the final week of preparations. But that wasn't the same as 19 lb in four days – on fight night Watson entered to a crescendo of roars, coming from the legion of Arsenal fans who had adopted him as their own as well as many neutral fans who backed him purely because of their dislike of Eubank. It wasn't unusual for a champion to be cast in the role of pantomime villain and, as Eubank would say years later, like him or loathe him they came to watch. It was just that, more often than not, it was more by circumstance rather than by design. In the early part of the twentieth century, Jack Johnson became the first black world heavyweight champion. Johnson's demeanour was at odds with what was expected of a black man in America in the 1900s. He dressed with style and expense and was often seen in the company of white women. Perceived as arrogant, Johnson became the focus of a campaign which saw every

half-decent white heavyweight positioned to challenge
'Papa Jack'. Even former champion James L. Jeffries was
lured out of retirement to see if he could bring to an end
the reign of Johnson. Booed relentlessly and also the target
of lawmakers who tried to put him in jail for committing
'offences' (which were barely worthy of the label), Johnson
was eventually relieved of his title by the giant Jess Willard
in the baking Havana sun in 1915, after seven years as
champion which demonstrated to later generations just
how intolerant and prejudiced the vast majority of America
was. Some historians have determined that Johnson invited
some of the treatment he received because of the way he
carried himself, a criticism levelled at Eubank more than
seventy years later. But race didn't play a part in the dislike
of Eubank in the 1990s – the boos were more in keeping
with those heard at professional wrestling shows, where
the promoters predetermined who were the good and bad
guys. The volume of the boos would not change Eubank's
demeanour before or during fights – he would always
give the impression of aloofness, his chin pointing to the
sky, face impassive, announcing that he was superior to
everyone, be it the opposing fighter or the fans. That wasn't
a reflection of his thoughts so much as his understanding
that self-promotion involved using all the tools available.

Eubank was smart, but even he could not have predicted
how his persona chimed with the growing sense of
frustration and restlessness prevalent in the country.
Margaret Thatcher may have gone but the legacy of her
years in power was there to be seen and felt. The recession,
at first denied by those in government, was taking grip.
Manufacturing output was down and unemployment was

rising towards two million. Inflation was at an unthinkable 9.5 per cent, while first-time home-buyers faced interest rates of up to 13 per cent. The optimism of the yuppie era was well and truly over and, to make matters worse for a great percentage of the population, the government had decided to join the United States in the Gulf War at the start of 1991. With all that, a young man wearing jodhpurs and a monocle was an unpalatable sight for many. Eubank's rags to riches story did not inspire – it just seemed to irritate. It mattered not a jot that he did plenty of charity work, was involved in helping homeless people in Brighton and had strong anti-war feelings that would lead to him being arrested years after he finished boxing. Eubank had made himself a target for hate. First the fans had put their trust in Benn to silence him, now they were trusting in Watson.

Maybe, just maybe, the common man had become tired of hating the Conservative government for everything that was wrong with his life (they had been in power since 1979) and found they could channel their energies into loathing a medium-sized fella who lived in back-to-back houses in Hove (Eubank had bought the property next to his house and converted part of it into a boxing gym). Elsewhere, the nation was delivering success in the sporting fields outside of the ring. In 1990, the gentrification of football began as a Paul Gascoigne-inspired England football team reached the semi-finals of the World Cup in Italy. Gazza's tears and Puccini's 'Nessun Dorma' brought England together and made it acceptable to go to football again. Not long after, BSkyB flashed the cash and a lucrative deal was formative in the creation of the FA Premier League, a foundation whose bubble shows no sign of bursting more than twenty years later. In 1992, in Nigel Mansell, Britain would claim the world's premier Formula One driver. The golf world feared a certain Nick Faldo, who had won majors at home and abroad. Failure on the cricket field was cancelled out by success with the oval ball, as the England rugby team went all the way to the final of the World Cup in 1991, losing narrowly to Australia.

Outside of the middleweight conundrum that captivated the country, there was also the looming menace of Lennox Lewis, a British-born heavyweight who had left the country for Canada at the age of twelve and represented his adoptive country at the 1988 Olympics, where he won gold, before returning to Britain to start his professional career. At the Olympics, Lewis had stopped American Riddick Bowe in the final and a rivalry between the pair had grown ever since. There was also plenty of talk about a charismatic lower weight fighter, born in Sheffield of Yemeni parents, called Naseem Hamed. And with television coverage granted to amateur boxing, a Welsh Italian born in west London called Joe Calzaghe was also making a name for himself.

In times of depression, beer and boxing could still provide comfort, and a sport still unfettered by modern nuance, and represented on this June night by Michael Watson, the very definition of old school, took centre stage as much as Eubank did. Watson's entrance into the ring was as low key as ever, Eubank's, to the strains of the same old tune was greeted by boos, the sign that hostility pervaded the air. At the sound of the first bell, Watson, in white shorts, moved towards Eubank, who remained stationary. 'I don't know why,' says Eubank. Faced with such an opponent, a boxer has two options. Apply pressure in the way he normally would or try and

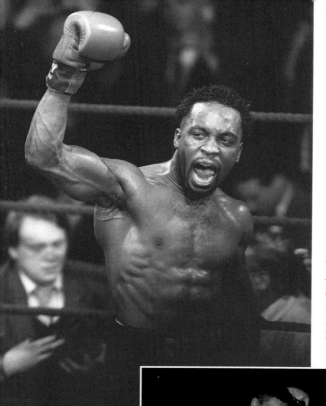

The Dark Destroyer – aggression and excitement, Nigel Benn at York Hall, Bethnal Green, London, January 1988. © Getty Images

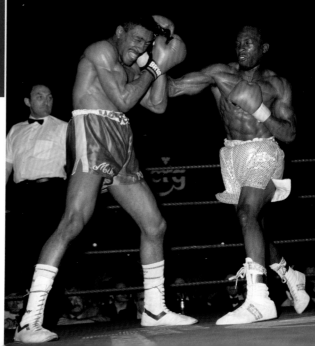

Covering up – Watson took Benn's best and then fired back. Watson beat Benn after the referee stopped the fight in the sixth round, Commonwealth Middleweight Championship, May 1989.
© Bob Thomas/Getty Images

After all the talk Benn and Watson found a mutual respect which lasts to this day. © Getty Images

Down but not out, Benn floors Eubank. But the challenger came back stronger to defeat Benn in the ninth round. WBO Middleweight Championship at Birmingham NEC Arena, November 1990

© Bob Thomas/ Getty Images

The pain in victory and defeat. Barry Hearn (promoter), Eubank and Benn, November 1990.

© Michael Fresco/ Evening Standard/ REX

Neither man ready to give an inch, Eubank vs Benn, November 1990.

© Brian Bould/ Daily Mail/REX

The Eubank entrance was one of sport's most iconic moments during the 1990s. Eubank defends the World Middleweight Championship at Earls Court defeating Watson for the first time, June 1991. © Bob Thomas/Getty Images

Eubank vs Watson, WBO Super Middleweight title fight at White Hart Lane, September 1991. © Getty Images

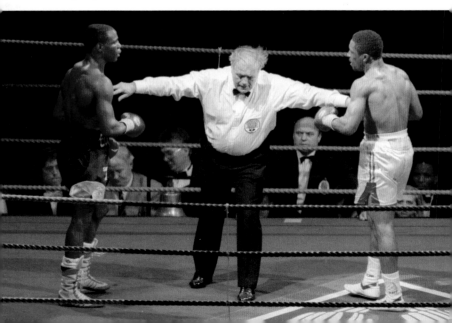

Eubank vs Watson,
September 1991.

*© Andy Hooper/
Associated Newspapers/REX*

Eubank got the
decision in the first
fight against Watson,
but the critics weren't
impressed. Eubank
successfully defends
VBO Championship at
arls Court, June 1991.

© Mirrorpix

Eubank's defining moment was quickly forgotten as Watson's plight became apparent.
Eubank vs Watson, WBO Super Middleweight Championship at White Hart Lane.

Eubank won the title after 12th round stoppage which left Watson with irreparable brain damage, September 1991. © Getty Images

Showing off – Eubank's knockouts became rarer after the Watson tragedy. Eubank vs John Jarvis, WBO Super Middleweight title fight, G-Mex Leisure Centre, Manchester, April 1992. © *Mirrorpix*

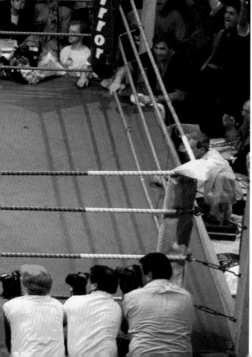

Benn looks down at Lou Gent.
Benn went on to win the title
in the fourth round. WBC
Super Middleweight World
Championship at the Royal
Albert Hall, June 1993.

© Getty Images

JUDGEMENT DAY

WBC SUPER-MIDDLEWEIGHT CHAMPIONSHIP

 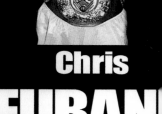

Nigel
BENN
WBC CHAMPION

Chris
EUBAN
WBO CHAMPION

SATURDAY 9th OCTOBER 1993
Manchester United FC, Old Trafford

DOORS OPEN
6.00 pm

FIGHT NIGHT PROGRAMME
£4

BOXING COMMENCES
7.30 pm

Fight programme for the hottest ticket in town. *Courtesy of Barry Hearn, Frank Warren and Don King*

Who won? Both of them. Eubank vs Benn, 2nd fight at Old Trafford, October 1993.

© Mirrorpix

Eubank's attacks in the rematch were sporadic, but they convinced one judge he had done enough to win.

© Andy Hooper/ Associated Newspapers/REX

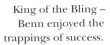

King of the Bling –
Benn enjoyed the
trappings of success.
Courtesy of Ambrose Mendy

American invasion – Benn's time
in the USA was brief and successful.
Courtesy of Ambrose Mendy

Boxing News didn't think Eubank
had beaten Graciano Rocchigiani
– so he rang up the magazine and
told them they were wrong.
Author's collection

DOUBLE DISASTER FOR SCOTS **PAGES 8-11** **FEBRUARY 11**

BOXING NEWS

Vol. 50 No. 6 85th year

EUBANK KEEPS HIS TITLE IN ANOTHER CLOSE CAL

ROCKY RIDE

WBO super-middleweight champion CHRIS EUBANK c
through an awkward title defence in Berlin at the week
against German GRACIANO "ROCKY" ROCCHIGIANI v
he gained another controversial points decis
HARRY MULLAN'S RINGSI
REPORT – PAGES 16-

**EURO
GLORY** Carl's Italian stunner - p-5
Jacobs' Paris triumph - p6-7

Eubank's first fight
on Sky drew
a negative reaction.
Author's collection

SPECIAL 32-PAGE COLOUR EDITION

JULY 15, 1994

BOXING NEWS

Vol. 50 No. 28 85th year £1.10 S.O.R.

EUBANK'S £10 MILLION ROADSHOW OFF TO A WOBBLY START

TOUR de FARCE!

Chris left with a credibility gap

SHUT-EYED Chris Eubank trades with Mauricio Amaral at Olympia. Eubank's supposed world tour spluttered into action as he scraped a decision over the enthusiastic but raw Brazilian.

Next stop is Cardiff on August 27 for a date with Irish southpaw Sam Storey, as Eubank's schedule of eight fights in 12 months for his new paymasters Sky TV takes shape.

...enn with Bob Arum and Ambrose ...endy in 1990. *Courtesy of Ambrose Mendy*

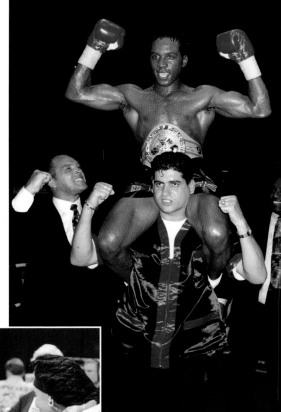

Benn with manager Pete
DeFreitas. © *Mirrorpix*

Benn proposes to the woman who
helped transform his turbulent
private life, Carolyne Jackson, after
losing the WBC Super Middleweig
title fight at Newcastle Arena, Mar
1996. © *Getty Images*

A fight between
Benn and legend
Roberto Duran
was discussed, but
never happened.

*Credit: Courtesy of
Ambrose Mendy*

Eubank lost twice
to cruiserweight
Carl Thompson –
his bravery won
over the hearts of
many. Eubank lost
on points after 12
rounds and then
spent the night at
Manchester Royal
Infirmary. WBO
cruiserweight fight
at Nynex Arena,
Manchester, April
1998. © Mirrorpix

The greatest achievement: Michael Watso[n] partially paraly[sed] following the fight with Euba[nk] completes the 26th London Marathon, Apr[il] 2003. © David Lof[t] Icon SMI/Corbis

Together agai[n:] Benn, Watson a[nd] Eubank at the Michael Watso[n] tribute dinner, Dorchester Ho[tel] September 201[1] © Daily Mirror via Mirrorpix

match his foe for dramatics and theatre. Watson was stuck somewhere in the middle. The confident box-puncher who walked through Errol Christie was replaced by an altogether more circumspect character. 'Watson's just trying to get the tension out of his shoulders,' remarked commentator Dave Brenner. His colleague Jim McDonnell noted that the opposite was true of the champion, who was 'feeding off the hostility generated by Watson's supporters'. The opening round was close, but the better quality of punches came from the champion, even if the quantity came from Watson.

Round two exemplified why attempting to knock Eubank off his perch was far harder than it looked. As Watson continued to pursue the champion, he was unable to close the distance between him and his opponent. Still tentative with his jab and right hand, he was caught on more than one occasion by a flurry of punches from Eubank, who looked the quicker and sharper puncher. His work rate may have diminished as the three minutes came to an end, but there was little doubt that the better shots, the eyecatching punches, were landed by the man in the amber shorts. Some experts believed that the bout's tempo suited Eubank, as the more orthodox counter puncher, with Watson more comfortable as the pursued rather than the pursuer. Many of those experts based their opinion on Watson's performance against Benn. Students of his career knew he picked his style depending on what was required. So far, his execution had been neither what he hoped for nor was capable of. Conscious of his energy levels, the first thing to go when you are weight drained, his application of pressure was sporadic, allowing the champion to flurry and take the plaudits.

For someone who described the sport as barbaric,

Eubank seemed to have no qualms about accepting the kind of punishment to his head which would render most men incapacitated in later life. He invited those punches by holding his hands low, his elbows tucked into his sides, as a way of avoiding excessive blows to his abdomen and kidneys. Those punches had taken him to the very edge against Benn and some sense of self-preservation had finally kicked in after two title defences. But it was the punches he took in the third round, landing on that jaw that seemed to be made from the material you'd find in one of Eubank's off-road vehicles, which meant this round went the way of Watson. At least in the eyes of the neutral.

That same neutral would have scored the next round in favour of Eubank, who seemed to hurt his man twice, first with a right and then with a left hook. The force of those punches seemed to take something out of Watson's legs, as he visibly hobbled back to his corner at the end of the round. Ahead after a third of the bout, Eubank increased the pressure in the next round, allowing Watson into punching range before landing a short, powerful right hand which disorientated Watson, forcing him to put those big gloves around his head. But this battle, a series of mini wars if you like between two men who both believed they were superior in the same areas, was edging the way of the champion. Watson had skin damage under his left eye and, although he had not been down, was looking like a man on his way to a slow beating. With a minute left in the round, Eubank hurt Watson again. Such was the champion's confidence, he now lunged in for the finish, throwing wild right hands – the kind you could see coming even if you were in the toilets – as Watson retreated to the ropes. At the bell, the pair walked past each other, with Watson seemingly intimating that, despite the punches he'd absorbed, he was still more than alive and also looking forward to the next seven rounds. Eubank would describe those first five as 'unquestionably' his. He was definitely ahead, but by how much only the judges knew.

Watson needed sustained success from now on if he was to wrest the title away from Eubank. But did he know it? If he had an obvious flaw it was in his total self-belief. That he knew he was better than everyone. He had not acknowledged the variety of skills that Eubank brought to the ring, and that by the very nature of his unique persona Eubank manipulated the minds of judges. They watched him, were captivated by him. Ask a person to judge a contest between a straight man and an eccentric and they will almost always notice the latter. The touch of theatre came exclusively from Eubank; if Watson was to match and surpass Eubank, he would have to do it through work rate.

The sixth round was crucial if Watson was to re-establish himself. With many now wondering whether the sustained beating he had taken at the hands of McCallum had left him damaged, he produced a sustained three minutes of work, moving forward, waiting for Eubank to throw and then miss, before countering with clean punches. 'Michael can't hurt Chris,' shouted McDonnell from the commentary box, but points in boxing are accumulated by the quality and quantity of punches, not by the perceived power. Watson was making Eubank expend energy, often in the futile quest to land 'Hollywood' punches. By the end of the sixth, the champion suddenly looked exhausted.

Both men seemed happy to rest in the following round, notable only for an attempt by Eubank to land the cheapest of cheap shots. As he released Watson's head from a clinch, he deliberately aimed the tip of his elbow at the head of the challenger and was immediately admonished by the referee, American Frank Cappuccino. In truth, Eubank should have had a point deducted, but the incident was illuminating in that it proved, not for the first time, that, although Eubank described his sport as barbaric, he was not averse to ensuring it justified that description. 'He has these little moments of madness sometimes, Chris Eubank, and that was one of them,' said Brenner.

'The harder shots are coming from Chris Eubank, the cleaner shots are coming from Eubank, the more work is coming from Michael Watson,' said McGuigan at the end of the round, pointing to the difficult job the American judges had. Round eight was no easier to score – Eubank began it with an impressive flurry of action. But that's all it was. After that, Watson stalked his man, throwing several jabs, landing with some, missing with others. The cheers were coming with each Watson punch, whether they were on target or not. This almost certainly made it harder for those men marking the scorecards. Eubank seemed to sense that his output wasn't what it needed to be and threw more punches in the next round than he had done for some time. It seemed to take Watson by surprise – he was unable to counter and ended the round looking like the man who had been underwhelmed during the first five rounds. Eubank's trainer, Ronnie Davies, was growing more animated with every second. The best judge of a fight is almost always a trainer. He knows what his fighter can do, how much punishment he has taken and how much energy he has left. He will have seen the weaknesses of both men and knows whose vulnerabilities are being exploited. Trainer and boxer had an agreement – Davies would slap Eubank in the face if he felt the boxer was becoming too passive or inert. One such moment was upon us. If Eubank was to win this contest without reproach or conjecture, he'd have to maintain the output of the previous round. He might have landed harder punches than Watson, but the challenger was tougher and smarter than most. You could hit Watson once, but, usually, he'd be out of range by the time the next punch sailed by. It meant that quite often action was at a premium, Eubank uncomfortable as the aggressor, Watson too cautious to commit to the kind of continued assaults which would cause the champion discomfort. The commentators could be heard frequently claiming that it was heating up nicely; in fact, it had just been simmering since the first bell and was showing no signs of coming to the boil.

Now the final three rounds – the championship rounds – were upon them. In the old days – when men were men, the cynics might say – fights lasted fifteen rounds and it was from thirteen to fifteen that the true champion would emerge. But the twelve-round distance meant that, quite often, a slow start left a fighter needing a knockout to win, so difficult would it be for them to take it on points. In the late 1970s, Liverpool light heavyweight John Conteh seemed on his way to an easy points win over Matthew Saad Muhammad until a flurry of knockdowns during the final three rounds swung the decision the way of the American. In a twelve-round fight, Conteh would have been safe. As it was, the decision loss would signal the end of his career at the highest level. In Earl's Court, Watson wasn't staring at the end of his career, but he was aware that the fight was drifting away. After weathering a mini assault from Eubank at the start of the tenth, Watson took over, applying steady pressure. It was not flashy, would never make a highlight reel but it was enough to make an apparently exhausted champion run like a disorientated gazelle. 'Eubank, sucking in huge gulps of air,' said Brenner. This was undoubtedly a Watson round – if he could win the final two, the worst he could do would be a draw, surely. 'Watson is slowly winning this fight,' shouted McGuigan during the eleventh round. The Irishman would also note that Eubank, having done virtually nothing for the first ninety seconds of the round, finished it strongly. One of boxing's oldest and truest clichés is that finishing a round strongly is as important as starting it as such. What was beyond dispute was that neither man could claim he had definitely won the stanza. 'I have to tell you, Barry, with one round to go, I have it dead level,' Brenner told McGuigan from behind the mic. Over on ITV, both Reg Gutteridge and Jim Watt now saw it as a fight that Watson could only lose. On Screensport, Jim McDonnell told his colleagues that someone at ringside had Eubank four rounds in front. This wasn't so much a case of who you rooted for as what style did it for you.

Round twelve summed up the entire fight – you could find ways to score it for either man. Eubank fought with desperation at times, swinging fast and wild, punches hard but lacking sophistication. Watson continued the path he had trodden for much of the fight – slowly, patiently, prodding forward, jab prominent, defence tight, perhaps lacking urgency. In his best win, he had absorbed the pace and then changed it to suit him. In his worst defeat, he'd never found the energy to match a relentless worker. Had he learned from the experience? Hard to tell. Here he was answering questions with a shrug, confident, it seemed, that he was doing his best and certainly better than his opponent. Yet if one man thinks you're winning and another doesn't, interpretation is all that's left. At the final bell, neither man had tasted the canvas as a result of a punch; neither had been so badly hurt that the referee had to make a decision about whether to stop the contest. If you were a Watson fan, and that seemed to be most of the crowd, you'd think he'd won. If you were in the champion's corner, you'd think he'd done enough.

There are bad decisions in boxing and there are controversial ones. Bad was probably the draw that Lennox Lewis received when he appeared to dominate Evander Holyfield at Madison Square Garden in 1999. But the sound of boos in the arena reflected the unpopularity of the decision, especially given that it had benefited an American in front of his own fans. A controversial one was the split decision given to Sugar Ray Leonard against Marvelous Marvin Hagler in 1987. American trainer Gil Clancy reckoned Leonard had done enough to win, especially as he'd had one fight in five years. Hugh McIlvanney, perhaps the finest boxing writer ever, believed Hagler had won and said that Leonard had performed an illusion, having convinced those watching that his little was worth more because of his underdog status when he stepped into the ring. Even the judges were miles apart in their evaluation of the bout – two of them scored it narrowly but to different fighters, while another gave the fight to Leonard by ten rounds to two. Hagler, having given so much to the sport, through his dedication and his desire to fight everyone, never came to terms with the decision and retired from the sport, permanently embittered by the way he felt he had been treated in what was to be his final bout.

Hagler would meet Watson some years later and was very complimentary about the way he worked and trained. One can only wonder how he would have viewed the decision that was about to be read out at Earl's Court – the arena had been bathed in light all night. Now, it felt darker and tenser. 'Judge Carlos Colón scores the contest 116 points to 113 points in favour of Chris Eubank. Judge John Rubin scores the fight 114 points to each boxer. A draw. Ladies and gentlemen, Judge Art Lurie scores the contest 115 points to 113 in favour of the winner and still the WBO middleweight champion of the world, Chris Eubank,' said the ring announcer. Mild cheers chased around the ring as Eubank followed, arms aloft, with Barry Hearn by his side, looking more than a little relieved. A familiar ritual around now would be the champion being interrogated by Gary Newbon, who, direct as always, told Eubank the decision was controversial.

'I fought like a dog this fight, I fought like a dog and I deserved to win. He was no way in front of me. I stayed with him and stayed with him. I was hitting him with clean shots, I was looking more classy than he was. He was aggressive, yes, but I was picking him off as he came forward. So, no, I won that fight, regardless of what people say. And Nigel Benn, let's do it man,' said Eubank. That was his opinion then and hindsight has not changed his belief. Such was the contempt for the decision from Watson's supporters that they chose to express their distaste by haranguing the champion as he left the ring for his dressing room, spit, coins and verbal abuse all hurled his way. It is to Eubank's eternal credit that he did not react to the provocation. In the ring, Watson continued to pace with menace, his eyes brimming with fury. Watson told me years later that Eubank, who had talked to him throughout the bout, had told him to come over after the final bell so he could give him the belt. It's a claim that has always been denied by the champion. Perhaps more simply, Jimmy Tibbs would say, 'He was robbed.'

Eubank's reputation as boxing's chief anti-hero was now assured and the tabloid press did as much as they could to play to that. A phone-in survey in the *Daily Mirror* found that nearly 90 per cent of those who watched the fight felt the belt was in the wrong hands. Jim Watt, conveying his opinion to more than ten million people, thought Watson won, although there was no criticism of Eubank. Watt, who knew a thing or two about how to pull victory from the jaws of defeat, felt that Watson dominated the second half of the fight. In the *Observer*, Hugh McIlvanney opined that Watson's performance was a 'triumph for honest orthodoxy over imaginative bombast . . . the scorecards came as a shock'. Years later, I spoke to McDonnell and Brenner about how they viewed the bout.

'He [Eubank] never won it,' said McDonnell. Brenner sided with Eubank, telling me he felt you had to take the belt away from the champion. The promoter of the bout agreed. 'I thought Eubank won it. Michael and I always disagree about it,' Hearn told me. 'He always tells me I know nothing about boxing. I sat there and I fucking scored every single round. I don't think Michael did enough. But it was close . . . I don't know how any fighter can score a fight he is involved in, because you get lost in the moment.'

Hearn admits at that stage of his promotional career that he wanted Eubank to win because he was the bigger draw. He was also the WBO's most prominent champion; the governing body was not recognised in America but the reigns of Benn and Eubank had given the fledgling organisation some limelight. By that stage, the champion had 'cult of personality'. A look back at the footage from ringside shows how magnetic he could be – even with the best seats in the house, plenty of customers would stand up to get a look at some of Eubank's moves. The posing, the quick punches, the posturing – they all added to the package. If he was bewitching for the paying punters, what effect could he have on the judges? Eubank did not fight in any kind of rhythm but his presence captivated. Judges are only human beings and it's not fanciful to suggest that some may watch a bout with one person in mind.

Brenner's assertion that a challenger needs to take the title away from a champion is a commonly held one in the sport. But judges can only score a fight round by round. They cannot go back to their cards at the end of the bout and decide to change things around, trying to make up for injustices. But in those closer rounds – and there were plenty of them in this fight – the man holding the belt may get the benefit of the doubt.

Eubank might have been eyeing up a rematch with Benn, but his next fight would almost certainly have to be a return with Watson. The title of the first bout, 'By Public Demand', would be more appropriate the second time round. The challenger would double his money this time as well, £200,000 representing the biggest purse of his career. And there would not be much time for either man to rest. The 21st of September would be the date, White Hart Lane the venue.

Scene III

For now, Nigel Benn was isolated. The controversial nature of the Eubank–Watson fight and the immediate rematch meant his name wasn't mentioned as a future opponent for either man. His thoughts were targeted on getting Eubank, although his loyalty to Watson meant he wanted the Islington man to win the return. Benn would keep busy, his latest foe being a boxer who went by the name of Kid Milo. His real name was Winston Walters but he could easily have gone by the sobriquet 'Tough Guy'. Milo wasn't the biggest of middleweights but, a year earlier, he had gone eight hard rounds with Chris Eubank, cuts being the only reason he didn't hear the final bell. He'd fought other Eubank foes such as Johnny Melfah and Simon Collins and had acquitted himself well, but Benn was a step up. Brave as always, Milo actually went straight at Benn on an intense night in Brentwood, and with disastrous consequences. Down twice in four rounds, Milo had to retire at the end of the fourth, with severe eye damage convincing referee Larry O'Connell to stop the bout.

Benn's demeanour was different now – the black trunks were gone in favour of bright blue and he was also intent on telling anyone who listened that 'the Dark Destroyer' days were over. Intimidation was no longer one of the weapons he'd bring to the ring. You could almost feel the disappointment as the snarl was replaced by a smile. Big changes were taking place in his life outside of the ring as well. The Milo fight would be the last time Benn had Vic Andretti in his corner. He'd now have Graham Moughton, who worked out of the Romford gym where many of the Matchroom fighters trained by his side. Despite his reputation as an 'up and at them' fighter, there were still certain nuances that he wanted to add to his fight repertoire. 'The technique Vic was trying to teach me was to roll with the punches, to keep my neck tight and not drop my head. Then Graham Moughton at the Romford gym was trying to teach me to draw away from my opponent's jab. It was all these different techniques,' Benn would say in 2002. The search for the perfect trainer for him continued and it would come to a head the following year.

If the start of the 1990s was remembered for the country being at war and the beginning of yet another recession, it was also notable for a new sound sweeping the nation. Dance music, which had been growing during the 1980s, was moving away from disco into a fusion of sounds like trance, drum and bass, acid jazz and hip hop. Clubs around Britain were alive to this new sound and being a DJ carried huge kudos. Nigel Benn was part of a new breed of boxer who trained to these sounds, eschewing the traditional *Rocky* anthems which had helped form the stereotypical image of boxers. The other aspect of the new wave of dance music was its association with Class A drugs, all of which were very much part of the club culture.

When not training, Benn could be seen at clubs, often in charge of the music. A story doing the rounds at the time was that Benn would get off the dais and circulate with the ravers and start shadow-boxing, in order to test just how intoxicated the dancers were. There was press speculation that he was one of those ravers, too, a charge he denied throughout his career. In 1996, after former minder Tony Tucker was executed as a result of drug deals gone wrong, Benn spoke about his friends consuming illegal substances.

'I can't stop them or hate them for doing it but I can stop them doing it around me,' he said. 'I've been offered every kind of drug but I will never take them. Drugs are everywhere. Six years ago I was at the Berkeley Square Ball, which is very la-de-dah, and this guy asked me if I wanted a "toot" [cocaine]. I asked: "What the hell's a toot?" I go to clubs to give people music they can dance to. If they want to do drugs, fine – just don't try to involve me.'

Years later, Benn would admit what many, but not all, knew. 'I never, ever, done cocaine. Just ecstasy,' he told me. 'I wasn't really a drinker. I can't drink brandy or things like that. One of my friends gave me this little ecstasy tablet and I was hooked. I was really depressed, took it and it really changed my life.' He can't remember exactly when that first hit was, but it was during that period when he was without a world title and still hunting a rematch with Eubank. And he was also wracked with guilt about his failed first marriage.

He also told me the shadow-boxing story was 'rubbish'. 'When I went clubbing, I was in the groove. Music was a passion of mine.'

Sometimes, things seem to work out well for everyone. What had been obvious about the first fight between Michael Watson and Chris Eubank was that neither man was at his absolute best. The middleweight limit was too much of a struggle for either man to make. Watson's frame had always looked capable of carrying another half stone at least, while the density of Eubank's muscle and his attitude towards roadwork meant a move up the weights was always likely. In 1991, the super middleweight limit was still relatively new – in fact, the WBO did not have a champion at that weight (the legendary Tommy Hearns had vacated it, as it had no worth in the USA). At the middleweight level, the WBO had installed Gerald McClellan as their number one contender, meaning he was entitled to a fight with the champion that year. If Eubank didn't fulfil that requirement, he'd be stripped of the belt, with ranking contenders numbers one and two (John Mugabi of Uganda) the men to fight for the vacant title.

'I told Eubank that we'd vacate the title rather than fight McClellan. Pound for pound, he's a horrible bastard and he's a nasty piece of work,' Barry Hearn told me. Eubank wasn't scared of the fight – that's the thing about boxers, they never are scared. Some may remember a steady stream of heavyweight contenders who seemed ready for the toilet before the first bell if they were fighting Mike Tyson, but these men don't train scared or frightened. They all have belief that, with both men wearing the same gloves and having trained responsibly, they have a chance to win. The ones with prescience and caution are the promoters and trainers. Hearn knew the dangers posed by the scrapper from Freeport, Illinois, who had been trained by the legendary Emanuel Steward. McClellan would prove just how good that advice to Eubank would be when he won the vacant title after knocking out the vastly more experienced Mugabi in 121 seconds at the Royal Albert Hall in November of that year. Hearn would also advise Benn in years to come not to fight McClellan, advice that would be ignored.

Of course, there were two other boxers who should have

fought for the WBO super middleweight title. But once it became known that Eubank and Watson would be moving up to that weight, the WBO conveniently dropped the two men, both from South America, from their rankings, in favour of Eubank and Watson. Despite his fondness for reminding everyone how dirty and corrupt boxing was, Eubank kept quiet about this little episode. It said more about how easy it was to manipulate the governing bodies – the WBO was still a fledgling organisation, which enjoyed a cosy relationship with certain promoters.

The first fight between Watson and Eubank had not been full of the extravagant hate and hype that had so disfigured each man's fight with Benn. After seven months or so as a champion, Eubank's standing as the man to beat meant his bouts were not hard sells. Even so, both men would act in very different ways in the build-up to the rematch.

Watson decided to part company with Eric Secombe, the trainer who had been with him from amateur through to professional ranks. Secombe had been informed by the fighter that Jimmy Tibbs would now be the chief trainer. Not surprisingly, being demoted hurt Secombe, who walked away from the camp, although he would attend the fight as a punter. Watson knew that his decision would be painful for some, but there was something very different about this version of Watson. 'He trained very hard for that fight. And he rested properly when he wasn't training,' Tibbs told me. There were only ninety days between the two bouts, so, after the contract signing, Watson began serious training at the beginning of August. Tibbs believed then, as he does now, in a six-week training camp. There was an intensity about Watson's work which suggested this bout was worth more to him than the previous one, or even the Benn and McCallum fights. 'These people are against me,' Watson kept telling himself. 'These people' were those who controlled the sport – in his mind there was something wrong about the decision in the first bout which wasn't just down to incompetence. 'I just couldn't get Chris Eubank out of my mind,' said Watson in later years. It's a tool that fighters often use – to think of *who* they're fighting rather than *what* they were fighting for. The recognition that he always craved was finally coming his way, quite often in the form of sympathy after the previous bout. The anger was now directed at Eubank. In an interview with South African writer Donald McRae ten days before the rematch, he gave vent to those feelings, which some interpreted as hate.

'Chris Eubank has no respect for anyone. There's something seriously wrong with his brain, with his way of thinking. Why should he attack boxing – the very thing that makes him a very good living, that has lifted him out of nowhere? Why should he describe boxing as barbaric? He would like to come from Eton but he comes from Peckham. He would like to be a white model but he's a black boxer. I think Chris Eubank is ashamed of his roots. Why else would he put so much pressure on himself, pretending he was born with a silver spoon in his mouth? The way he speaks, the words he uses, that's not the way Chris Eubank speaks to his own mother. It's sad but I have to say that I've never seen another black man try so hard to look and sound white. I don't understand it – I just think he's a very weird and confused guy. Our fight is for a world title and me getting some justice after the last decision – but it's also a battle for the security of our families, for the future, for respect. Deep down, in his heart, Eubank knows all this.

'If this one comes down to a war, he'll finish the worse for it. I've been to bleak places in the ring, places he has never even touched. Last time, I was drained by making middleweight. This time, I'm stronger and I'm gonna do it for me but for every other fighter out there, I'm going to do it for the sport of boxing – I'm gonna strip Eubank of everything. These days, they tell me it's not enough just to be a boxer. But, man, that's what I am – a fighter. I ain't no Chris Eubank.'

In none of his previous twenty-eight bouts had Watson made a fight seem as personal as this one. The whole Eubank act had riled him beyond the point of rationality. If he had, in the opinion of some, cut corners in his preparation for the first bout, this time he sparred hard rounds against future WBO middleweight champion Chris Pyatt and hard-hitting light heavyweight Gary Delaney. Watson would say in press conferences, in response to how much he wanted victory before the two stepped into the ring, that he was 'prepared to die'. It's the kind of phrase a sportsman can use without fear if his profession is golf or tennis, but, when used by pugilists, the neutrals and those involved in the sport recoil because it has echoes of an era in which death in the ring was all too common.

In the 1940s, Sugar Ray Robinson, the consensus choice as the greatest fighter who ever lived, fought and knocked out an Irish American fighter named Jimmy Doyle. Robinson tried to pull out of the contest after having a dream in which he killed Doyle. Persuaded to fight, Robinson's punches did in fact render Doyle unconscious – he would never wake up. His death had a profound effect on Robinson, who, when asked if he was worried about the pain he was inflicting on

Doyle during the fight, gave an answer that resonates to this day. When the coroner asked if he figured to get Doyle 'in trouble', Robinson said, 'Mister, it's my business to get him in trouble.' Those cold, hard, brutal words defined the sport for years: Robinson, one of its most stylish and astute performers, admitting that the notion of killing a man to win wasn't anathema to him.

Sugar Ray was generally too classy to invoke that kind of soldier mentality before a fight. His dashing good looks and reputation meant he was treated with respect for much of his career, especially once it became apparent the reflexes weren't what they once had been. Respect. Boxing may be about money and glory, but how a young man longs to be looked in the eye and thought of as *something*. Popular in Brighton as a bit of a sideshow, Chris Eubank wanted more than that for his endeavours. A handful of the English press were happy to indulge him and his eccentricities and wrote kind words about him. 'His is a genuine talent, able to command a platform. Having engaged people's attention, he is also capable of making his points shrewdly and with purpose,' wrote Nick Halling, familiar to boxing fans today as the commentator of many of Sky Sports' live fights. 'Eubank has proved to be both smart and articulate, the antithesis of the punch-drunk bum.'

It is also true that Eubank could not understand why he was so despised by so many. He hadn't been able to work out why, after calling Benn a 'fraud' and saying he had 'no time for such people', that 'the Dark Destroyer' had so much contempt for him. Eubank felt it was possible to play the hype game and also believe that nothing he said would be taken personally. The problem was, given his love of the limelight and how readily he would hold court, things would slip out which would give him cause for regret. In one of those press conferences, he described the fight as a 'kill or be killed' situation. In its way, it was as volatile as calling the sport a 'mug's game'. The winding-up of Watson would continue throughout the weeks preceding the fight. Eubank would appear on Terry Wogan's weekday chat show, parading his belt and reminding Watson who had walked out of the ring with the championship. He also grew tired of the incessant criticism, seemingly aimed at him, because of the decision in the first fight. He called Watson a 'whingeing child' and stormed out of a press conference, with Barry Hearn looking as surprised as anyone to see his main man lose his cool.

Some form of anger was seeping out of Eubank. He was preparing his mind for the size of what lay ahead. 'Michael Watson is strong. He will not give in without a severe beating. I have the same feelings welling up inside me as I did before I fought Benn in Birmingham. I think it could be that tough – but I prevailed then and I will prevail now . . . We await our fate together, Michael Watson and I. Soon it will only be the two of us – face to face. Then, we will find out whose heart breaks first,' he said in one of his final interviews before the fight. Anger and also vulnerability – this time, he would not have the cloak of invincibility around him, the championship belt which allowed him to play unskilled matador to whatever animals there were in his backyard. The fear, as it became apparent, manifested itself in some final, personal insults directed at Watson at the last press conference before the fight.

'You lost the last fight and you'll lose again. You're a loser – go and ask your bank manager,' said Eubank. 'I was only running on half a tank and I still beat you. And I will beat you again,' he reiterated before storming out. Watson, whose choice of pre-fight insults was usually conservative, in keeping with his devout religious beliefs, poked fun at his opponent's accent and lisp. Eubank's trainer Ronnie Davies spoke on behalf of his now absentee fighter. 'That was no promotional gimmick. He is genuinely upset. Michael wound him up. It's unusual for Chris to react like that. He doesn't like Michael and he's fed up with his continual whingeing.'

All the hype, the dislike, the hate, was a reminder, before the action even started, of one of the sport's most famous quotes, from one of the sport's most vicious practitioners: 'Boxers go to dark places that no one else inhabits,' said Roberto Durán. The training, the sacrifice and the dedication. They all remind you what's at stake – the glory and the despair. Thank God they don't make winner-takes-all bouts. The intensity would be too much for the viewer, let alone the participants.

Rematches rarely surpass the original. There's an argument that the third Ali–Frazier fight was the best fight ever, but that ignores the sustained quality of the first bout, which pushed both men to the limit. In the old days it was common for men to fight each other on more than two occasions. Henry Cooper had five fights with the Welshman Joe Erskine. Sugar Ray Robinson took on Jake LaMotta six times, winning five of those contests. Sam Langford, a brilliant boxer who operated during the early stages of the twentieth century, fought fellow black fighter Harry Wills seventeen times, as both men struggled to get world title shots because of the colour of their skin.

Immediate rematches are rarely sought and it is even rarer

for them to live up to the first bout. Sugar Ray Leonard's fifteen-round brawl in Montreal against Durán in 1980 was one of unremitting intensity. Durán won, but later that year, in a rematch, he quit after eight rounds, apparently helpless to defend himself against Leonard's speed, now utilised from long range. '*No más, no más,*' Durán is alleged to have said as he turned his back on Leonard: 'No more, no more.' Six years later, Evander Holyfield, after a dozen fights, beat the durable cruiserweight world champion Dwight Muhammad Qawi after fifteen rounds which left the challenger so dehydrated he had to spend the night in hospital. In a rematch the following year, Qawi didn't get past the fourth.

Earlier in 1991, Mike Tyson's ring rehab continued with a seven-round stoppage of the particularly dangerous Donovan 'Razor' Ruddock. A rematch was ordered on the grounds that many felt referee Richard Steele had stopped the fight too early. Barely four months had passed before the return, which was an altogether more brutal and cranium-sapping affair, with Ruddock lasting the full twelve rounds, despite suffering two knockdowns. It was hoped by many that Eubank–Watson II would have some of that energy and sustained action, with almost everyone agreeing that the first chapter of their rivalry had delivered controversy but not much in the way of quality.

Even so, if White Hart Lane could be filled to its 35,000 capacity, Barry Hearn put the gross income at £2 million. 'This is a fight with great commercial appeal and it is a bonus the first meeting ended controversially. This is business and a business fight. But here we have a case of unfinished business.' A further sixteen million people were expected to watch the fight on ITV. Punters might have been expected to flock to television sets to see a Eubank–Benn rematch, but the polar opposites of the two men boxing on this Saturday, and the baggage being carried into the ring as a result of fight number one, all added up to a potent cocktail.

The problem of staging a boxing fight in a football stadium is that you get a different clientele. While drinking at a sporting occasion might be more controlled now, expecting the majority of the 20,000 plus audience to arrive sober, let alone stay that way through the first five fights before the main event, was naïve. Impatience, frustration, maybe violence – all those emotions were stirred up that evening. Dave Brenner recalls there was 'a nasty atmosphere in the crowd that night. You were scared for your safety and were desperate for the show to end so you could leave. It was a thoroughly nasty evening – it reminded me of Hagler–Minter.'

The night Marvin Hagler beat Alan Minter at Wembley Arena, on 27 September 1980, was one of the ugliest in British sporting history. Before the bout, Minter, the world middleweight champion, was alleged to have said 'no black man will take my title'. After three shockingly one-sided rounds, which saw Minter's face reduced to a mass of crimson welts, the referee was forced to stop the bout and award the title to Hagler. As he celebrated the final part of his journey from humble, hardworking, and often ignored and avoided contender to champion, Hagler was pelted with beer cans and bottles by irate 'fans' who had shown up in the expectation of seeing a 'lynching'. The handful of Hagler fans who had made the journey from Brockton, Massachusetts, testify to this day of feelings of genuine fear for their lives, as they watched policemen scurry to the ring, escort Hagler out through a secret tunnel, leaving them at the mercy of those tanked up and looking for trouble.

Efforts to contain drunkenness in future fights were made as a consequence, but there could still be the odd skirmish ringside. There had been trouble at Tony Sibson's fight with Frank Tate a few years earlier and there always seemed to be a chance that if a boxer with a particularly strong, regional support came from distances further out, that combination of beer and travel could combine to bring a sense of menace to arenas and stadiums up and down the country. With the distaste for Eubank now reaching its peak – he did have fans of his own, but their voices weren't as brash and bold as those of his detractors – there was every chance things could turn nasty before, during and after the fight.

Scene IV

'The sport has to be resurrected'
                    – Michael Watson, September 1991

'I don't regard him as anything. Who is he?'
                    – Chris Eubank, September 1991

As an Arsenal fan, Michael Watson chose to use the visitors' changing room at White Hart Lane, home of his team's bitterest rivals, Tottenham Hotspur, as his preparation room. For him this would be a case of third time lucky, or so he hoped. Now twenty-six, he had challenged for a world title twice and failed on both occasions. He'd said already that winning the belt was secondary to beating

Eubank. That determination extended to his approach to the ring that night. He could usually make his way to the squared circle with only a few noticing when he put one leg over the middle rope. This time, the thumping beat of LL Cool J's 'Mama Said Knock You Out' echoed around the stadium. It made people wonder whether Watson, who had never lost his focus in the face of Benn's barrage of intimidating insults and snarls, had let Eubank get to him. People had seen how Benn had gone in against Eubank full of hate and left the ring battered, bruised and defeated. Would the same thing happen to Watson? On a night that was already dark – it was nearly ten o'clock – and with a mild breeze, the tone was set, as it had been all week after those volatile exchanges during the press conferences when Eubank had walked out. One look into Watson's face was enough to make you realise where his head was. Eight pounds heavier he might have been than the last time he fought, but in the hard angles which led from his jaw to his ear there was a determination, an anger, which was impossible to ignore. This would have to be his night.

As he danced around the ring in a red robe, gladiatorial instrumental music replaced the rap. It had become the preamble to the arrival of Chris Eubank. For the first time in ten months, he walked to the ring as a challenger. His face impassive, as always, his body told a better story. His arms moved freely as he walked, the strain of weight making apparently a thing of the past. When he arrived at the ring, the noise of the music and the gentle jeering stopped as he assessed how best to make his entrance. Standing on the edge of the ring, he started some vigorous shadow-boxing, perhaps teasing the crowd and Watson into thinking the trademark vault into the ring had been erased from his repertoire. Seconds later, in he sprang. His eyes fixed on a place in the distance, would the Eubank whose courage and fire had thrilled against Benn finally resurface?

Some believe you can read things into the way a boxer reacts when his name is read out. Watson looked anxious, as if this was another delay in his pursuit of destiny. Eubank, arms held in front of his body, seemed to have gone into a different world. As his camp held their hands up at the announcement of his name, he remained impassive, preparing to go from Eubank the personality into Eubank the fighter. When the two men were read their instructions by referee Roy Francis, a veteran of the British circuit but officiating in his first world title, there were no histrionics or name calling. They touched gloves without being forced to and returned to their corners. Reg Gutteridge, once again commentating for ITV with Jim Watt, told viewers that Eubank was the bookies' 2-1 favourite, which was broadly in line with how most in the sport felt this fight would go.

At the end of the first round, Eubank strutted back to his corner, as had become his fashion. Once the act was over, he took in massive gulps of air. It wasn't so much a statement of his lack of conditioning as the pace that Watson had set. 'A force of nature,' Jim McDonnell, who was at the fight, told me. For that first three minutes, Eubank matched that work rate, engaging Watson in what seemed like a hundred mini wars, all of them carrying more fire, more danger and more intensity than the first six rounds of their previous fight. 'A good, action-packed first round,' said Jim Watt as replays showed Watson digging in a succession of right hooks to his opponent's ribcage. All of those were thrown with, as Mike

Tyson used to say, 'bad intentions'. Eubank's own punches were no less powerful or sharp, but as he would say again and again, 'with every punch I landed, he kept coming forward'. Scoring the round seemed academic – there was no way either man could keep going at this level. As Hugh McIlvanney noted in his fight report, 'From the first bell, Watson made it plain that he was wagering everything on a commitment to sustained pressure.' It was sustained pressure that many felt was the only way to guarantee victory against Eubank.

The greatest three rounds of middleweight boxing were between Marvin Hagler and Thomas Hearns in 1985; the sheer fury and energy expended by those titans left the viewer wondering whether they needed pacemakers, let alone the participants. The opening three rounds of the second Eubank–Watson bout had a similar intensity – round two began with Eubank, no doubt under orders, channelling as much power as possible into a right hand. It landed flush on Watson's chin and its sheer force moved him off balance. But he didn't go down or even cover up as he had done in the first fight. Instead, he continued to chase Eubank around the ring. It was hard to work out why this bout was so different from the first. Was the ring smaller? Had Watson been training with Linford Christie? Did Eubank, usually so evasive, have rocks in his boots? The pair might have been fighting in a Wendy house and still had enough room for their trainers to sit in. At the end of the third round, Gutteridge admitted he needed a breather, the action being too sustained and incessant to pass comment on in detail. His colleague Watt noted that, while Watson had been fighting more recklessly than normal, there were signs that the pace was starting to wear Eubank down. He had thrown more and better punches for three rounds than in any of his four previous world title fights and yet, after those nine minutes of action, he slumped on his stool. He may have posed and pranced on his way back to the corner, but there was no doubting his level of discomfort. He admitted later that from the end of that round onwards he was in survival mode.

Watch the fight again and you'll notice that Watson returned to a theme of the first fight and also Eubank's meeting with Benn – utilising a body attack to make his opponent suffer. While it may have been possible to give all three of those opening rounds to Eubank (and some did) there was little doubt who had suffered the most internal damage. Watson would say much later that it was 'one of his easiest fights'. As the bell sounded for the start of the fourth, Eubank took great gulps of air that would have kept an elephant alive. He knew, better than anyone at ringside, what he was facing. 'He's so strong,' he told Ronnie Davies.

In the fourth round there was no ambiguity about the scoring. Eubank's punch rate slowed dramatically, while Watson's remained high. Eubank was holding his left hand at his waist, protecting his already tender abdomen. At the pace Watson was fighting, he couldn't help but hit Eubank with a succession of right hands, taking advantage of that lowly held left. He also opened a cut under the left eye, as a result of those rights. By this stage, if you didn't know Eubank and were unaware of his reputation and his almost limitless courage, you feared for his safety. There seemed no escape for him, unless he decided to run at the bell. It's doubtful that anyone would really have blamed him if he had.

Round five was the first one in which either man exhibited

signs of weariness – Eubank had saved his most desperate expressions for his corner – as more punches missed than landed. There were a couple of clinches, a sign that one or both boxers were happy to take a break from the action. At the bell, they exchanged a look, not for the first time. Watson's seemed to say: 'I told you I was better than you.' Eubank's expression was one of defiance: 'And I'm still here.' Their common foe, Nigel Benn, was ringside, speaking to Gary Newbon.

'Nigel, why are you yelling for Michael Watson?' asked Newbon, out of shot. Benn was wearing a shirt and luminous yellow jacket, a sure sign that he was firmly in the forefront of fashion in the nineties.

'They've both beaten me . . . but I've got a lot of respect for Michael inside the ring and outside the ring and . . . no person more than me would like to see Michael win the title.'

'Do you think Eubank is winning?'

'No, no,' Benn replied with a dismissive shake of the head.

'Why do you think Watson's ahead?'

'His aggression, he's coming forward, he's connecting with good shots. I mean, I'm so happy that he's actually changed his tactics and has come out and been so aggressive.'

'Can he keep this pace up, though?'

'Can Eubank last this long? Who knows,' countered Benn. 'I've got to hope he does. Nobody hopes that Michael wins more than me. Come on, Mike!'

If, for the previous five rounds, Eubank had moved away, as much as he could, from Watson's fire, in round six it seemed as if his moves were less voluntary. More than once Watson's flurries to the body caused Eubank to stumble towards the ropes. A sustained attack in the former champion's corner was the most trouble anyone had seen Eubank in since he'd fought Benn. 'He looks like he's trying to pinch a rest. He'll be glad when the bell rings,' said Gutteridge as the round came to an end. Even so, Eubank still managed a little bravado at the bell, standing in front of his corner, hands together, before turning and sitting down. Some may have marvelled at the audacity but a great many more were not fooled. If Eubank were to finally fall, he'd do it on his terms.

Watson's white shorts were now touched by a colouring of crimson – but that reflected the damage he was inflicting. And his pace, which had dipped ever so slightly in round five, was now back to the intensity with which he had begun the fight. In round seven, he threw over seventy-five punches, the number you may expect a flyweight or featherweight to output at the start of the fight. The majority of those blows were power shots, aimed at Eubank's head and body. His use of the jab was purely incidental, thrown as a range finder. And Watson was doing to Eubank what no fighter had done before – landing with combinations. Even when Benn had had his moments a year ago, he had been most successful with single shots. In close, Watson was switching his attack from body to head and then back again. The variety and velocity were too much for Eubank to bear.

After seven rounds, Watson was ahead on most scorecards. That suited the majority of the crowd, who had chanted their man's name lustily throughout. The cheers were most frequent when it looked as if he was scoring punches. There seemed almost an element of surprise in the reaction of the crowd – no one could believe that Watson was making his victory march look so easy. As trainer Jimmy Tibbs said to me, 'He was walking it – doing what he liked with him.'

Even so, there was no chance of taking liberties with Eubank. If the Brighton man was allowed just a little room to plant his feet down and throw serious punches that could hurt, Watson knew there would be trouble. But because he was permanently on the move, he could roll and slip any punches that came his way. And once Eubank was on the retreat those right hands that he liked to throw, either straight or over the top, had less power. There were just twelve minutes of action left and many now believed that Eubank needed a knockout to win.

Eubank would claim later that he felt Watson was intent on prolonging the beating. 'He was beating me up with malice,' said Eubank in his autobiography. That's difficult to believe, but what does seem apparent is that Watson was enjoying his work, enjoying making Eubank miss and enjoying showing the crowd of 22,000 or so who was the better man. At no point had he seemed desperate or lacking in composure. Just determined. Very determined. Eubank, though, *was* desperate. Round nine began with him throwing a handful of those haymaker right hands, all of which sailed past Watson's chin. At the start of the fight, Eubank had spoken to Watson – neither would say what – but by now the man who would never use one word to explain himself when fifteen could suffice had become monosyllabic. Watson remembers his opponent 'crying' when he was hit in the body.

What must have worried Eubank by now was that his strength, his power, thought by many to be his true advantage, had not been a factor. Watson had walked through all those punches and seemed unperturbed. By the start of round ten, Eubank had convinced himself he could no longer win – he had merely conditioned his body to absorb the punishment that was coming his way. He was having the odd moment of success but it was almost like watching a football team celebrate the one goal they've scored to the other team's five. Certain reporters, with their penchant for boxers rather than pressure fighters, were being more generous to Eubank than others. Crucially, Eubank himself was under no illusions about who was winning. 'The integrity of the fighter' (his words) was what kept Eubank on his feet and still wondering if there was any way he could win.

There were several occasions in the tenth round when it seemed he would fall to the floor through exhaustion. His efforts to repel Watson's raids frequently led to him throwing wild counters, which would miss, and this would be accompanied by the unedifying sight of his body following through, his balance now all but non-existent. 'When Eubank misses, look where he goes. He's not an attacking boxer,' said Watt. The other man was, always ready to rumble, his hooks and cuffs sending Eubank all over the ring. As the bell sounded for the end of the tenth, Eubank's legs looked stiff, the belief having drained from his body. Watson may have been tired as well, but he still skipped back to his corner, knowing that all he had to do was control the last two rounds. By now, the crowd was expectant. Watson's fans had waited patiently to see their man win the world title they felt he deserved. The Eubank haters had waited, with less patience, to see the *bête noire* of British boxing get the strapping they'd wanted to see.

The only thing that Watson hadn't done in the previous ten rounds was land the knockout punch, the one that made the judges' scorecards irrelevant. Should he chase it, mindful that leaving his fate in the hands of three other men was not a safe bet? Or would Eubank force him into a change of plan? These were the championship rounds and at the start of the eleventh, Eubank, whose cut by his left eye had become less serious but the swelling around it now causing him problems with vision, looked sharper. There was snap, menace and power in his punches. At times during the previous ten rounds, he had looked like a man harbouring a sense of self-pity. Bad enough to be the target of all the jeers but far worse for them to be replaced by punches. But, for once, a right hand forced Watson to cover up. His head twisted, he stepped backwards for the first time. Fortunately for him, there was no composure about Eubank's work. A fusillade of blows came Watson's way but he leant back and let Eubank flail away, the punches hitting air and rope. Watson's head was cleared, but Eubank, usually so smart about the other man's weaknesses, punched himself silly, the last vestiges of energy slipping from his body. And now Watson could sense the end. His right hands targeted Eubank's head. These were concussive shots – 'He's in trouble,' shouted Watt – and Eubank was being battered. He had stopped throwing punches and there was an argument to suggest he should not have been allowed to take more punishment. Around twenty punches landed in the next thirty seconds, a final combination that sent Eubank to his knees, voluntarily, by the look of it. The fight seemed to have only one possible conclusion.

Barry Hearn, at ringside, had spent most of the night encouraging Eubank forward. But now, even he knew there was nothing left to see. 'He bashed him up,' Hearn said about Watson's performance that night. 'When Eubank went on his knees, after Michael dropped him, my very first thought was "Hmm, Watson–Benn rematch". I'm always thinking business. Don't make me a nice person but I didn't have a second – Eubank has had his time and he's been completely outclassed and dropped so I thought "Move on". It's a bit Don Kingish, but it's the practicality.'

Dropped he may have been, but Eubank would get up. No one doubted that. The most idiosyncratic British world champion might also have been the bravest. The full extent of the beating he'd been taking should have been obvious to anyone at ringside when he spat out blood on getting up. Eubank says that the moment he hit the canvas, the strength that had been draining from his body returned. That his senses were alive. It's what makes a fighter go from good to great. How they react when things go against them. 'Skills pay the bills' is one of boxing's most popular refrains. But when the skills have been neutralised, what's left is instinct. What sets boxing apart from every other sport is how your mind reacts to the pressure of a beating from an apparently unstoppable force. The great heavyweight Evander Holyfield best exemplified this when describing how his mind worked when the younger, heavier and more powerful Riddick Bowe battered him around the ring in the tenth round of their first encounter the following year.

'He was laying a lot of leather on me. He had me from pillar to post, but even while he was hurting me, I thought, for the first time in the fight, that I had a chance of winning. He was spending a lot of energy, and I thought I could catch him when he tired.'

Holyfield lost, but no one would ever forget how he nearly came back from the brink.

At White Hart Lane, Chris Eubank had less time to think

about what to do next than he should have had. Under WBO rules, a fighter is given a mandatory eight count by the referee after being knocked down. Experienced he may have been, but Roy Francis got caught up in the moment and counted up to four before allowing Eubank to continue. There were less than ten seconds remaining in the round. Enough, surely, for Eubank to survive. Maybe his corner could revive him sufficiently for an assault in the final round, where he'd need a knockout to win. All three judges had him behind, by varying amounts.

Eubank walked forward and Watson came to meet him. Years later, he'd tell boxing writer Steve Bunce that he was already dreaming about the riches he could now bestow on his two daughters, so certain was he of victory. He'd been dominant in the eyes of the majority and had been more than a match for everything Eubank had done. So far.

All night he'd countered Eubank's best shots with a jab and then a right hand. Sensing victory, he loaded up the power in his right hand, perhaps dreaming of the knockout punch. But for the first time that night he wasn't prepared for any retaliation. It came in the form of a right uppercut. The punch was a short one, but it came with Eubank's forward momentum. The force of the punch, landing on the tip of Watson's jaw, forced him off his feet and towards the corner from which he had just walked. If he had just landed on the canvas, things may have turned out – is better the right word?

I remember years ago, when I was just starting out as a reporter, interviewing Sir Henry Cooper. I asked him for his prediction on an upcoming bout. After he'd told me, he added: 'I just hope whoever loses, if they get knocked out,

I hope it's clean. Just one shot.' The clean knockouts look scary, but more often than not the fighter gets up, shakes his head and then asks his trainer what happened. Michael Watson might well have been knocked out cold if his head hadn't hit the third rope. Bad enough to have taken a punch with the force of a speeding car but now the whiplash effect of the rope against the back of his head left him in a state of distress that only a medical expert could explain. Watson would also get to his feet quickly, as the bell rang to end the round, but his legs looked stiff, as if they were being powered by his hips. His eyes were looking at Eubank, or at something in the distance. It was hard to tell. When you focus on a boxer's legs, you realise how thin they are and wonder how they could possibly support a man for as long they do. That it takes so long for them to fail is the miracle.

Jimmy Tibbs rushed out to collect Watson, to do what he could to stimulate his fighter's senses. He was three minutes from the title and Tibbs knew how much it meant to Watson. The crowd were stunned. What happened, they were thinking. The punch had been so short and quick, you'd need a monitor to spot it. But there was no doubt that the man most of them wanted to win was now in some sort of trouble. How? *How?* He'd been winning as he pleased. And he'd been doing it to persistent, tribal shouting of his name: 'Watson, Watson!' The atmosphere now was not so much cold as confused and anxious.

'Are you all right?' Tibbs asked Watson, once he had him sitting down in the corner. The boxer nodded. He seemed to know what was going on, but, like many a fighter, he was having difficulty getting his body to obey him. As he got ready to answer the bell, Watson's mouth seemed either incapable or unwilling to accept the gumshield from the other man in the corner, Dean Powell. No one knew it at the time, but Watson was struggling to get oxygen into his brain. His central nervous system, already scrambled by that right uppercut, had other problems that it needed to fight off.

In the other corner, Eubank was still weary, still bruised, but for the first time all night he had a purpose. He looked over at his opponent. Watson was still looking at him, or at the very least that was the direction in which his eyes were pointing. When the bell went, Watson remained where he was rather than join Eubank in the centre of the ring for the obligatory touching of gloves at the start of the final round. Referee Francis dragged him by the arm and forced the issue. And now it was obvious that there was no strength in that body. His legs had no power – if he was to fall now he'd never get up. Eubank sensed the moment and started punching. Frantically and without much skill, he threw punch after punch at Watson's head. Instinctively, Watson brought his arms up and blocked virtually all the blows. He was moving from the hip, allowing the ropes that were his enemy to be his friend, aiding his weaving and rolling. But he couldn't move. Eubank had him pinned. Soon, one of those punches had to land. Watson had not thrown one of his own since the round began. With twenty-nine seconds of the round gone, Watson was an open target. Referee Francis, who had been monitoring the stricken fighter since he'd had to pull him to the centre of the ring, put his body between both men and waved his arms to signal the end of the fight. Eubank, improbably, incredibly and impressively, was the winner. For all the posing and pontificating he had demonstrated, unequivocally, that his fighting heart was as true as any of the great champions'. And his boxing brain, his nerve, were as flawless as those of men like Ali and Leonard. How else could he still have plotted an escape from where he was? However spurious the WBO title, he was now a two-time world champion. And it was his fairly and squarely.

As Francis took Watson, whose eyes had a dream-like quality about them, back to his corner, Jimmy Tibbs was already in the ring. 'At first, I was angry,' says Tibbs about it. In his mind, Watson had 150 seconds to survive and take the title. 'They all want to be champions. That's why they come into the gym in the first place,' he'd tell me. In the 1990s, and for many years before, boxing was not, in any way, safety-first. It was about the winning.

For now, the winning and losing had been decided. But still there was fury. Watson's legs might have been stiff and he was not throwing punches, but could he still have held on and won? Tibbs wasn't alone in thinking there was an escape route. Then Francis, in his thick London accent, uttered the words that must have haunted Tibbs for years.

'He's hurt, Jim. And you know it.'

Still Tibbs didn't really believe it. And then Watson sagged in his arms. And soon it became apparent to those near the drama, including the trainer, that this wasn't exhaustion.

In the ring, Eubank had been confirmed as the new champion and was now being interviewed by Gary Newbon.

'From round six, he was too strong for me . . . but I knew I could go the distance and I knew he would tire at this pace. He kept up a phenomenal pace. When I caught him, I knew that was it. I didn't know whether he would revive in between rounds. He didn't. I'd like to thank my brother Simon for taking me running,' said Eubank, before embarking on a monologue in which he thanked his wife, the newspaper the *People* and the association that had voted him best-dressed man in the United Kingdom.

'He hit me with a couple of good shots. He was very, very strong. I want him tested, I want him tested to see if there was anything in his blood.' Newbon pressed him – did he mean drugs?

As Eubank answered, saying he wanted Watson's urine tested, a fight broke out. The champion's concentration was broken and he would not answer Newbon again. He would say later that he never thought Watson was on drugs, but he wanted to know where his strength had come from – it certainly had not been there in the first fight.

What was happening outside the ring was now pivotal. Newbon wrapped up the interview and handed control of the programme back to Jim Rosenthal. Newbon was trying to get to Watson, to see what was happening. 'I didn't realise how serious it was, because I couldn't get near him. It was pretty ugly that night, the atmosphere,' Newbon told me. The alcohol-fuelled fight that had broken out started because of a feeling that Watson had been robbed of the chance to win. But that sense of injustice wasn't helping. It wasn't helping the image of the sport but, much more importantly, it was preventing people being able to attend to their man, who was now struggling.

Only one doctor was around to try and aid the stricken boxer. The chaos that surrounded the evening clouded his thinking. With Watson sinking into unconsciousness, he was held up by friend and DJ Tim Westwood. The fight had officially finished at 10.54 p.m., and no expert medical attention had been given to the boxer in the five minutes after Roy Francis had waved his arms in the air to call the bout off. With no stretcher on the scene, the doctor placed a briefcase on the canvas and rested Watson's head on it. There was still fighting outside the ring and it only started to ease when police, aided by Nigel Benn, calmed the situation. It wasn't perfect but it was enough for Tibbs, Westwood and another friend of Watson, Kamal, to carry the boxer out of the stadium and into the tunnel. He was carried past his mother, who was assured her son was suffering from exhaustion. A series of lies were told to other loved ones to keep them calm. By now, blood was forming on the surface of Watson's brain. Those who had been at ringside, who had watched what happened, knew the seriousness of the situation. This wasn't a one-punch knockout where the stricken man comes round after a few minutes in the abyss. As Watson would say later about slipping away, all he knew was darkness.

There is no escaping the fact that boxing is dangerous. You may debate its purpose, how to achieve victory and the fact that many noted boxers have triumphed at the highest levels of the sport by putting a premium on defence while hitting their opponent cleanly but without fury. But there is no way around one aspect of it – it requires, as its purpose, for one man to hurt the other. Serious injury to boxers is a permanent risk. And when you see it, you don't forget it. My night was in Sheffield, nine days before Christmas 2000. Local man Paul Ingle was defending his IBF featherweight title against Mbulelo Botile, a South African boxer who, on any given night, would have given Ingle a pretty hard fight. On this evening, he toyed with Ingle. The problem was that the champion had struggled with his weight making – the rumour had been that he'd lost a stone in the week before the fight.

After ten rounds, Ingle was a battered wreck. Sitting next to Claude Abrams, the then editor of *Boxing News*, I tried to work out with him how many rounds Ingle had won. I was much more generous to Ingle than Abrams was. In the eleventh, Ingle was dropped. We all seemed to know that was it. There was no sense in Ingle being allowed to fight another round. He was weak, groggy and distressing to look at. But there he came, on legs as sturdy as blancmange, ready to take his final blows. Ingle had fought eleven hard rounds with Naseem Hamed, wore camouflage shorts and had a reputation for fitness. Then you remembered his record – he was always in hard fights. Those were the boxers you worried about. How many times can you take yourself to the brink?

Ingle was put out of his misery twenty seconds into that final round. Mercy. Except, he didn't get up. For several minutes. He remained on the canvas until a stretcher took him away, his family distraught as he was carried past them. The bout was the chief support for another world title fight that night – Joe Calzaghe would defend his super middleweight title, the same one that Chris Eubank held, against Richie Woodhall. As the fighters approached the ring, I remembered promoter Frank Warren trying to muster a clap of sorts for these two warriors. He was obligated to do so, but it was impossible not to think he wanted to be anywhere else. His face ashen, his head no doubt full of weariness, knowing he'd have to debate the sport and its morals the following day. I wrote for the BBC website that during the Calzaghe–Woodhall bout 'news filtered back from former British champion

Kevin Lueshing that everyone feared – Ingle had suffered a blood clot on the brain'. Most at ringside had seen it before – the dates and names change but the fear, the worry, the dread doesn't change. Trainers liken their boxers to sons. They know their personal life, their niggles, their personal worries. And writers aren't so different. 'We're not supposed to get attached to them,' Abrams told me once.

More than a decade later, Ingle has made a recovery. Not a full one. But he is alive.

The best medical minds talk about patients who have suffered severe brain trauma needing to be treated within the 'golden hour' after suffering the injury. Treatment during that period offers the victim the best chance of survival and then a full recovery. Key during that first hour is that he is offered oxygen support. The fight had ended at 10.54 p.m. and Watson did not get to a hospital until 11.22 p.m. It was only then that he was provided with oxygen support, without which he would have died. The problem for Watson was that the hospital, the North Middlesex in Edmonton, did not have the facilities to perform the operations he'd need on his brain. At 11.55 p.m., the boxer was put back into an ambulance and sent to St Bartholomew's Hospital in central London.

A scan at the North Middlesex had confirmed that Watson had a blood clot on his brain which was denying his body sufficient oxygen and was also growing at an alarming rate. There was no time to waste. The pupils in his eyes had dilated and at around 1 a.m., more than two hours after the fight had been stopped, he was taken into the operating theatre for a procedure to reduce the increasing pressure around his brain caused by the blood clot, which was now the size of a saucer.

He'd be operated on for over ninety minutes, a procedure which involved a section of the skull covering his brain being temporarily removed to give access to the clot. For such an operation, two surgeons, two anaesthetists and two nurses were involved, and despite the serious and complicated nature of the operation, no one doubted that the boxer would require further such treatment if he was to survive.

By now this was no longer just a boxing story and Fleet Street had descended on Barts aware that Watson had begun his second fight in twenty-four hours. At around quarter past six that Sunday morning, consultant neurologist Peter Hamlyn spoke to journalists about Watson's condition. If many expected him to confirm that the boxer had lost his life, the news they received was indeed of a funereal nature. The word critical was used – and Hamlyn also admitted that he could make no definitive statement about the likely direction of Watson's responses to treatment.

In the following twelve hours, there would be more cause for concern. The pressure inside Watson's skull increased again and another operation was required. This time, after the excess fluid was drained from Watson's cranium, Hamlyn chose not to replace the temporarily removed piece of skull, so that in the event of further procedure being required he'd be able to operate more quickly. It was clear that Watson's condition would need to be carefully observed for some time. Hamlyn was also aware that even if Watson did make it out of intensive care, his quality of life would be questionable. Even so, there was no reason, as yet, to switch off the ventilator that was keeping him alive.

Watson's recovery would be a long journey and it began with the smallest of incremental steps. He was, twenty-four hours after the fight, in a coma, watched by nurses, doctors and family. His mother, who had gone through a similar agonising procedure with her other son, Jeffrey, some twenty-five years earlier, remained vigilant. Faith had played a big part in Michael Watson's life, although he would later admit that it hadn't always done so in his formative years. Now, that faith was paramount to his recovery; his mother's prayers then, in the months and years to come, would give him enormous strength. The serious nature of Watson's injury would be summed up by Peter Hamlyn years later: 'He was iller and more severely affected than any other person I've ever encountered. He was closer to being dead than anyone I've seen.'

Outside the recovery room, the merits of boxing were being questioned. Even without round the clock news coverage, debate raged far and wide as to whether civilised society should allow such an apparently barbaric sport as boxing to continue to flourish. Respected figures like Frank Warren and Mickey Duff were advising on safety measures such as regular doctors' checks during a fight as well as a change to the ropes around the ring that had almost certainly caused the whiplash suffered by Watson. But neither man could come up with a coherent argument about how to change the basic nature of boxing – to prevent it being the pain game. As Harry Mullan wrote in the *Sunday Times*:

'Sometimes, there is no easy explanation with which to salve our consciences, only the bleak fact that a man died because he was a boxer. Such a case was the death in 1986 of the Scottish welterweight champion Steve Watt, an apparently fit and well-trained boxer at the peak of his prowess. The post-mortem showed that Watt went into the ring that night with his brain already severely damaged from the repetitive, percussive damage caused by a busy and competitive career, first as an amateur international and then as a highly-ranked contender for the British title.'

Deliberately or otherwise, the latter part of that quote hinted at the punishment Watson had taken in his fight with Mike McCallum. Had that beating left his body and senses more vulnerable? There was no way of knowing. Regardless, those who had worked with him were struggling to deal with their own consciences.

'I think there are times when any sane person asks himself "what are we doing in this business?" and that was a very good time to ask that question,' said Barry Hearn. 'Going to see him in hospital was not easy, because you do feel partly responsible, there's no doubt about it. If I hadn't put them both in the ring, it wouldn't have happened.' Hearn was also the target of criticism from the sections of the press for allowing the 'hate' angle to become such a pivotal part of the promotion. The effect on Hearn personally was bigger than he would admit – those around him recognised the extreme stress he was under and how he took most of the criticism on his own shoulders, rather than allow others at Matchroom to handle the fallout. But Hearn never did get out of the sport and, despite going to see Watson regularly for several weeks in the immediate aftermath of the fight, his visits dried up as he sensed that he was being held responsible for Watson's predicament.

Another man struggling to come to terms with everything was Jimmy Tibbs. Boxing had been his life since the 1960s and, while there had been elements of his life that, at best, could be described as unsavoury, he had been a dedicated

Christian for over a year, despite the doubts of those closest to him. 'How long is this going to last?' his wife asked her husband when he informed her of his conversion. It had been his decision to send Watson out for that twelfth round. Whether or not it would have made any difference if he'd retired the boxer when he walked back to the corner after taking that uppercut was something he'd never know. More than likely, the damage had been done when Watson's head hit the ropes. When Tibbs reached the hospital and saw Watson's condition, Peter Hamlyn assured him that it was not his fault. He has kept those words in his head ever since, but the doubts continue.

'I was absolutely distraught. No one realised how seriously injured he was until we got back to St Bartholomew's. I was ready to call it a day. I thought . . . Seeing that happen to a young man like that,' Tibbs told me. Before he got the chance to hang up his spit bucket, Tibbs was visited by friends he had made through his newfound faith. They convinced him to carry on, saying that he could do more for their shared faith by training young boxers. Eventually, he would return full time and his future would be linked with Chris Eubank.

But as he contemplated his future he was not to know what lay ahead for the boxer he had trained to within a second of victory, only to see glory replaced by defeat, despair and then tragedy. Tibbs, along with the rest of the sport, held his breath as Watson clung on in a way he never did in the ring. He, along with the boxer's family and friends, had been told that even if Watson did come out of the coma there would be a heavy price to pay. It was likely that he would be in a vegetative state for much of his life and would require constant help to feed himself, dress himself as well as go to the bathroom. As it was, he already required a tracheotomy to enable him to breathe. How, then, would boxing defend itself? As it was, the sport's most famous, most active practitioner, Mike Tyson, had been charged with the rape of a beauty pageant contestant in Indianapolis. A savage business for savages, cried the many who had always believed the sport had no place in a civilised society. The abolition of the sport would be discussed in parliament, although the chances of any binding resolution were minimal given that there would be a general election the following year. What no one could ask with legitimate prior knowledge was whether Watson would be one of the voices calling for the sport to be cast adrift. Those who knew him well would probably assume that he'd never even thought about it. But as someone who had campaigned for greater control over his career, Watson would no doubt have some thoughts as to the rights boxers had when they were in the ring. After all, the medical attention afforded to him that night came after a delay and there was a link between his current plight and the speed at which he could be treated given the failure to arrange for medical professionals to be on site.

Rod Douglas had suffered the same injury on the same side of his brain when he lost to Herol Graham in 1989 yet he had left hospital within days of his injury, the speed and success of the surgery allowing him to lead a normal life, even if he would never fight again. At the time, John Morris was head of the British Boxing Board of Control, the body responsible for providing the medical supervision for the fight. He would say a year later of the Board's evaluation of their performance that evening and their subsequent action: 'We made very few changes. However, we did sharpen up the reaction time. My own feeling, after more than forty years' involvement in boxing, is that the safety and welfare of boxers is the first consideration. If it isn't, we're in trouble. Boxing cannot afford mistakes.'

One of those mistakes meant that one of the fighters they were looking out for was battling for his life. A month after the bout, Watson began to show signs of recovery, although he could neither open his eyes nor speak, the occasional blink or slightest of movements on his right side being the only movements that enabled doctors to judge his progress. By November, two months after the fight, he was moved out of the ICU unit where he been taken after surgery and into a recovery ward. The signs were encouraging.

At White Hart Lane that September night, Chris Eubank sat in his dressing room after the fight in silence. It wasn't just the dark clouds that rendered him monosyllabic. The extent of the beating he had taken meant he could not stand up. Barry Hearn insisted he stay in a wheelchair until after he had himself been to hospital. There were bruises consistent with the savagery inflicted on his body, but Eubank would heal. Sort of.

The Eubank ride had been fun, that was unquestionable. He was twenty-five years old and the WBO super middle-weight champion. His presence and personality had helped galvanise boxing. Plenty of people could stomach his pontificating as long as the fans kept turning up. And Eubank had enjoyed most of the journey, the successes as well as the setbacks, regarding those as character-building. Away from the ring, away from the cameras, his personality was vibrant, his company engaging. But now, he had been rendered as silent as Watson was immobile.

For someone who had spent so much time explaining his dislike of the profession from which he earned his living, the plight of Michael Watson was the nightmare Eubank knew he might one day have to endure. Other fighters had been involved in similar situations. Barry McGuigan fought a Nigerian boxer called Young Ali during the early stages of his career. Ali was knocked out in six rounds and, like Watson, fell into a coma. He remained in it for five months before hearing the final bell.

'I still see the wee man in my dreams. Both of our wives were pregnant. He never knew it, but he had a son, too,' said McGuigan. 'It had a dramatic effect on me. I really didn't want to fight on but I did, and in my next fight I honestly pulled my punches. I had the guy in trouble and he was expecting me to finish him off but instead I hesitated and he nearly took my head off with a left hook. I realised I had to get the job done but I cried in the dressing room afterwards.'

But McGuigan learned to fight hard. Hard enough to win a world title and defend it. Eubank was already a world champion – what could the sport offer him that he did not already have? And having spent most of the past year being one of the most reviled men in British sport, he knew that, while there would be a degree of sympathy for him, it would be limited for a man who had severely injured a rival while also picking up a significant sum of money. His torment would continue as, post-fight, the tabloids sought to stoke up the animosity between the two men, claiming that Watson didn't want Eubank to see him. It seemed an unlikely claim, given how hard even the most basic form of communication was for Watson. There were people who remember the stricken boxer refusing to see Eubank, blinking his eyes twice to signify that he was an unwelcome visitor. The effect on Eubank was unquestionable. In the face of the biggest physical beating of his career, Eubank had none the less found a way to win. And now he was being asked to hold his head high while those in the cheap seats threw stones at him. What to do next? Eubank would find a way to visit Watson shortly after the fight. He saw the extent of his injuries. And he left contemplating retirement. Others noticed a change in his behaviour. In the end, Eubank would decide to carry on, but it was not a decision taken lightly. And it might not have been the best one.

'It finished Eubank as a fighter. He never, ever gambled to try and stop someone again in his whole career. And not because he was worried about hurting someone. He was worried about someone doing it to him,' said Barry Hearn.

If one former foe found his connection with Watson fraught with emotional anxiety and resentment, another showed there was a side to him that few knew existed. Nigel Benn had been at ringside that night, cheering on the first man to beat him, not just because of his dislike for Eubank but also because of his admiration for Watson.

'I visited him in hospital a few days later and tried to talk to him and comfort his girlfriend. It hurt to see him in that condition,' Benn wrote in his autobiography. Their friendship would not end there. 'The Dark Destroyer' would keep in contact during the difficult days of recovery, through to the brighter days.

'Nigel is one of the most caring men in the world,' said Watson's mother, Joan. 'His warmth and generosity to Michael have been a tremendous help. He's not boasted about it. He just gets on with it – and Michael loves him.' A few years after the fight, Watson's house was burgled. Benn replaced the stolen TV, video and hi-fi and tried to prevent the press from finding out, although they eventually did, from Watson's mother.

'When you see Michael and Nigel together you can understand what mutual respect and love is all about. No matter how busy Nigel is he's always managed to find time to help Michael. If other people haven't seen how warm and loving a man Nigel can be, then I'm sorry,' continued Joan Watson.

Compassion notwithstanding, Benn wasn't dissuaded from the rigours and dangers of a ring career after watching his friend suffer such serious injuries. In fact, watching Watson that night had galvanised him. He had observed the movements of his two conquerors and had been seriously impressed by the way Watson had approached his task that night. The intensity of his attacks and improved fitness had taken him so close to victory. It was clearly the way to beat Eubank, as long as you were prepared for those counter-attacks that would almost certainly come at the end of the bout. Benn would change trainers again. Brian Lynch, Vic Andretti and Graham Moughton had all brought him to a certain point, but Jimmy Tibbs would take him to the level he wanted to go to.

Act IV

Experts on brain injuries and their effects on victims will tell you that no two cases are the same. Michael Watson may have suffered the same accident that befell Rod Douglas – a subdural haematoma – but the two men suffered their injuries in very different circumstances. Douglas had had a much milder ring career – fourteen fights with just the one punishing evening. Less than eighteen months before his fateful night with Chris Eubank, Michael Watson had suffered a horrendously prolonged attack at the hands of Mike McCallum. Frequent blows to his head would have led to some permanent bruising around the brain.

The other problem for boxers is that frequent blows to the frontal lobe of the brain can have a far-reaching impact. They create a sense of fearlessness and also take away quite a few social phobias. An absence of fear might be considered no bad thing for a boxer, but it also probably means that he is the last man to know when his time is up.

Anyone who saw Watson that night at White Hart Lane would have noticed that fearless streak. Now it would be tested to the extreme. His recovery from brain damage of the utmost seriousness would be on a number of levels. Firstly, in order to recover, Watson would have to work as hard as he had done in training for any of his fights. And even if he did put in the hours, there were no guarantees that he'd have a life worth living. Watson had gone from being three minutes and ten seconds away from fulfilling a lifelong dream to being left in a vegetative state. More than a few people I'd spoken to say that, prior to his accident, Watson had more than a trace of resentment in his DNA. The belief that his was a talent never fully appreciated. Would that affect his efforts to recover? Until Watson started to talk again, no one would know. In January 1992, he was transferred from Barts to Homerton Hospital in Hackney, recognition that there was a degree of progress in his recovery, although there was always a chance that he might succumb to his injuries at any time.

At Homerton, Watson endured hours of repetitive physio-therapy in order to give him back some sense of flexibility. At this stage, he still had limited vision, did not speak and communicated mostly through the pointing of fingers or the raising of an eyebrow. That was encouraging, in the sense that he could understand everything happening around him. Now he'd be asked to find feeling in his limbs, through a series of physiological exercises which would arouse one of the few senses he still had. Pain.

'The brain is like a fingerprint – it is made up of neural networks which are made up of the way we are and the way we think,' says Alice Everett, who, as brain injury adviser at Addenbrooke's Hospital in Cambridge, has seen dozens of patients attempt to recover from injuries similar to Watson's. 'Physio is just repetition – part of it is natural, building up strength and building up the pathways in your brain that have been damaged by the accident. To move your arm, you have to tell your arm to move, as well as train it to move. It's a mental and physical thing.'

All the while, Watson would go through the routine. Unable to dress himself, needing to sleep with a bedpan. His life before the bout had been one of seeking the one big fight that would change his life. Now, it was a steady stream of smaller bouts that required enormous physical and mental courage. To make matters harder the entire left side of his body was immobile and impervious to manipulation. Even so, he would continue to work. In fact, twelve months would pass before there was any real sign of improvement. Before that, he would speak his first word, calling out the name of one of the nurses who looked after him. In pain. Those who knew him best, who made sure they were by his side as often as possible, still shudder at the memory of what Watson put himself through during those long sessions at Homerton. They knew he was in pain, they could see it in his face, but he never complained. Those around him included friends from way back, not necessarily boxing people. The exception was Nigel Benn, who managed to sneak in, without any fanfare, and check on his friend and former rival.

In May 1992, Watson was taken back to Barts for another operation, this one to close his skull. Shortly afterwards, he was visited by Muhammad Ali, who was facing his own battle with Parkinson's. 'Boy, you're nearly as pretty as me,' said the former three-time world heavyweight champion. Those present at the meeting recalled the effect Ali had on Watson. For the first time since his accident, he smiled. And then he raised his right fist in the air to touch Ali's.

It was, according to Watson, the only uplifting thing that happened to him that year, but it may have provided the motivation required to get through the hardest days. The physical impact for Watson of Ali's visit could not be underestimated. 'It's hard to predict recoveries – but determination does mean a lot. If people are self-motivated then they can achieve so much. You have to push yourself,' says Alice Everett.

Religious faith also helps and now Watson leaned heavily on his god. 'I can do all things through Christ which strengtheneth me – Philippians 4:13. No verse in the Bible better exemplified Watson's thinking. Again, there are those who believe faith can help, and certainly Watson's friends who weren't necessarily spiritual believe it did. But they do not underestimate the power of sheer bloody-mindedness either. Watson had both in abundance. And with every little battle he won he'd rely less on faith and more on himself.

The year 1992 was as low and high as Michael Watson had ever been. He was still entirely reliant on others to bathe, feed and clothe him, but by the end of the year he was allowed to leave hospital and spend Christmas at home with his two daughters. Most patients in his condition can remember things like their first home, their primary school teacher and their friends and family – Watson remembered

the street and the house where he lived in Chingford –
but the minutiae of their day-to-day lives are much more
difficult to recall. It is only with the help of those around
him that he is now able to remember what was happening
in his life. He knows now that for his first Christmas back
home he was wheelchair-bound, confined to the house he
owned and unable to spend too much time with anyone,
so tired was he after performing the simplest of tasks.
It was a struggle that he undertook in private. After the
initial months following his accident, when details of his
recovery were in every newspaper and on several television
news bulletins, Watson had gone back to the obscurity he
had dreaded so much when he fought. His close circle of
friends kept a close eye on him, but the sport of boxing
carried on as before.

Watson's goal was to go home for good. He would need
permanent care, but the hope was that he would come to
depend upon it less and less. Twenty-one months after the
accident, during which time he was introduced to fans at
Highbury, then the stadium of his beloved Arsenal, Michael
Watson was finally allowed home. But rather than it be his
crowning moment, he would find being in his house harder
than hospital life. He still could not walk and talking was
painfully slow and energy-sapping. There were financial
issues as well. Watson had not made any money for two
years and would need to have his house modified in order
to allow him to live with convenience. A benefit, organised
by Ambrose Mendy, raised around £86,000, which was spent
entirely on equipment to help Watson to navigate around
the house.

Enough people would tell Watson that the British Boxing

Board of Control had been negligent in their provision of adequate medical care on that night at White Hart Lane, but he would need to pursue his grievance with them before 21 September 1994, when the three-year limitation period would end. In an interview with the *Sun*, he said: 'I now know every second counted. Just about everything that was done was wrong, and I will pay for the rest of my life.' He was seeking a million pounds for damages. Crucially, the BBBofC would contest the action vigorously. A payout of such an amount would have bankrupted them.

It had already been shown earlier in 1994 that nothing was going to change the inherently dangerous nature of the sport. Bradley Stone, a promising bantamweight, was knocked out in ten rounds by fellow British fighter Richie Wenton in a tough battle at Bethnal Green. Stone walked away from the ring in apparent control of all his faculties, telling people he would take a year off from the sport. Three hours later, while talking with his girlfriend, he collapsed, fell into a coma and died two days later. Like Watson, who visited him in hospital, he had suffered a blood clot on the brain.

As a result of what had happened to Watson, the BBBofC had made changes to the medical care available at ringside. At the start of 1995, Nigel Benn would fight American Gerald McClellan in London. The man from Illinois collapsed after being counted out in the tenth round. He was immediately attended to by one of four anesthetists present and taken to hospital as quickly as possible. But McClellan remains in a state of blindness and has little brain function.

By now, Michael Watson's recovery was visible to those who had been with him since before that fateful night.

He could, with assistance, take a few steps, even though he remained wheelchair-bound. He would go to church and speak to hundreds of people. There were moments when the darkness could set in, but it was almost always short-lived. He was starting to go out more and more and the public reception he would receive almost always lifted his spirits. What would sap them was the torturously slow process of taking his fight for justice to the law courts. Incredibly, the case would not be heard in court until 1999, a full five years after the writ was served and eight years after the accident. The only benefit to the delay was that it had allowed Watson time to heal further, with regular memory exercises helping him to piece together what had happened to him on 21 September. He'd watched that fight countless times on video without being able to remember any of it. Now, slowly, it was coming back. Every aspect of what he had gone through was an ordeal and the therapy, which required him to focus the mental side of his body, was just as demanding. There was additional pressure. The BBBofC could not afford to lose so they hired the best: two leading barristers and a neurosurgeon were brought in to counter testimony from Peter Hamlyn. The Board's team would also try to insist that Watson did not have the right to legal aid, but he argued successfully that he was incapable of earning a living. He had little money left as it was. Colin McMillan, the former world champion who had known Watson for years, was at the forefront of organising a benefit to raise much-needed funds for his friend. 'We'd heard that Michael had been told he would never walk again. And when we had the benefit, Michael turned up and took a few steps.'

The court case was set to commence on 8 June 1999 but shortly before it did so the BBBofC made an offer of £180,000 compensation. Watson asked for an additional £40,000 but the Board would not budge. So it went to trial, with the BBBofC arguing that Watson's injuries would have been the same, regardless of the adequacy of medical provision on the night. Watson memorably gave testimony; he was wheeled into court and then walked twenty, very slow paces, to his seat. He had already filed a twenty-four-paragraph statement detailing his injuries and the progress he had made with his life since.

The hearing was supposed to last six days but it ran until 22 June. In the end, Judge Ian Kennedy ruled, three months later, in favour of Watson, saying that the Board owed the boxer (and all future boxers) a duty of care. The date the verdict was reached was 24 September, almost exactly eight years after the fight. The stress of the whole case took a massive toll on Watson, not least because he knew that it was not the final moment of victory. I remember lining up an interview with him just a couple of days after the verdict, but was told just a few hours before he was due to arrive that he was simply too tired to attend. The interview was due to be held under camera lights, a format I would learn in later years does Michael no favours.

The legal costs that the BBBofC were saddled with forced them into administration and the process dragged on for another two years before an unlikely mediator forced the issue. Frank Warren had never promoted Michael Watson, but a duty to boxing and boxers meant he got involved, essentially making sure that the BBBofC would pay Michael £400,000 as part of a long-term settlement. His boxing career had been one long journey for respect, in the end earned in the most tragic of circumstances. Now, in his quest for justice, he'd gone down a similarly long but significantly more arduous route. But the victory was his.

Act V

Scene I

Chris Eubank would fight on. As he said, it was what he did. But it was also the way to stay in the news. His involvement in an accident as serious as the one that had befallen Michael Watson added a sense of fatalism which was probably the only element missing from the Eubank package. The act remained the same – the vaulting over the ropes, the preening in the ring and the impassive stare. But, privately, he had changed. Ebullient with his friends before the tragedy, Eubank had become more introspective. Watson's condition remained critical and Eubank felt responsible. Despite those feelings of regret and anxiousness, he now had to continue fighting.

Matching Eubank had not been the easiest of tasks for Barry Hearn. Before he fought Watson, any number of top professionals had called the champion out, but instead, Dan

Sherry and Gary Stretch had been the challengers. Neither presented either a realistic challenge or box-office potential. The one fight that everyone wanted to see was a rematch with Nigel Benn, but Hearn wanted the anticipation for that fight to build. In order to safeguard that bout, Eubank would be matched with challengers not expected to beat him, and certainly without the ability to seriously hurt him. Thulani 'Sugar Boy' Malinga was a perfect example of that. The South African had mixed at the highest level for a few years and rarely beaten anyone of note. At the age of thirty-six, and with six defeats in thirty-nine fights, he was expected to pose Eubank very few problems. His record of thirteen stoppage wins from thirty-three victories did not suggest he could punch that hard either. The fight would take place on 1 February 1992, four months and ten days after the Watson fight. The venue was the scene of one of Eubank's greatest moments, the NEC Arena in Birmingham, where he had beaten Benn. And those in the auditorium were firmly behind the Englishman. Eubank had always craved more popularity than he had – the irony that he had to almost kill a man to gain sympathy and support cannot have escaped him.

What was the difference between Eubank before and after Watson? It was hard to tell over those first five rounds against Malinga. The challenger moved in circles and selected his punches well, a strategy that always gave Eubank fits. 'So far, Eubank's doing very little in this contest,' said commentator Dave Brenner at the end of the second round. But in round five, Eubank finally managed to hurt Malinga, dropping him with a single right hand. Instead of forcing a stoppage, Eubank allowed Malinga to survive further rounds, taking a split decision on points. Afterwards, he was accused of having lost the instinct that boxers have when their opponents are in trouble, a charge he denied. But the safety-first attitude speaks volumes for his sense of self-preservation. It was hard not to believe he had other things on his mind, as he indicated in his post-fight interview. 'I don't know if you're looking on TV but please, Michael, recover.'

Perhaps the best explanation I've ever heard for how a fighter changes after he was involved in a ring tragedy came from former world featherweight champion Gabriel Ruelas. In 1995, Ruelas was considered one of the premier featherweights in the world and he showed most of his skills in an eleven-round stoppage of Colombian Jimmy Garcia. Thirteen days after the fight, Garcia succumbed to brain injuries sustained in the bout. Ruelas had visited him in hospital and had spoken to the stricken boxer's family. Garcia's mother asked to look at Ruelas's hands, to see the 'fists that killed my son'. Ruelas would never be the same again. Once noted for his variety of defensive and offensive skills, he would be stopped himself four times before retiring at the age of thirty-three. Years later, he would describe his state of mind after the Garcia fight.

'That took away my anger. You need anger to be successful as a fighter. You need that hunger to be a world champion. I don't have that any more . . . You have to be hungry in boxing, like I said. And after Jimmy I wasn't. My trainers noticed it in training, when I was sparring. I would back off and not hit my sparring partners hard. And you can't afford to do that, you can't afford to be like that – to feel sorry for your opponent. Boxing is the hurt business after all. It was very hard. It is even now. It feels like just yesterday.'

There was definitely a lack of hunger in Eubank's work

that night. As he himself remembers, winning the fight meant he could afford something luxurious for his house. Away from the ring, there were further reasons for darkness. Shortly after the Malinga fight, he was involved in an accident on his way to Gatwick Airport to catch a flight to Jamaica. Losing control of his Range Rover, he drove the vehicle on to a building site, killing a labourer. 'I saw this fellow there, and I couldn't do anything,' he told a Magistrates Court in Sussex. It was established that he had not been exceeding the speed limit, but was still ordered to pay costs and had his driving licence endorsed. Then there was the stigma. A man was dead. Over the next few months, he would find the word 'murderer' sprayed on to his house on numerous occasions. The show had to go on, but the performer was not at peace.

He was back in the ring within three months. This time, the venue was Manchester's G-Mex Leisure Centre. The scheduled opponent was tough American Lindell Holmes, but he pulled out and was replaced by compatriot John Jarvis. His record was an impressive one – twenty-five wins from twenty-eight fights, with only seven of those going the distance. What was also notable was his durability, which had been called into question with those three defeats all taking place inside the distance. In fact, in his last fight, nine months earlier, he had been knocked out in three rounds by the then IBF champion Darrin Van Horn. It was a case of different year but same ending for Jarvis, who took a full-blooded right hand and went over – hard. Eubank's response to the knockout was in keeping with what had once been expected of him – strutting, posing in the middle of the ring. He appeared to have no concerns about inflicting pain on this occasion.

One of the consequences of his fight with Watson had
been that post-fight interviews were, for now, conducted
outside the ring arena. Dressed in a light blue vest, Eubank
answered questions with humour and also a little edge.
When asked about a potential rematch with Benn, he
warned that it would only happen if he was paid a million
pounds after tax. Benn was the mandatory challenger for
the WBO title, which meant that, theoretically, he would
have to get a title shot by the end of the year. Benn had
waived his right to the fight, for now, to allow Eubank to
defend his belt against another American without much
chance of victory, Ron Essett. And it was then, when asked
further about Benn, that the fighter inside Eubank truly
came out.

'I've nothing more to prove to Nigel. I've beaten him
once, there was no controversy or luck involved . . . If you
don't pay me what I want [and the fight doesn't happen], I'll
sleep easily, knowing my name stands over his.'

Once again, the gauntlet had been thrown down to his
nemesis. But exactly how could promoters find that sort
of money for Eubank, an amount unheard of for British
fighters boxing in their own country?

Knowing the only way he could get to Eubank was by
going up a weight division, Nigel Benn became a super
middleweight. Having watched his mate Watson come so
close to stripping Eubank of his unbeaten record and then
coming up tragically short had not put him off. Revenge
was all he could think about. There are plenty who believe
the move up in weight – Benn would carry an extra 8 lb –
was detrimental. He was not a big middleweight and could
possibly have got down to the light middleweight limit, so

ferocious were his cardiovascular workouts. But not many people have ever persuaded him to change his mind.

American Lenzie Morgan was selected for his first super middleweight bout on 26 October 1991, with the venue being Matchroom's arena of choice in Brentwood. Morgan's record was littered with some of the better super middleweights and light heavyweights around the world. Crucially, though, he rarely beat any of them. He was around six inches taller than Benn and a couple of years younger. And he was tough. If Benn's first fight in America, against Jorge Amparo, was a wake-up as to how hard this business was at the top, his first at a new weight was no different. Punches that in the past would move and disorientate seemed to bounce off Morgan. Ten rounds came and went and, although Benn would take a points decision by a single round, he never looked in serious trouble. Barry McGuigan reasoned that the extra pounds helped him take better punches, if not throw them. Interviewer Gary Newbon would incur Benn's wrath by, in the fighter's mind, failing to show him respect for the change in his style. It was a reminder of the volatility that always lurked beneath the surface with Benn; the eyes darkening and the sure knowledge that, if he was pushed further, he could explode. While Eubank appeared to be able to keep all those emotions hidden, Benn's demand to be understood in the way he wanted was expressed in the severest of terms.

Eighteen days before Christmas 1991, Benn reassured his fans that there was still dynamite in his fists when he took on Buenos Aires middleweight Hector Lescano. The visitor had rarely fought outside Argentina and was out of his depth and weight class, a flurry of punches to body and head ending matters in the third. Hearn's ability to build a fight was demonstrated in Benn's next outing, against former Eubank foe Dan Sherry. The Canadian tried his best to bother Benn, but, again, he was not a super middleweight. Even if he had been, it was his bad fortune to walk on to a savage right hand in the third round of their contest at Alexandra Palace in north London. All those details about the context of the knockout were irrelevant in terms of hyping of a Benn–Eubank rematch. The challenger was healed and apparently hitting harder than ever. That fight took place on 19 February 1992 – Benn's next fight would be against recently beaten 'Sugar Boy' Malinga.

'He was my bogeyman,' says Benn of the Zulu, who frustrated and teased him for ten rounds at the NEC in May that year. At the time, he would say, 'He gave me a hell of a fight. I underestimated him and paid the price', but in fact he paid no price. Virtually everyone at ringside believed Benn had lost – in fact the only person who didn't was referee Paul Thomas, who gave the decision, by a round, in favour of the British boxer. 'A bit of a hometown decision,' says Benn of that night.

But the restlessness inside him, which was his default setting for much of his youth and still raised its head intermittently, threatened to derail his career. His problems with his first marriage and the lack of direction in his career – when would Eubank fight him? – were submerging him. There wasn't much in the super middleweight division to keep him interested. Iran Barkley was the new IBF champion and there was little interest in seeing a rematch. The WBA title was held by Panama's Victor Córdoba, a tricky southpaw who was bound to make Benn look awful if they fought. That left the WBC champion, Italian Mauro Galvano. Benn had bided his time, waiting for Eubank to grant him a rematch. If and when the fight took place, he wanted to be paid the same as or more than his rival. But that would never happen if he was a challenger. If he came into the rematch as a fellow champion, only then Benn could expect parity.

It's no exaggeration to say that fighting in Italy was every visiting boxer's nightmare. The word was that you needed a knockout for a draw if you were taking on an Italian in his own country. The Mexicans do their best to create an atmosphere of genuine hostility, but, equally, they are respectful if a foreigner shows courage and the ability to fight, rather than hide. Those attributes were likely to count for nothing against Galvano, whose connections with the Italian underworld meant that in 2012 he was sentenced to six years in prison for crimes such as extortion. In 1990, another east London boxer, Mark Kaylor, had lost his European title to Galvano in a fight the Englishman knew he had little chance of winning. Galvano was tricky and known as a spoiler, someone who would knock you out of your stride before instigating his own plan. Very few people outside Italy would willingly pay to watch him fight, but in front of his own people he was a hero.

Few gave Benn a chance of winning. But since he had watched Watson come so close to beating Eubank, he had an eye on how he would do what his friend could not quite do. He wanted to change trainers and he initiated the move to bring Jimmy Tibbs on board, initially for the Galvano fight, but with the bigger picture being to make him a better boxer for when he took on Eubank.

An East Ender, Tibbs had always known about Benn, from his early days as an amateur with blistering power through to his professional career. He'd watched the performance against Malinga and noticed how Benn's head kept popping up after he'd throw a punch, making him an easy target. Although Tibbs had a reputation, unfairly he insists, for working with boxers who had upright, classic British styles, he could offer wisdom to anyone. And it was that conditioning and pace that he had instilled in Michael Watson which encouraged Benn to make contact with him.

'A man rang me up and said someone is going to ring up – they want you to train someone. And I thought, "Not another six-rounder!" I don't mind training six-round fighters, but they cost so much money, if you don't have a promoter,' recalls Tibbs. 'Anyway, it was Nigel's mate, Ray Sullivan ['Rolex Ray']. He said, "would you be interested in training Nigel Benn?"'

Meanwhile, Benn rang the Tibbs household and asked the lady of the house if Tibbs could come to Tenerife, his new training base, to train him. 'Of course he can. I don't care where Jimmy goes to train!' Mrs Tibbs told Benn. The whole family had known of him for years – Benn had trained with Tibbs's son, Jimmy Junior – and weren't intimidated by his volatile reputation. 'He was always polite,' adds Tibbs. He was also a phenomenal trainer, according to the venerable cornerman. 'He was a dream to work with. He never missed a morning run, was always on time. He might get a little excited every now and then but you wouldn't want to take that away from him, because he needs to take that into the ring with him.'

'He loved his boxing. If you told him to do something,

he'd want to know why. And then he'd say "show me how to do it". And I'd show him how and how other fighters did it, and Nigel would say "I'll do it better than him".' Tibbs also realised there was an issue with Benn and sparring and would make arrangements to combat that, encouraging his charge to hit the pads harder and move his upper body more, making him a slighter, more elusive target. There would be sparring, but not every day, and Benn would never spar for more than nine rounds on a given day. The pair were together for three and a half years and Tibbs doesn't recall them having a single argument. Even now, after a career in the sport that has lasted over fifty years, his eyes sparkle at the mention of Benn's name and that era of boxing. And those days in Tenerife were also particularly special. Benn would also say that, in retrospect, if he had had Tibbs in his corner on the night of that frenetic fight against Watson at Finsbury Park, he might have had a chance of winning. 'The best trainer I ever had,' Benn told me.

The Galvano fight would be the first time Tibbs appeared in Benn's corner and the last time Benn fought abroad. Prior to the bout, he was unbeaten on his travels. But for this assignment he was a massive underdog. 'A cornered Nigel Benn is a fearsome beast,' remembers Jim Rosenthal of those times when the experts thought he had bitten off more than he could chew. At just twenty-eight and very much in his prime, the time was right for Benn to pull off a surprise. The date was 3 October 1992 and the venue was the Ice Palace in the Italian town of Marino. On his way to the ring, Benn was the target of coins and spitting from racist sections of the crowd. It was unlikely to upset a man whose upbringing on the streets of east London was as tough as anything he experienced in the ring.

Galvano's strategy was to hold Benn by the back of the neck whenever possible, in order to smother his power. But during the first round, a couple of big right hands landed on the Italian's chin. The champion responded by landing an elbow by Benn's left eye, while the American referee, Joe Cortez, was temporarily blindsided. Cortez's mantra was that he was 'firm but fair' but he was probably one of the weaker world referees, allowing Galvano to hit low constantly and butt and elbow Benn. But while the Italian might have had the edge with the roughhouse tactics – Benn was no angel himself – he could not cope with the challenger's power. Straight right hands and uppercuts continued to explode on Galvano's chin, forcing him to fight more defensively. By the end of the third round, the champion's left eye was bloodied and closing. Sensing their man was going to get a steadier beating, the Italian's cornermen asked Cortez to examine the eye and looked for a technical draw, hoping that the official would rule the cut was the result of a head butt. 'This is a real try-on by the Italians,' said Jim Watt in the commentary box. If, under WBC rules, a fight was stopped before three rounds because of a cut caused by a clash of heads, the referee was obliged to call the result a draw. But Cortez never inspected the cut – it was the Italians who had decided their man had had enough, which really meant a retirement. Galvano did not come out for the start of the fourth and Benn assumed victory and started celebrating wildly, unaware, it seemed, that the Italians were looking to pull a 'stroke'.

Barry Hearn sensed what was going on. He remembers

the evening as follows. 'I won Nigel the world title and he never wanted to acknowledge it. I could see there was a stroke going on. The Italians didn't look disappointed or unhappy. I went over and I was told "no contest, we keep the title". I spoke to Cortez and said, "Joe, you've done a hundred and fifty odd world title fights, don't fuck your career up over this." So I then got hold of the phone and I said I was dialling [Jose] Sulaiman [late head of the WBC] and you're all out of a job. I went potty. And then Cortez said, "It was a punch." So I told him he had to stick to that. And so we won the title.'

Benn had run the gamut of emotions in the space of three or four minutes and it was all played out on live television. He'd refused to be interviewed by Gary Newbon when it looked like he would not be getting the title. Then he had fumed, asking Newbon, 'What do you expect me to say?', and then, when he was given the decision, he hugged the interviewer. It was Benn in a nutshell, hostile one moment, teddy bear the next. He revealed that the name of his deceased brother Andy had been sewn into his shorts and dedicated the victory to him and one other person.

'The other person who gets that belt is Michael. Michael, I hope you're watching. That is your belt and no one can take it away from you. That's from me to you, with my love, Michael.'

To complete the haul of men who had beaten him, Benn then reached through the ropes to greet Chris Eubank, dressed in a navy suit and sporting sunglasses. The two exchanged what passed for handshakes, before Benn had, for one of the few times, the last word:

'Now we can do business.'

Scene II

In 1992, the biggest draw in sport was facing up to at least three years in prison. The former world heavyweight champion Mike Tyson had been convicted of raping Desiree Washington and was given a ten-year sentence. Four of those years were suspended and under the laws of the penal system in Indianapolis, where the crime had been committed and Tyson was housed, he would be entitled to a day's parole for every day he served with good behaviour. Even so, the earliest he would be released would be some time in mid-1995. There was thus a void at the top end of the sport.

Tyson's behaviour notwithstanding, boxers, especially heavyweights, were incredibly grateful to the self-styled baddest man on the planet. His reign as champion and even his subsequent fights as former king had generated so much money that fighters were being paid bigger sums than ever before. The number of noughts on the cheque had risen to seven by the time of his incarceration and he could expect as much, if not more, when he returned. The revenues were being generated by pay-per-view television, a rapidly growing phenomenon in the United States at the start of the 1990s.

While gate receipts generally cover the costs of a promotion, and in some cases can help generate a slight profit, television money had always driven the size of the purses that could be paid out. In America, pay-per-view or closed circuit television had helped put together such events as Sugar Ray Leonard's memorable comeback win over Marvelous Marvin Hagler in 1987, as well Tyson's ninety-one-second defeat of Michael Spinks a year later. The cost of paying for a fight to be broadcast into your home in America has usually been around the $50 mark. In 2007, Oscar de la Hoya fought Floyd Mayweather Junior in a bout purchased by 2.4 million households, generating nearly $140 million in revenue. With fighters represented by agents who are, generally, far shrewder than those who managed during the sport's infancy, their knowledge of their own worth has grown substantially during the past twenty-five years.

Pay-per-view had not hit Great Britain by 1992, but, just as television programming in the USA had been affected by the power of cable networks HBO and Showtime, both of which were major players in boxing, so BSkyB were starting to flex their muscles in the world of sport. Their primary target had been the national game, association football. That year, the product now known as the English Premier League was born, offering clubs in the higher echelons untold riches compared to what they had received in the past. There was money on the table and soon some of the best players in the world, who had plied their trade in more lucrative markets such as Italy and Spain, were finding the lure of the lira and the peseta easy to ignore when sterling was thrust in their faces.

With dedicated sport channels, BSkyB could offer more depth to their coverage than terrestrial television, which had to justify itself to the licence fee payer. In the end, that would help the organisation to get their fingers into virtually every sporting pie that had previously been the preserve of the BBC, ITV or even Channel 4. In 1992, those days seemed far off, but for now certainly people in television whose jobs had rarely involved having to fight off rivals were now getting a little twitchy. Their principal concern was that they could not offer the money that promoters would expect from Sky. 'We knew the game was up once Sky bought the Premier League,' says Trevor East, Head of ITV Sport at the time, who would eventually work for his rivals as more and more sport disappeared from terrestrial television.

Tyson's drawing power had increased his own financial strength and it was no different for Chris Eubank. 'He got the ratings,' said Gary Newbon, who had a dual role as ringside reporter and executive. It didn't matter that 'Simply the Best' was involved in a series of bouts that were tactically sound, rather than offering heavy hitting violence. The other side to that was that, in Eubank, ITV were dealing with a man who knew his worth. He had done since he had embarked on his professional career and with every thrilling win over Benn or Watson the interest in this unique boxer grew. His demands for a purse in the region of a million pounds for a Benn rematch were unprecedented but also realistic. This would be a bout with global appeal, if marketed correctly. And if that happened, television revenues would be huge.

Eubank also knew that Nigel Benn had made a name for himself in America during that year after he was beaten by Michael Watson. And in the absence of Tyson, the likes of HBO and Showtime were searching around to find value in other weight divisions. Traditionally, middleweight boxing was the second most prestigious division, made glorious by Sugar Ray Robinson during the 1950s, and some of that lustre was seen again when Hagler dominated the 1980s, his bouts with Leonard, Roberto Durán and Thomas Hearns all doing fabulous business around the world. The current vintage of American middleweights looked promising. Michael

Nunn, a stylish southpaw who had looked the natural heir to
Leonard, had been a world champion and then moved up a
weight and would soon dethrone Victor Córdoba to become
a two-weight champ. There were others – Roy Jones Junior,
who should have been Olympic champion but for a violently
corrupt interpretation of scoring at the Seoul Olympics in
1988, and James 'Lights out' Toney, an engagingly outspoken
fighter from Michigan who had inflicted the first defeat of
Nunn's career and was now finding a move up in weight a
necessity.

Benn and Eubank had been content, wherever possible, to
continue their careers within the cosy confines of their own
country. Eubank's diet of faded American fighters happy
to travel for a low-risk contest, with the outside chance of
winning a world title, kept the champion comfortable, in and
out of the ring. The forecast for Benn in his first six months as
WBC champion was no more challenging. But soon the pair
would be faced with a choice: stay on easy street or challenge
themselves against the men regarded as the best, Nunn, Jones
and Toney. It had suited all parties to keep things domestic,
but now some on the other side of the Atlantic had begun
to pay attention, specifically a man notorious for being the
sport's most prolific shark. Don King.

The man with the electrifying hair had always been
regarded as an opportunist. He fondly told a story of how, in
1973, he walked to the ring with world heavyweight champion
Joe Frazier and left it minutes later with the man who took
the belt from him, George Foreman, having inched his way
into the winner's corner during the six minutes of violent
destruction inflicted on Frazier.

As more than one boxer has told me over the years, in his

prime King could deliver the fights, and even after 'getting screwed' by him they were richer than they would have been if they had stayed patiently with their original promoters. Now, with meal ticket Tyson temporarily unavailable – King stayed in touch with the imprisoned fighter, making sure he knew who he would be fighting for when he was released – King channelled his promotional duties into other fighters. The great Julio César Chávez headlined shows on both sides of the US/Mexican border and King also tried to get his fingers on the heavyweight title, which had been wrestled from Evander Holyfield by Riddick Bowe, who was not aligned to either King or his promotional rival Main Events.

Always creative, King would later strike up a relationship with Frank Warren, who had spent much of the early 1990s recovering from being shot and then rebuilding his promotional empire. Key to Warren's success was the emergence of the colourful and talented Prince Naseem Hamed, who would become, arguably, Britain's most high-profile boxer.

For now, King was the gateway for Hearn to the American market he had not yet explored. He'd been able to take Eubank as far as he had because he had what he liked to call 'fuck you money', an expression he had learned from rival promoter Mickey Duff. Even so, he did not have enough of it if he wanted to put Benn and Eubank together and pay them what they wanted. The fight would probably be held at a football stadium, with Wembley the obvious stage for two boxers based in the south. But getting the money was still an issue – Hearn had already agreed to pay both fighters a million pounds, a significant amount given that Britain was in the middle of recession, precipitated by Black

Wednesday, the day in September 1992 when the pound was withdrawn from the European Exchange Rate Mechanism, a move which would cost the country £3.3 billion. The Conservative government had, against the odds, won the general election earlier in the year to retain power for another five, but the state of the nation, depressed since the start of the decade, had not changed. Interest rates soared to 15 per cent and the property market, which had been buoyant during the latter stages of the 1980s, slumped. Repossessions rose, as people struggled to make monthly mortgage payments, while those in negative equity had difficulty purchasing new houses. In sporting terms, the rise of Sky, part of media mogul Rupert Murdoch's empire, was perfectly timed, giving a financial boost, initially to football and then subsequently to other sports, including boxing. But on a wider scale, Britain would not feel fundamental change until 1997, when a new Labour government, led by Tony Blair, and taking advantage of improving global financial conditions, stormed into power.

Before King came on the scene, Hearn was only due to receive £25,000 for the international television rights for the rematch. With King on board, however, the figure rapidly rose to nearly a hundred times that. A contract was drawn up which saw both fighters aligned to King after the fight, whether they won or lost. The only way they'd escape the man with the startled hair would be if the fight was declared a draw, a result that had become less and less common in the sport.

Scene III

Chris Eubank's right hand knocking out John Jarvis would come to be seen as a landmark moment. He'd fight three more times that year and not come close to stopping anyone. For his next bout he would box Ron Essett, the American he should have faced on the night he beat Jarvis. The bout against Essett was in Portugal and on an extraordinarily humid evening Eubank retained his title by decision. 'That was an awful night,' remembers Dave Brenner. 'Just a dreadful fight.' Essett was one of the sport's nearly men – he'd challenged for a world title twice before and come up a little short. He was just as unsuccessful against Eubank, who struggled in the heat and was sluggish. The judges awarded him the win by margins of eight, five and four points and there was no clamour for 'Simply the Best' to return to Iberia.

Stiffer competition would come in the form of another American, Tony Thornton, in Glasgow. Thornton endeared himself to fight fans by combining a ring career with a full-time job as a postman. In front of a raucous and passionate crowd at the Scottish Exhibition Centre, Thornton forced the pace for twelve rounds and threw and landed more punches. But it was yet another of those bouts that seemed open to interpretation. The commentary team of Brenner and Barry McGuigan were unanimous in their feeling that Eubank had done enough to win the decision, oblivious to the boos that rang out around the ring as the champion actually ran away from Thornton in the final round. Eubank's sharper punches had dominated the early rounds, but there was little doubt that he lost most of the final four, with Thornton's pressure leaving the champion an exhausted and occasionally dispirited looking figure. Even so, with many at ringside believing Thornton had done enough for a draw at worst, Eubank won a decision by margins of five, three and two points.

There would be one more outing for Eubank that year, against the Paraguayan Juan Carlos Giménez at the G-Mex Leisure Centre in Manchester. Like both Thornton and Essett, Giménez did not have an especially intimidating record as a puncher, the majority of his wins coming in South America and against a cluster of fighters with no marquee value. His style was basic at best, his arms whirling in a continual cycle of uncultured hooks, which never troubled the champion. Even though Giménez would end his career as a cruiserweight, he looked much the smaller man against the impressively chiselled Eubank. There was no hint that this was a close fight, with the champion able to lean back against the ropes, absorb the best that Giménez had and throw combinations once the Paraguayan had punched himself out. Another unanimous decision went the way of Eubank, who was adjudged to have lost only a couple of rounds.

It was impossible to ignore the change in Eubank's ring performances. The grand entrances and showmanship remained, but now, when the bell rang, he appeared cautious. While Hearn believed a sense of Eubank's own mortality restricted his performances, the fighter thinks otherwise. 'I lost the ability to finish,' he said years later. He was no longer the figure of hate he had been before the second Watson fight but he was also struggling to provide value for money. Boxing experts could see the merit of victories over the likes of Malinga, Thornton and Giménez, but with

knockout victories at a premium there was a growing air of
restlessness among casual fans. They wanted to see Eubank
in a fight against a man they knew. There would, of course,
be no third fight with Watson. But there had to be a rematch
with Benn.

Like Eubank, Nigel Benn would also cram one more
fight in before Christmas 1992, a defence of his title
against Welshman Nicky Piper. It had all the hallmarks of
an easy night for the Londoner. Piper was basically a light
heavyweight who was voluntarily shedding half a stone to
make the championship weight. To compound matters, he
wasn't considered that tough, having been knocked out in
three rounds by Carl Thompson. In fact, the most sellable
quality he possessed was his brain. Piper had an IQ in
excess of 150, qualifying him as a member of Mensa. Piper
was also one of a growing breed of fighters who advocated
taking control of their own careers. Although Eubank
is normally credited with the change in the perception
of fighters, he, Benn and Watson were all unique in the
way they dealt with managers and promoters, sometimes
going to court to make sure they could dictate the course
of their careers.

In the future, Piper would play a prominent role in the
Professional Boxing Association but while he fought he
managed himself and was one of the more accessible men
on the circuit. On the night in question at Alexandra Palace,
he utilised his considerable height and reach advantages to
nullify Benn's power and one of the judges had him holding
a points advantage after ten rounds. Points don't always
tell the story of a fight, however. Advised by his corner that
Piper would be drained by fighting at an unnatural weight,

Benn targeted the challenger's ribcage and abdomen. By round eleven, the Welshman was ready to fall and after suffering a knockdown and then several painful punches, he was mercifully prevented from carrying on by referee Larry O'Connell.

The next destination for Benn was Glasgow and a mandatory rematch with Mauro Galvano. It was a fight that had to happen. The Italian fought as he had the first time round, holding and spoiling and falling well behind on points against a curiously flat Benn. The only moment of real excitement came in the twelfth and final round when the champion was hurt by a big right hand. The problem for Galvano was that it happened with just seconds remaining and Benn survived to hear the final bell and collect a unanimous decision. 'Survived' being the operative word – at the sound of the final bell, he stormed to the centre of the ring, expecting to find Galvano there; so disorientated had he been by that final blow that he believed the bell was summoning him to another round. Benn would admit afterwards that his legs had gone. What was evident was that the longer a Benn–Eubank rematch was delayed, the bigger the chance was that one of them might lose a fight in the build-up. Defeat for either would have a detrimental effect on the long-awaited bout. Negotiations for the fight had started but a deal needed to be in place as soon as possible so that the fighters could focus on something more tangible than just the next defence of their title.

Chris Eubank would defend his title against another fading American fighter at the start of 1993. Lindell Holmes had a wonderful pedigree at world-class level. He had been a world champion and had fought most of the leading

contenders for the past five to six years. He was also way past
his prime, approaching his thirty-sixth birthday by the time
of this final world title challenge. In fact, he'd have just one
more fight after taking on Eubank before retirement. The
date was 20 February 1993 and the venue another favourite of
the champion's, Earl's Court in west London. With Eubank's
increasing reluctance to end bouts quickly and engage in
the trenches, and his opponent's age, this fight was billed
by some as a contest between a man who wouldn't and a
man who couldn't. Ever ready with the bombast, Eubank
promised to punish Holmes's first mistake with 'cold, clinical
precision'.

With an impressively sculpted upper body, Holmes looked
like a young man but his reflexes told a different story.
When Eubank attacked, Holmes did not have the ability
to counter and would have to wait until the champion had
punched himself out before launching his own attacks.
The pattern would become a familiar one and neither man
was ever in any serious danger of a knockout defeat. The
anomaly with Eubank was that no one could ever be certain
as to how easy it had been for him as he took this fight by
a unanimous decision by margins of two, five and eleven
points. The questions remained: would Eubank seek a more
dangerous opponent next and what about his stamina? He
was visibly puffing and panting in most rounds, the exertion
of throwing power punches leaving him drained. It was how
he trained, he explained. It was all about power, he'd say,
and that he wasn't the only man currently fighting who had
an energy issue.

As for the opposition and its quality, that would never
be answered satisfactorily. Eubank could claim, with some

justification, that Benn's opposition was hardly threatening. Piper and Galvano were not superior to the likes of Holmes or Thornton, but the difference was that Benn did all he could to make those bouts exciting and give value for money. In most of Eubank's contests, it was the opposition that forced the pace and threw more punches. And it was also the case that, for more than a year, he had coasted as a world champion, making comparatively easy money against a string of opponents who offered no threat. If Barry Hearn felt that his man was unwilling to take risks for fear of what might happen to him, he had no reason to worry about the current opposition posing serious danger to either his health or title. After an incredibly tough first year as world champion, which had begun with wresting the title from Benn in a bout that left him urinating blood for days, through to the Watson rematch that put him briefly in a wheelchair, Eubank had needed the time to heal and take stock. He had fought five times in 1992, more than most world champions in that era and considerably more than any of those currently operating. He had now had eleven world title fights in less than two and a half years. And he had not lost. An unbeaten record can play on the minds of many a fighter. The pressure of maintaining it builds and builds until that inevitable first defeat. And once a fighter does lose for the first time, that sense of invincibility disappears, perhaps forever. Maybe that didn't affect Eubank that much. After all, this was a man with 'unquestionable physical and emotional ruggedness', according to *Boxing Monthly* editor Glyn Leach. And, certainly, Eubank had known what it was like to be on the verge of losing before being able to find a way to win.

One more examination of that ability would come later in 1993. Glasgow was the venue for the second time in twelve months as Eubank entertained the challenge of Northern Irishman Ray Close, who had earned his challenge by virtue of winning the European title in Italy, against slippery Italian southpaw Vincenzo Nardiello. At just twenty-four, Close was the youngest man Eubank had defended his title against and by virtue of that had the most energy. Of the men who had challenged Eubank in the past two years, only Michael Watson had given the clearest indication of how to beat him. It was, surely, to set a pace that the champion could not operate at. Skilled at stealing rounds by fighting in flashy bursts, Eubank had snatched victory from defeat's jaws on more than one occasion. Boxing and indeed sport are made up of what ifs, and you can't help wondering if Eubank would still have been undefeated if Watson had not had the temerity to knock him down during that fateful eleventh round at White Hart Lane. It did not seem likely that Close could inflict similar pain on the champion – he was a grafter and did not have a reputation as a particularly hard puncher.

That graft gave Eubank problems from the start as Close set a pace that was both frenetic and consistent. Whatever those at ringside thought – and there were many who believed that Close needed to land three punches to every one of the champion's in order to remain ahead on the scorecards – Close had a lead going into the final two rounds. But a left hook from Eubank at the start of the eleventh changed all that. Close got up and survived the round, before winning the twelfth, but the knockdown in the eleventh meant the round was scored 10-8 in Eubank's favour. That was enough to earn him a draw on the card of one of the judges, with the other two officials siding with challenger and champion. In the event of a draw, the man with the title retains the belt and so Eubank once again found a way to keep the gravy train rolling. A rematch with Benn still seemed miles away, but at least there was potential for it to happen. And Eubank had shown enough in the Close battle to suggest that some of his old hunger had returned.

Even so, Eubank had now had seven fights since the Watson rematch and there had been little to suggest that he was boxing for any reason other than money. He'd knocked out one man but for the rest of the time he'd prevailed by taking the long route, against a group of fighters handpicked to ensure that he was never in danger of being hurt. He would not be defined by these bouts, only against opponents who offered something else. Opponents such as Benn, who everyone knew would bring spice, hate and hype to the ring.

Nigel Benn had said he changed his training camp to Tenerife to get away from the distractions of London. In truth, his Canary Islands base was no less fraught. 'Sex, drugs and rock 'n' roll' was how he would later describe his lifestyle during those heady days and Tenerife could and would serve as the epicentre for all of that. Benn was treated like royalty on the island, as were a handful of other boxers who set up camp there, including, in later years, Frank Bruno. Benn's ability to party was matched only by his knack of making sure he never missed training as well as displaying no ill effects from the wear and tear of his social life. A reliance on vitamins as well as those long runs in the altitude of Tenerife's famous Mount Teide which allowed him to lose himself meant he was able to cling on to his fitness and mental well being for a little bit longer.

Recently, some have suggested that Benn battled his demons during those years, but those who knew him believe he mostly ignored them. His ability to turn on the charm when he needed it to get him out of many tight situations and, if that didn't work, the other side of his personality, the intimidating persona, would also serve a purpose. Virtually everyone who speaks of Benn confirms that Jekyll and Hyde nature. Or to put it in simpler terms, he can be whoever he wants to be, depending on the situation. Until he had a date for a Eubank rematch, he was also lacking a real focus. As always, the inner anger would be realised in his training and world title defences, but the one thing he really struggled to deal with, that first defeat to Eubank, would be an itch that he could only scratch when he got his nemesis back in the ring.

That was reflected in the way he fought. Since he had hooked up with Jimmy Tibbs in the summer of 1992, he had fought with measured aggression (in the first fight with Galvano), with the air of a champion (against Piper) and like a man going through the motions (in the rematch with the Italian). Absent from that list was the one kind of fight with which he was synonymous – a tear-up. But one of those was on the way. With so much vulnerability evident in his last bout, Benn was matched, sensibly, against journeyman Lou Gent, who had no real right to be in the same ring as his fellow Londoner. But the ratings can be manipulated if the occasion demands. Gent held the WBC international middleweight title, which gave him an automatic top ten spot in the governing body's list of contenders. There were almost certainly twenty or thirty men more deserving of the chance to fight Benn and the fact that Gent had won just three of his last six didn't seem to bother the capacity crowd at Earl's Court on a tense June evening. It didn't bother ITV, either, who were also showing the fight live on a Saturday night. Why? Well, in Eubank they had a guy who apparently everyone wanted to see lose (although the cheers for his name which seemed to multiply with every fight seemed to suggest popularity and loathing in equal measure), and in Benn they had someone who could lose at any moment. And if you're selling sport to a Saturday night TV audience, predictability is not a valued asset. Apart from that, it seemed the preamble for Benn–Eubank II had gone on for too long. As the wait continued, the viewers needed entertaining.

The sales pitch for this bout was that Gent, a natural light heavyweight, would enter the ring maybe a stone heavier than Benn, having gorged himself after making the weight the night before. The challenger's father had bet on his son to stop the champion in any one of the twelve rounds. If there was fear in the Benn camp, it wasn't obvious. He told those close to him that he saw fear in Gent's eyes. The first two rounds were pretty even, as the balding, tattooed Gent forced the pace. But at the start of the third, Benn landed a left hook that illustrated the challenger's problem. Having slimmed down to make the weight, he had neither the strength nor the power to discourage the champion. He went down from that hook, got up, fought back and then went down again. From the start of the third through to the middle of the fourth, he was floored five times, on each occasion falling heavily but getting up without much difficulty. By the time of the fifth knockdown, Benn had worked out that Gent's abdomen could not take the punishment, each hook south of the ribcage causing the challenger to wince. Referee Larry O'Connell signalled enough was enough after Gent hit the canvas for the fifth time and promoters on both sides of the Atlantic breathed a sigh of relief. The big fight was already being talked about as an event in October at recently crowned Premier League champions Manchester United's Old Trafford. Now all that needed sorting was the money. Given the animosity that lingered between Benn and Eubank, it wasn't just a case of how much they would be paid as who would get the most.

Scene IV

'Judgement Day' was the title of the promotion that saw Nigel Benn and Chris Eubank square off for the second time, nearly three years after their first bout. At stake would be the WBC super middleweight title that Benn held, but after the initial negotiations Eubank's belt would not be. By the time the fight was staged, both titles were on the line in what was, at the time, a rare unification bout and the first between two British fighters in their own country. October the 9th was the date and the venue was Old Trafford. Eubank had never professed any great love for football whereas Benn had always been marketed as an East End boy, a West Ham man, like his cousin Paul Ince, who was now playing for Manchester United. Privately, Benn would admit to being only a casual football fan and that if he did have a team it was the one at whose ground he was about to fight. 'Judgement Day' seemed to reflect the nature of the rivalry and it also mimicked the subtitle of one of the most popular films of recent times, the second of *The Terminator* films.

Benn had managed, through his adviser Peter DeFreitas, to negotiate a million pound purse for the rematch, a couple of hundred thousand more than his opponent, who was paid less because the value of his belt wasn't as high – the WBO still had no credibility in America. There was also an increasing darkness around Benn – the criticism of the way he fought, his vulnerability and the fact that he wasn't knocking people out as regularly as he once had. And, of course, he was about to fight Eubank. When his hatred for the WBO champion was put to one side, the cold, hard fact was that he had lost their first fight, without controversy. On paper and in the opinion of virtually everyone, he could not claim to be the better man. All those criticisms, which were entirely valid, irked him in a way that only his opponent otherwise did. His training for Eubank was done in secret, in Tenerife, with no deliberate leaks to the press about either his condition or his mood. Behind closed doors, Benn was taking things very seriously indeed.

'Nigel wanted revenge. When we finally got the chance for revenge, we trained really hard,' says Jimmy Tibbs, who, despite talk in the media that he would be dropped from the team, remained Benn's cornerman for the bout. 'I said to Nigel, "What you've got to do to this guy, you just can't go out there and hope to slug him out. And knock him out in three rounds. It might happen, but it probably won't. You've got to be in front of him and make him work for three minutes of every round. Bobbing and weaving, bobbing and weaving."' It was an extension of the strategy that Benn had been employing since he'd taken Tibbs on a year earlier. The difference was that the opposition was superior.

In contrast, Eubank was delighting in the spotlight, the place in which he was happiest. As he had done before previous fights, the Brighton man would hold public training sessions, hitting the pads held by trainer Ronnie Davies and pontificating at length about the fight game and his opponents, past and present. It was a reminder of one of the inner battles that Eubank faced – he might have hated the sport that made him, but he loved the sport that had made him a star. And now he had a contest which, everyone hoped, would take him out of his comfort zone and bring the best out of him. In the first Benn fight, he had demonstrated a champion's heart and the knack of knowing when to strike. And against Watson, he had shown in their second fight an unbelievable ability to take punishment and still think clearly, even when defeat seemed on the cards.

To handle a star, you need to be either patient, tolerant or understanding. Ideally all three. That summed up Ronnie Davies, who Eubank used as cornerman for his fights as well as camp manager. Davies admitted in the build-up that their relationship had not always been as easy as it seemed. 'There were times in the past when he used to drive me mad. He was working in my gym and telling me what to do and that caused some terrible slanging matches,' said Davies. 'But he's a perfectionist and in the end turned out to be right. He now gets his own way, deciding what time he trains and when he runs. In fact he's a dream to train and I don't really train him, no one can. He comes out with moves I've never seen.'

Davies also had to be aware of where Eubank had taken him in the sport. During his own career as a lightweight during the 1960s, his best ever purse was £175. Now he was earning thousands more without having to take any of the punishment. And because Eubank insisted that everyone associated with him had to dress in the style he approved of, Davies was also the owner of some custom-made designer suits.

The fight game in Britain was booming – just a week prior to 'Judgement Day', WBC heavyweight champion Lennox Lewis defended his title against national hero Frank Bruno in the first ever all British world title fight in boxing's glamour division. The bout was staged in Cardiff, at the city's much loved rugby stadium, the Arms Park. The fight had plenty of bad feeling, maybe more than the Benn–Eubank rematch, ostensibly because Lewis called Bruno an 'Uncle Tom' in the build-up, in reference to the challenger's amiable countenance and ability to poke fun at himself in interviews and regular appearances in pantomime, which ran counter to the image of black fighters in Britain at the time.

Lewis would win inside seven evenly contested rounds on a night that suggested problems for the promotion the following week as well as boxing in the future. Cardiff on an early October evening was cold, especially with the bout taking place in the early hours of the morning and in an open-air stadium. One of the enduring images of the night was Lewis wrapped in a blanket between rounds, in order to prevent his muscles seizing. And the stadium, which could hold around 60,000 spectators, wasn't even half full. Just over 25,000 made it that night but the cost of the tickets did not reflect the demand. And the undercard, as it was, provided unremarkable entertainment, the exception being the professional debut of a heavily hyped former amateur star called Joe Calzaghe.

More worrying were those empty seats. A fight between two London-born men should not really have been taking place more than 200 miles away from the place where both had entered the world. Making matters worse was the time of the fight – shown late so that TV audiences in the USA could watch at their convenience – as well being screened on satellite TV in Great Britain. A week later ITV devoted nearly three hours to their coverage of the Benn–Eubank rematch, with an audience of over sixteen million turning up the volume. A fraction of that number would even be able to watch the heavyweights duke it out and, whereas four years earlier, six million had tuned in to see a preview of Bruno's challenge for Mike Tyson's title, this time round there was no preview to be found on terrestrial television. For all its uniqueness, Lewis–Bruno had failed to fire the imagination of the common man.

The likes of Barry Hearn and Don King must have been slightly concerned about the wisdom of making two London-born middleweights scrap it out 200 miles away from the nation's capital. But in 1993, Old Trafford held around 45,000, and by the night of the fight over 40,000 tickets had been sold, with terrace tickets going for a much more reasonable £25. Hearn and King were also aware that this fight needed no 'Uncle Tom' type of insults to increase the hype. Fight fans had been waiting nearly three years for something they'd have paid for several times during that period. Still, on the night before, to the surprise of no one who lived in Manchester, it rained. With those sitting on the seats erected on the Old Trafford turf exposed to any rainfall, the expected downpour could well dampen spirits.

As it transpired, the rain stayed away. The fight was

broadcast just after 10 p.m., inviting a mainstream audience, and the temperature was around 50 degrees Fahrenheit in the ground and likely to be higher in the ring. And those who were watching at home were probably feeling the heat as well. In a departure from the normal broadcasting format, ITV had recorded a preview programme for the bout, with both boxers brought together in the studio to be interviewed by rising celebrity Jonathan Ross. An audience, comprised, it seemed, of stars from showbiz and sport were in attendance. For a brief moment, Ross interviewed both men together, asking them why they didn't like each other. Eubank professed to having no dislike for his fellow champion, a claim that would be undermined by a quote from him in which he said, 'Nigel, you're not the man you portray yourself to be. I always said you were a fraud and I don't mean to be impolite.' For Benn's part, he would tell Ross, 'Chris has beaten me and I respect him as a boxer. He punches hard and I respect him. As a person, I don't like the way he conducts himself.' At no time was there any chance of an unscheduled confrontation. Both men smiled and displayed the charisma that seems to have bypassed so many athletes before or since. At one point, when answering a question about how hard Benn punched, Eubank reeled off a series of stats about his opponent. After a moment, Benn got up from his chair and walked over to Eubank, who stood up to meet him, but Benn simply made as if to put some money in his rival's hand, as if saying thank you. Then, for one of the few times during their rivalry, the two men exchanged a grin. People always expected Benn to lose his cool when Eubank was standing next to him. There were stories of him threatening to do

Eubank harm when, by chance, they bumped into each other in lifts before both fights and that only the presence of Barry Hearn or Ronnie Davies prevented a brawl. But Benn knew that when the cameras were on he had to keep his fists to himself, unless the pair were in a boxing ring. Benn had not mellowed with age but he understood that if he started something in a studio he risked losing some of the support and goodwill he had.

After a few more questions, Ross interviewed both men separately. Sir Henry Cooper was invited to pass comment on the fight and said simply that there seemed to be too much anger in this one, perhaps forgetting how much dislike there had been between him and Joe Erskine back in the 1950s and 1960s. There was also a prescient moment when Barry McGuigan said he felt that Eubank was slightly misunderstood, describing him as a 'genuinely good guy'. There was time for an excerpt from *Spitting Image*, which mocked Eubank, and also a sparky satellite link-up with a gym in Miami. Sitting in a seat there was actor Mickey Rourke, who at the time was having the occasional fight at middleweight, while also hanging out with some of boxing's cognoscenti. As it happened, he had got to know Benn when the Englishman was based in Florida after losing to Michael Watson. Rourke was there to add a little glitter, as well as sell himself, but the real reason was to introduce an acquaintance of his, the IBF super middleweight champion, James 'Lights out' Toney. While the WBA champion Michael Nunn, in theory, awaited the winner at Old Trafford, it was Toney who was regarded by many as the one to beat. He had knocked out both Nunn and Iran Barkley on his way to winning world titles at middleweight and his current division. And he had done all this at the age of just twenty-five. He also had victories over Mike McCallum and Doug DeWitt and was a candidate for boxing's mythical 'pound-for-pound' title, the unofficial award for the boxer considered the best at any weight. He was also a boxing writer's dream, because he could and would say anything to his opponents. Benn and Eubank were about to become his latest targets.

When asked by Ross who he thought would win in Manchester, Toney's response was simple and to the point: 'I don't care who wins. I'll fight either one of them. In fact I'll fight them on the same night if you want.' Benn and Toney exchanged a few words, although it proved to be lightweight compared to the treatment Eubank received. As the WBO champion pondered his choice of words, Toney lashed out again: 'When I see you, I'm going to beat you and your momma's ass. There are no fighters in England. They're all bums.'

In later years, Eubank would rue the exchanges, although it should be pointed out that he was merely the recipient of the barbs and not the giver. He believes that his association with such behaviour deprived him of the kind of endorsements and sponsorships which could have made him even more of a crossover star. But his response at the time was fascinating. When asked by Ross to explain why he had been so quiet, this was his reply:

'This is one of the many aspects as to why I don't like this sport. This is what I've got to be dealing with here. The guy is talking about my mother. I don't need that. I've never said anything about Nigel I couldn't justify. This, I can't sleep at night, when people talk to me like this.'

It was part of the Eubank persona no one could

understand. He had traded barbs with Benn and Watson, with some of the insults quite personal. But when the brash American Toney did the same, he took offence. Eubank had said many times that he did not like hype, that it demeaned the sport. But it made him rich beyond his dreams. People wondered why he couldn't just accept it and move on. After all, very few expected him to go to America and fight Toney, especially after the series of less than threatening opponents he'd faced in the past year.

At the end of the show, Benn and Eubank were encouraged to shake hands, which they did. Just as had been the case three years earlier, when the pair signed a contract on television, Eubank avoided eye contact with Benn. It was something he always did, especially with 'the Dark Destroyer'. It wasn't a slight – Eubank had no interest in seeing the fury in Benn's eyes, especially given the pain that he'd gone through that night in Birmingham.

While the public remained fascinated as to why there seemed to be so much animosity between the pair, such contempt for each other, the boxing press treated it as more or less another fight. Reporters covering the sport would have heard such talk many times before. It predated Muhammad Ali, although 'the Greatest' was probably the finest exponent of it. Even so, they struggled to get to the bottom of why, even after a first fight which had forced both men to go to places they hadn't gone to before, there was still dislike.

Eubank wasn't the only one who thought boxing was a nasty game. There is video footage of Benn saying almost exactly that as he prepared for their second fight. Eubank's opinion stemmed from the way his brothers had been treated during their careers, frequently used as opponents rather than promoted as potential stars, Benn's from his numerous rows with promoters as well as the experience of missing out on a Commonwealth Games appearance. Both men had got into trouble on the streets. Eubank's regular brushes with the law in London led to him being sent to the United States by a despairing father. Benn was made to join the army, again after personal intervention from his father. Both men took charge of their own careers, Eubank essentially managing himself, while Benn went to court in order to gain independence from his manager. They would both say that boxing had enabled them to secure their children's futures. And although Eubank's dress sense was both unique and bold, it would not be true to say that Benn didn't enjoy wearing expensive designer gear, although his style then was more in keeping with that of a footballer.

In the ring they could both hit hard and, while Eubank relied on boxing skill to set his pace, his love of 'the sweet science' was at odds with what he would say about the sport. Being a boxer allowed him to be Chris Eubank the showman, the extrovert he had always been. It was an outlet for him in the same way it was for Benn, who could channel his aggression and hatred into combat. If as a teenager Eubank had had a reputation as a master of petty theft, Benn was known throughout those neighbourhoods in Essex for having an 'intimidating' personality. The resentment came from how both men conducted themselves in the eyes of the other. Both spoke with a lisp, but while Eubank had taught himself to speak in a certain way, pausing to find the right word, Benn's conversational skills tended to be more off the cuff. And neither man could understand why the other disliked him. Eubank would often say 'if you dislike me, dislike me for the right reasons. And as far as I can see, there are no right reasons.' A self-made man, he may have seen something of himself in Benn but knew the difference was that he had learned to control his emotions and had also given himself an education in the USA. Why, with all the money at his disposal, had Benn not sought to better himself? Benn couldn't see what was wrong with himself – yes, he liked to party hard, but he also trained hard. Since losing to Watson, he had not taken any shortcuts. And both men gave to good causes. Eubank worked hard for charity and helped the homeless in Brighton. Benn paid special attention to a small child with disabilities and made sure he was always ringside. And he had gone out of his way to help Michael Watson. From his point of view, he was no less a man than Eubank. And yet Benn was called a 'fraud' by a man who dressed like a country gent and drove a Peterbilt. It wasn't just the words that hurt; when the pair met, in or out of the ring, Benn always felt that Eubank looked down on him.

The similarities had not been so obvious during their first meeting, because they were coming from opposite sides of the track. Benn had been champion then and Eubank strutted in from nowhere and took his rival's title. During the intervening three years, both had struggled with certain things. Eubank's involvement in the ring tragedy that nearly cost Watson his life had stripped him of the sense of fun that he brought to proceedings. Benn's inability to get himself back into the middleweight picture until beating Galvano, and the continual battles in his private life, saw him retreat further into the darkness. But while Eubank continued to box for money, to maintain his standard of living, Benn fought on for revenge. He'd never have the chance to fight Watson again and part of him acknowledged that a victory in that rematch might have been beyond him. But Eubank was different – it was personal and, also, he didn't think the WBO champion was better.

What was not debated was the reality of the dislike between the two men. It was not manufactured, something created by a series of stage-managed exchanges. The feud brought out the worst in both of them. Benn became more confrontational than normal and Eubank projected greater arrogance. The problem for Eubank was that it encouraged him to take his opponent lightly this time round and the worry in his corner was that he had been reading the papers too much and believed it when some writers said that Benn was past his best, based on a year which had not been his most impressive. Against Piper, Galvano and Gent, Benn had shown little to fear. And Eubank was telling everyone who would listen that he had suffered from a lack of motivation since his second bout with Watson. It was a case, apparently, of needing the fear again. But was he really fearful? Benn was afraid of one thing – of losing to the man he hated losing to the most, again. He also seemed relaxed, but inside there was fury. Nearly three years had passed since that night in Birmingham. He had never questioned the validity of Eubank's win. 'He prepared like a champion, and I didn't.' This time, with the man he considered the best trainer he'd had in his corner and a different, less hectic strategy, he was confident he would change things round. The reward of fighting Michael Nunn was secondary – all he wanted was revenge. That was all the motivation he required.

At the final press conference, Benn said nothing. He didn't show up. Was it hate or hype? No one really knew but it all seemed slightly childish. Was it that he loathed Eubank so much he couldn't stand to be in the same place as him? You could only guess but the situation meant that anyone at the press conference had to face up to a twin ordeal. Don King's pre-fight shtick was known around the world. It was seldom revealing and whether or not anyone had ever told him, he carried on regardless, whether the listening crowd showed interest or not. 'The Marquess of Queensberry is smiling over me now,' King said. 'I can feel his spirit.' And then came the sermons of Eubank. He had been a breath of fresh air when he first burst on to the scene, but now the same reporters had heard enough. The sound bites weren't choreographed in the way they might have been had he been sponsored by a sportswear company. Eubank's pressers would normally include some kind of 'increase the peace' comment and his musings on the state of the world. After that he lectured journalists about the articles they wrote, and he was asked why he had agreed to a rematch with a man who had hurt him so badly three years earlier that he had begged to be taken to hospital. 'When women have babies the pain is excruciating. At the time you say "Never again" but afterwards, because of what you have produced, you forget the pain. I use that example because I am a woman's man' was the response. Even King rolled his eyes. Eubank managed to hold court for nearly ninety minutes. Of the rematch and what it meant to him in terms of his game plan and how it would affect him, these were his comments: 'Fighting Nigel will give me that kick. He punches like no other fighter. My mind will be more alert and I will be more alive than I have been for a long time. I relish the thought of getting into the ring with him again. I almost relish the thought of taking another one of those big punches, of sucking them in and coming back with my own.'

It was the theatre of the sport that still appealed. The idea that when he got into the ring people had come to see *him*. And he could define himself – boxer, entertainer and tough guy. More often than not, he would not have to prove the toughness, but against Benn and Watson he did. Now it was Benn's turn again and Eubank was sure that, having beaten him once, the mental advantages were all his. The moment he hit Benn with a right hand with all the force he could muster, it would surely be all over. That was his mindset. He had not considered that Benn had improved. Or that he had a game plan different from the first fight. For Benn, this was the moment he had been denied for three years. Being the underdog suited him – against DeWitt, Barkley and Galvano he had not been favoured but had come through. What drove him was the fear of failure and the look on Eubank's face. That perceived arrogance, which he took to be a superiority complex. It didn't matter how he won, as long as he did.

Scene V

'Only educated to a certain extent. Under different circumstances he would be a bouncer on some door in the West End and he'd have three kids from three different women. I'm a superior person to that'

– Chris Eubank speaking about Nigel Benn in 1992

'I don't fucking like you'
    – Nigel Benn to Chris Eubank at a press conference
                                   before the rematch in 1993

With Don King, Barry Hearn and Frank Warren, who walked to the ring with Benn and who would soon be promoting him again full time, involved in the promotion for 'Judgement Day', the show had more to it than previous ones seen in a British ring. For a start there was another world title fight that night, featuring the impressive welterweight Crisanto España, a Venezuelan based in Belfast, defending his WBA title against Canadian Donovan Boucher. The South American would win in ten rounds, clearing the way for the main event.

Devoting three hours of air time to the bout – including the pre-recorded interviews with Jonathan Ross – on prime time was the biggest indication of how big the rivalry had become. The biggest sporting entity in the country at the time was Manchester United, but beyond that it was hard to see past Benn and Eubank. What made it even bigger was the fact that it was a global event taking place in England. Nearly five years earlier, Frank Bruno's failed challenge for Mike Tyson's world title had captivated the country, but that fight had taken place in Las Vegas and was shown live on the still emerging Sky. And no one really thought Bruno could win. Benn versus Eubank was a much more balanced contest between two men who had become household names by virtue of their regular exposure on terrestrial TV. Barry Hearn had said in private to Trevor East, head of ITV Sport, that he didn't need to take his boxers to America because there was enough money to be made in the UK. Delaying the rematch for three years had proved to be the right decision; it had stimulated demand and increased anticipation. The live and television audiences were massive and it was hard to think of a boxing event in the UK that had such pre-eminence.

With over 40,000 fans in attendance, controlling every aspect of the promotion was a near impossibility. Matchroom's John Wischhusen admits it had gone beyond his control with half an hour to go as he paced back and forth from the stadium tunnel to ringside. 'It all got so out of hand. It wasn't falling apart, but getting people to sit down was one problem. The police were trying to get them to sit down, I was getting half a dozen different messages and in the end, I just thought, this is going to happen. It had a momentum of its own. They are going to fight.' Writing in the *Guardian*, John Rodda said: 'The security was totally inadequate to cope with spectators from faraway seats who drifted down to the outer ringside and stood in the gangways for the main event. Even when the police arrived they seemed unable to dislodge all of them, and there must have been some very disgruntled punters in very expensive seats who had to stand to get a view of some of the rounds.'

It had already been decided that Eubank would come out first. The American ring announcer was Jimmy Lennon Junior, whose father had been an MC during the fifties and sixties. His signature phrase was 'It's show time' but for now it was his job to inform the expectant crowd that on his way to the ring was Chris Eubank. Making his way from the home dressing room, Eubank was still out of view when instrumental gladiatorial music started to play. Those expecting and hoping to hear Tina Turner's familiar throaty lines would not to be disappointed. Wearing a red robe with yellow trim, Eubank looked happy, as if this was yet another moment he had been waiting for, rather than it being forced on him, and this time no one stopped the music early. There had been rumours that the somersault into the ring would be jettisoned for this one, but the show was as important as the performance for Eubank. 'The ego has landed,' proclaimed Reg Gutteridge as the WBO champion vaulted in. The reception for Eubank was mixed – there were cheers, but there were boos, too. He'd almost become the professional wrestler who was generally the bad guy, but his gimmick had become so good it was impossible not to admire him. The essential difference between wrestling and boxing is that the grappler knows what's going to happen when he steps through the ropes.

Eubank began shadow-boxing, as was his custom, while his music was silenced by the sound of the chimes of Big Ben. The WBC champion had used those tones at the start of his career and they were making a return now. The next thing you heard was dance music, something that Benn had no doubt heard or played during his stints in Tenerife. Then he appeared, with former manager Frank Warren leading him down the path to the ring. Whatever issues had existed between the pair previously seemed to have been settled for this night and in the future. Benn was in white satin, sporting a skull cap against the weather. But he looked relaxed. And, it must be said, smaller than Eubank. Benn's status as one of the country's most popular fighters was reinforced by the reception he received that night: cheered from the moment he appeared until he walked into the ring, with sections of the crowd already in unison to 'There's only one Nigel Benn'. He was also the underdog. In his mind, with so many

behind him, Benn said to himself, 'I dare not lose'. Three
years earlier, the former squaddie had been tipped for an
early win. This time the smart money was on Eubank to win
late or by decision. Boxing odds are notoriously unfavourable
for the punter, unless you pick a round for the bout to end
in, but there was one other bet worth considering – a draw
would pay you thirty-three times your stake. Draws used to
be commonplace in the sport, when fights were judged by
the majority opinion of news writers or by the sole arbitrator,
the referee. But that was at the beginning of the 1900s. Two
exceptions of recent vintage stood out. In 1989, Thomas
Hearns floored Sugar Ray Leonard twice during a twelve-
round contest, only to receive a tie. The fight was also a
rematch, with Leonard having won the first by knockout,
despite being behind on points. No one, including Leonard,
seemed to think he deserved a share of the spoils second
time round. And in September of that year, Julio César
Chávez, the most dominant fighter in the world, appeared
very fortunate to earn a draw against Pernell Whitaker, with
few writers prepared to give him more than three rounds
over the course of the twelve they fought. The draw suited
Chávez's promoter, Don King, who could continue to sell the
Mexican's undefeated record, which was now approaching
the one hundred mark.

With instructions given to both boxers by referee Larry
O'Connell and the only warmth between the two camps
coming from the opposing trainers – Tibbs and Davies
shook hands in the middle of the ring – both men were
ready to go. Three years earlier, Benn had just stared at
Eubank in preparation for the first bell. This time, as the
WBO champion went into character, Benn mimicked

him. Those who knew the Essex man recognised his way of showing he was ready. Others, including TV analyst Jim Watt, felt Benn had a few too many smiles for the crowd, as if the showmanship should be left to his opponent. No matter: style before rounds would win nothing. This was going to be a battle of pride, skill, courage and stamina.

With his head shaved and robe off, Benn looked wiry in comparison to Eubank, whose frame looked brimming with muscle. There was speculation that, with twenty-eight hours between the weigh-in the previous day and the fight, Eubank might have added nearly 14 lb to his body, which had scaled 12 stone, in accordance with the super middleweight limit. Benn had weighed in at 11 stone 13 lb, and some of that could be accounted for by the thick gold chains he wore around his neck. Plenty of people outside his camp thought his best days belonged at middleweight, but, twenty years later, Tibbs told me that by this stage of his career Benn was a super middleweight.

That wiry frame did not lack strength, as it was Benn who moved Eubank into the corner and threw punches into his stomach. What was also apparent was that the WBC champion was not nearly as reckless as he had been in Birmingham. At the NEC, perhaps conscious of his weight-drained state, Benn seemed to gamble everything on an early stoppage. At Old Trafford, the first round was circumspect, a reconnaissance mission if you like. Tibbs had instructed him to bob and weave and make himself a more difficult target. At the same time, he wanted Benn to throw punches, just not wild, heavy ones. There were no power shots from the man in the white trunks, just little hooks to the body and clubbing rights to the head, when the pair were in a clinch.

Eubank spent the opening 180 seconds mostly on the retreat. His jab flickered out impressively on occasion and his movement, in a clockwise circle, was elegant and controlled. But, like Benn, he was wary of overcommitting. He did not throw combinations apart from one moment midway through the round, when it seemed that he had Benn pinned on the ropes. When he realised that his opponent could weave his way out of trouble, Eubank retreated. What was also noticeable was that he had his trunks pulled up so high that the top was less than six inches below his ribcage. Eubank wore two groin protectors, so the chances of him getting hurt were minimal. Even so, a left hook from Benn to belt line drew a warning from referee O'Connell as the bell sounded. This time there was no eyeballing from either man, allowing Eubank the chance to hold centre stage and pose for all four sides of the stadium although, if you were in the stands, you'd need binoculars to see what he was doing. There might be no denying the bond between Eubank and Ronnie Davies, but there was frustration etched all over the trainer's face as he waited for his man to sit down, almost certainly because he'd seen a different Benn from the one he'd helped Eubank beat three years earlier. By the time Eubank did sit down, Davies had about twenty seconds with him, not enough time to get the message across. Davies had been worried about Eubank's attitude to the contest, the fact that he seemed overconfident. Having seen a less reckless Benn than three years earlier, he was already wondering whether this was going to be a more difficult night.

Round two saw both men relax a little bit. While it was Benn who, inevitably, forced the pace by moving forward constantly, Eubank was looking to land counters in order to draw Benn's sting and put him off his strategy. 'Benn is not getting his punches off,' said Jim Watt. All the bobbing and weaving seemed to distract him from what he was there to do – hurt his opponent. For the opening minute, Benn struggled to land anything of note, while Eubank impressed the judges with his jab and ring generalship. But then Benn came back with some power punches, which drew a roar from the crowd. A judge can be as neutral as he wants to be, but the fans' response can make him question what he is watching. Nothing that landed seemed to hurt Eubank or Benn, a surprise given the agony that both had suffered three years earlier. In fact, during the final twenty seconds of round two, Eubank landed with consecutive right hands, the type that had had Benn wobbling three years earlier. This time, Benn tapped his hands together as if to say, hit me again. At the bell, the pair were caught in a clinch and the expectation was that one of them might say something to the other. But Benn simply walked through his opponent and towards his corner.

If the action had not so far surpassed the first fight, the atmosphere had. Despite Old Trafford being an open-air stadium, the noise stayed in and the singing continued all night, mostly in favour of Benn, but interrupted more than occasionally by 'Euuuuuuuuuuuuuubank'. And there was enough action to keep both camps interested.

Those expecting war to break out may have been heartened by what they saw midway through the third round. Benn was warned again for hitting Eubank low, who responded by doing the same. But the pattern of the fight was not changing. Each man was showing huge respect to the other. Neither landed a punch of note in round three until the end, when Eubank left his chin exposed long enough for Benn to dare to throw a left hook. The punch would have had more impact if the thrower had not been on his heels and the receiver had not had one of the best chins in the sport. A follow-up punch or two might have had Eubank in more trouble, but the two boxers clinched until the end of the round.

The lack of action in comparison to that night in Birmingham was attributed to three separate factors. Neither man seemed desperate to put himself through the physical agony they had both endured then. There was also the fact that Benn was not making himself as easy a target this time and Eubank always struggled against fighters who were elusive. And though neither would admit it, the thought of what had happened to Michael Watson must have inhibited them. Benn might have been working to a plan based on Watson's performance in the rematch but he wasn't being reckless. And there was so much at stake – neither man's ego could stomach disappointment at this stage, with so much time in the fight left. Far better for each to stand back and wait for the other to commit.

A glimpse at the scorecards at that moment showed that the lack of intensity suited Eubank. Two of the judges were American and one of those, Carol Castellano, had given the WBO champion all three rounds. The other, Chuck Hassett, scored rounds one and three to Eubank, giving the other to Benn, who, according to the only English judge, Harry Gibbs, only won the third round. It would not have come as a surprise to Benn that Gibbs sided with Eubank – British officials have a reputation for favouring boxing over aggression. But given that American judges are famed for the opposite, to have lost all three rounds was a worry for 'the Dark Destroyer'.

They'd all agree on calling the fourth for Benn. On two occasions, he'd land right hands which moved Eubank to the ropes, off balance more than hurt, but looking in discomfort. The WBO champion punched less and covered up more, mindful of what had happened the last time he'd fought Benn, who didn't commit himself entirely to attack. And there was yet another warning for punching low for the WBC champion. Not one of those blows had hurt Eubank; in fact, they seemed legitimate enough because of how high his trunks were. But with neither Tibbs nor Benn having raised concerns about what was an acceptable height for body punches, they were leaving themselves at the mercy of referee O'Connell and the possible deduction of a point.

Round five threatened, like the previous four, to be more explosive. It began with Eubank landing a hard jab which rocked Benn back to his corner. The WBO champion ripped more punches at his opponent with mixed success, but the sight of Benn pinned against the ropes, ducking and weaving away from blows and then nodding to his corner that he wasn't in any trouble, could not have assured his supporters that he was in control or that his strategy was working. By the end of the round, he was chasing Eubank again but without too much success. Both men were throwing more punches than they had done in Birmingham, but there were, as Jim Watt noted, 'more missing'.

No round had felt pivotal as yet but the sixth delivered the moment all Benn supporters had feared since Larry O'Connell's first warning for low punching. A point was taken from the Essex man for another blow that landed low. Benn could have few complaints – he'd been warned three times already and whether those punches were low or not, they were hard. As big a worry was how little he had impressed the judges up to that point. Without the point deduction, Benn trailed by a point on the cards of Gibbs and Hassett and five points on Castellano's. His controlled aggression had not been a success. Even in that round, when he had responded to being pushed out of the ring by landing half a dozen solid punches, he had not done enough to win it on any of the cards.

I remember thinking, when I watched this fight live, that scoring was pretty difficult, as very few rounds saw either man putting together sustained periods of domination. Watching Eubank flick out a series of impressive looking jabs, some of which landed, but quite a few of which missed, may have been enough to convince the purist that he was bossing it. Proof of whether those shots were landing or not seemed to belong on Benn's face, which was unmarked. Equally, if he had landed any of his power punches cleanly, the chances were that Benn may have been floored or been in more trouble than he'd shown so far. Likewise, Benn's stalking of Eubank should surely have been worth more if he'd have forced Eubank to cover up as regularly as he had done three years earlier. But that had not happened as yet. The wincing which had been so evident at the NEC when Benn landed those terrifying body punches had been replaced by the mild discomfort of being hit low. It would be an exaggeration to say both men were pulling their punches, but their strategies indicated a fear of going to that dark place again.

Those who thought Benn had regressed as a fighter

were re-evaluating. He was definitely less fluent and more cautious, but he was, in general, following Tibbs's orders to put pressure on Eubank. Beating Eubank meant so much to him, he had in fact changed his approach. People thought that Benn would only be satisfied by knocking out Eubank, but it was slowly becoming evident that victory would be welcome in any way it came. There seemed less idea as to what Eubank's strategy was, except that it was not that different from the way he'd been boxing for the past twelve months – ever since the Watson fight, in fact. Years later, he would admit what many people believed was obvious, that he had underestimated Benn and found that his opponent was 'on his game that night'.

It would not be the first rematch that failed to live up to the original. The light welterweight pair of Aaron Pryor and Alexis Arguello fought a classic fourteen-round battle in 1982, during which both men hurt each other on regular occasions. Pryor would win by stoppage in the fourteenth but both men were praised for their efforts in a bout voted best of the year. In 1983, their highly anticipated rematch saw much more trepidation, with Arguello much more defensive, before being counted out in the tenth round. Going back further than that, Rocky Marciano and Ezzard Charles waged a fifteen-round war in 1954 which the former won by decision to retain his world heavyweight title. Later that year, Marciano would beat Charles in half the time, with the challenger's body perhaps mindful of the pain he'd gone through just three months earlier.

The other side of that coin is two fights between Muhammad Ali and Joe Frazier. Their first meeting in 1971 was a classic, where both landed and took heavy punishment before Frazier won a unanimous points decision. They'd fight for a third time four years later, in the famous 'Thrilla in Manila' in which the punishment they both suffered was even more severe. Ali described it as the 'closest thing to death' even though he won, with Frazier's trainer Eddie Futch pulling him out before the start of the fifteenth. The brutality of that fight could be explained best by the fact that both men became spent forces, their bodies weakened by repeated beatings at the hands of the some of the greatest heavyweights who ever lived.

That was not the case for Benn or Eubank. The latter had been in a few harder fights than his opponent but, for the last two years, Barry Hearn had ensured that his opposition did not put him in the situations he'd been in for the first Benn battle or the Watson rematch. For Benn, avenging one of his two defeats had meant modifying his style, to the point where he was taking fewer risks than anyone could remember. And he had no sense, at this stage, that he was behind on all three cards. The instructions before the fight had started were to put the pressure on his opponent, to make him work hard, with the hope being that Eubank's notorious stamina issues would become the decisive factor. For the first six rounds, the WBO champ had tried to match his opponent's work rate – he had attempted the same when he fought Watson the second time and struggled as the bout wore on.

Round seven suggested that neither fighter was prepared to make radical changes to his plans. Benn pursued his man, Eubank made sure that neither man was ever within punching range and you could only pity the judges. It was impossible to spot any clean punches being landed;

if there was one conclusion to draw, it was that Eubank's accuracy wasn't something to behold. Against an opponent he couldn't miss in their first battle, he was frequently left punching at air, bemused, it seemed, by the fact that Benn was moving his head from side to side. Both men slipped to the canvas as well, with Eubank's loss of balance causing many in the crowd to believe that he had been floored by a punch. A Benn left hook had grazed the top of his head, but Eubank was already on his way down by the time the punch had connected. The noise remained incessant, mostly in favour of 'the Dark Destroyer'. A lustily sung 'Nigel Benn, Nigel Benn, Nigel Bennnnnnnnnn' punctuated the air and certainly gave the neutral the idea that he was ahead. On British television sets, Jim Watt was telling viewers that he had Benn winning the fight and that the quality of Eubank's work was not of the highest calibre.

The fatigue that many suspected Eubank was suffering from became very apparent in the following round. Stuck in a clinch for nearly twenty seconds, he was unable to mount any kind of retaliation as Benn continued to pound right hands against his neck and the side of his head. Later in the round, Eubank staggered towards his corner as the result of a Benn right hand, but his uncoordinated appearance owed more to exhaustion than pain. While it was hard to confirm superiority for either man, Eubank's problems seemed more obvious. He had trained for a fight where the opponent would be a statutory target. Having to think the fight through and force the pace to suit him were not things he was comfortable with. His entire strategy in his pomp was to position himself as a matador – it was why the first fight against Benn had remained his finest performance from start to finish and why Watson had given him so many problems. Benn had fought recklessly three years earlier, whereas Watson's innate savvy and ring generalship meant he could think three or four moves ahead, especially against less skilled boxers. The other problem for Eubank was the class of opponent he'd faced for the last two years; more often than not, he had not been tested, had not had to operate at his highest level. And now, it was showing. Fighting was the way Eubank stayed fit and sharp, but he had been tackling men whose best days were behind them, whose hunger had long since turned into expedience. And on this night, against an opponent whose need for victory and redemption was greater than any of those, he was struggling for direction and inspiration.

With four rounds remaining, the noise of the fans, who were probably four to one in favour of Benn, seemed to indicate that the WBC champion was in charge and heading for victory. Neither man had enjoyed a moment that seemed to swing the fight in their balance, but the fact that Benn continued to move forward and had yet to look as dazed as he had in Birmingham meant the moral victories were being won by the man from Ilford. One wonders what the spectators would have made of the fact that Benn was behind on the cards of all three judges after two-thirds of the bout.

Protect yourself at all times, say the referees before the start of a bout. Nigel Benn would discover the true meaning of that in round nine. After dodging a hook from his opponent, he watched as Eubank lost his balance and ended up with his face on the ground and his legs in the air. His heel managed to hit the back of Benn's head – it was almost certainly the most trouble the WBC champ had been in. Referee O'Connell allowed Benn a few seconds to recover before inviting both men to continue. Eubank held out a conciliatory glove to Benn, as if to say 'sorry, it was an accident'. What he was about to do wasn't. As Benn responded by putting his glove out as well, Eubank threw a right hand at his unprotected chin. The punch missed, with Benn ducking, and Eubank then found himself on the end of a left hook, possibly the best shot of the night. But what Eubank had done, by trying to sucker his opponent, wasn't anything to admire. It was at odds with what he liked to call 'the integrity of a fighter'. And it hinted at desperation. For much of the rest of the round, he was on the receiving end of little hooks and jabs. The crowd, which in the main had been behind Benn since the start, roared their approval as their man went forward and landed shots. Sentiment was with Benn as well. Beaten three years earlier but always, it seemed, a warrior, he was apparently earning the chances for revenge.

It had felt like a Benn round and Eubank's trainer Ronnie Davies gave his man the slap which was part of their routine – it meant that he needed to fight harder. He did in the tenth, but to no avail. He got caught by a lovely left hook, which seemed to hurt him, and from that point he found himself on the front foot but beaten to the punch. Eubank had been too passive for too long and it was a statement of intent. As Jim Watt would say towards the end of the round, 'I've got Benn in front. He's always been busier and he has the last word in a lot of the exchanges. And Eubank has not had the accuracy that he usually does.' Eubank's psychology was to pose at the end of a round if he felt he might have lost it or been hurt

– and that's what he did at the end of the tenth. It was part of the package. It made people wonder whether he actually was in danger and it might influence the minds of the judges who were struggling to separate the pair on their scorecards.

However much most of those viewing the fight might have agreed with Watt, the three people whose opinions mattered the most didn't. By the end of round ten, Harry Gibbs had Eubank in front by two points, having given Benn just one of the last three rounds. Carol Castellano, having given Eubank five of the first six, had now gone against him for four consecutive rounds. Even so, she had the WBO champ ahead by a point. Only Chuck Hassett disagreed – he had the fight even. If Eubank won one of the last two rounds on the judges' cards, he was the winner. Which was easier said than done – the officials had only agreed on three rounds so far.

There was no way Eubank or his corner could know how the judges were seeing the fight, but informed opinion around ringside could be passed round. The BBC's radio commentator John Rawling had Eubank ahead, as did the American television commentary team. But the majority of ringside reporters had Benn in front, albeit by a small margin.

Eubank started the eleventh the way his corner would have wanted. He cornered Benn and unloaded. Jabs, hooks, crosses were all aimed at Benn's head. The majority glanced off the WBC champ's head, as he ducked and weaved. But he did not exchange punches. Eubank took a lead in the round. Benn would come back later and land some right hands but he seemed tired. He had been busier for the first ten rounds, that was unquestionable. He also had a history of fading late in fights, when the fire had gone out and he realised he couldn't knock his opponent out. And as Eubank proved when he beat Watson at White Hart Lane, he was always thinking about how he could win.

Eubank was warned for the third time by O'Connell, this time for holding Benn's arms in a clinch and then hitting. Again he escaped punishment. Benn's body punches continued to look questionable, but he had not been warned since having a point deducted. But as the round came to an end, one was left to wonder how, after all the hype, hate and history, there had been no knockdowns, no cuts and no swellings.

Eubank had recruited his old amateur trainer Maximo Perez for this bout and he and Davies had taken turns in giving instructions between rounds. For this final round, it was the man who had been with him for his professional career who spoke. 'You've got to stop him, you've got to stop him,' said Davies. The former lightweight is too loyal to his fighter to suggest something that his charge might disagree with, but his words suggested that he felt his man was behind and that only a knockout would do. In the other corner, Jimmy Tibbs, who felt he'd had no reason to reproach his fighter, said simply. 'This is the biggest round of your boxing career!'

In the stands, it was felt that this fight was close, but if there was a winner it was Benn. He merely had to survive a Eubank onslaught and avoid a knockdown in order to get the decision. Looking around, there didn't seem many Eubank supporters who felt their man had a chance. The momentum and sentiment were with Benn, who had been written off beforehand by so many and was now so near to closing a chapter of his career. In his mind, he could accept that Michael Watson was a better fighter than he was, because he actually liked him. He didn't like Eubank and had hated losing to him. For Eubank it was not so simple. He didn't hate Benn – he just didn't rate him as a boxer or as a human being. And he had struggled with himself throughout. 'As a champion in my own right, I knew I was more emotionally intelligent than Benn . . . but I just didn't have the focus that I did in our first fight.' And yet, Eubank knew what was on the line – his title, his unbeaten record and the knowledge that he could walk away with that superiority over his nemesis.

Benn had looked weary the previous round but he began the next round in explosive fashion. A fusillade of blows to Eubank's chin had the WBO champion on the run. From the stands, it seemed the Brighton man was on the verge of being stopped. He wasn't responding with punches of his own and looked disconsolate. But Benn had thrown a lot of punches in that opening minute and was now happy to conserve what little energy he had left. Eubank's responses so far after ninety seconds of the round were inaccurate, but he was now on the front foot. But he kept missing and getting countered. It was what he had done to opponents for the last three years, but in this final act of the fight he was getting a taste of his own medicine. He had talked to Benn throughout the fight, without much response. But now, in a clinch, the pair exchanged words. No one could tell what they were saying, but there didn't seem much in the way of agreement. 'A couple of cocky characters,' said Reg Gutteridge on ITV, summing up in a single phrase why there was so much enmity inside the squared circle. With a minute left, Eubank hurt Benn with an uppercut and then threw everything in an attempt to end the fight. But just as it had been throughout, finding the second, third and fourth punches was beyond him. Rarely had he ever missed as much as he did on this night. At the final bell, both men celebrated, but it was the reaction of the two corners that spoke the loudest. Tibbs, chief second Dean Powell and Benn looked triumphant. Davies, Perez and Barry Hearn seemed less so.

The wait for the scorecards to be announced seemed interminable. While we waited in Old Trafford, viewers got to see the opinions of those at ringside. Michael Nunn was due to fight the winner and refused to put his weight behind either man. Don King boasted, as he would given his status as co-promoter, that 'the fans won'. It was left to Hearn to give an opinion.

'I've never seen a fight as close. If I'm going to go for anything, I'm going to go with the draw. That's my honest opinion. I can't divide these two.'

Barry McGuigan also had it as a draw, having given Eubank both of the last two rounds. Jim Watt had given the fight to Benn, despite also giving those last two rounds to Eubank, while Reg Gutteridge believed the WBC champion had already been tipped off that the victory was his, as he went to each side of the ring and celebrated with the fans. Eubank sought his foe out for the customary post-fight hug, which he finally got after lots of posturing from Benn. After almost exactly four minutes, the scores were revealed by Jimmy Lennon Junior, who, twenty-nine days earlier, had told a packed crowd in Texas that Chávez and Whitaker had drawn.

'Judge at ringside Harry Gibbs scores the bout 115-113 Chris Eubank. Judge at ringside Carol Castellano scores the bout 114-113 Nigel Benn,' started Lennon Junior. At this point, Benn and Eubank stood opposite each other. Gutteridge told the nation that this 'looked like being a draw'. Lennon Junior continued. 'And judge at ringside Chuck Hassett scores the bout 114-114 even, a draw. The bout is even, a draw.' A smattering of boos rang out at ringside, but no more than that. Benn slammed down his right glove on Eubank's and then marched around the ring, before storming out of the ring.

'I was genuinely mad. But it was a bit of theatre, a bit of theatre. You know it!' he told me. But then he expanded. 'But there is very, very little theatre in boxing. Back then, I was peed off, so it wasn't really theatre. What you see is what you got with me. I was very angry so I could put on a bit of theatre. Especially with Chris.'

And what about the decision?

'I've seen worse decisions than that in boxing. As long as I've got that belt around my waist and a million pounds in the bank, I'm happy.'

It didn't seem like that at the time. Benn storming off put his trainer in a predicament. 'Gary Newbon said "Jim, do you mind doing an interview? Cos Nigel's gone!" I thought, I've got nothing else to do. Chris was going to run it down. So I said my bit, Chris went to interrupt me, and Gary said "hold on, you've had your say. Now let Jimmy have his say." I said we won by a round, two rounds. If they don't take that point away from us, for punching low, he's won the fight. But I didn't worry too much because we had the belt. It would have been nice to have the two.'

Crucially, Tibbs can't remember Benn pleading for a third fight.

On the ring apron, Eubank was asked his opinion. 'It was close. I thought I might have nicked it on the boxing. He was punching hard. He was scoring with shots. He's not the man I thought. I thought I would knock him out, I thought his resilience would go. What a good fighter he is. I'm glad to have got the draw and now we can do it again.'

Twenty years later, speaking to ITV in a programme dedicated to his life, Eubank was more candid. 'Even though he hit me low and lost a point, he still did enough to win the fight. And a fighter knows [when he's lost].' Of course, given the rivalry that existed then between him and Benn, there was no way he'd admit to having lost. And there seemed little reason to admit to it now, except that a cynic might say that Eubank can admit to anything now, because the record books will always show that he did not lose.

A further examination of the scorecards revealed some more surprises. Judge Castellano continued her theme of scoring the last six rounds in favour of Benn – even the eleventh was given to 'the Dark Destroyer'. And all three judges scored the last round for Benn, which most gave to Eubank. If they hadn't, Eubank would have won. And Tibbs was right – the point deduction for low blows stopped his man from winning. The only surprise was Gibbs giving the fight to Eubank by two points, but, then, the veteran Englishman had previous when it came to swimming against the tide. In 1971, he was the referee and scorer for a British, Commonwealth and European heavyweight title fight between the champion Henry Cooper and Joe Bugner. Cooper was beloved, having given great service to the British fight game and for his come-forward style, despite his moderate size and brittle skin, which was frequently lacerated. The fans disliked Bugner in equal measure, because his style was overly cautious and because he wasn't considered British, having been born in Hungary. Cooper later acknowledged that for many of the fifteen rounds he wasn't at his best. Even so, he came on strong during the later minutes, only to lose a decision by the smallest of margins. The decision was widely derided and Cooper retired immediately. He would hang around boxing for years, as an analyst and friend to up and coming boxers. But what he refused to do was speak to Gibbs, studiously avoiding him until six months before the official's death in 1999, when they shook hands at a charity event.

There would be further consternation about Gibbs's scorecard given that he lived not too far away from Barry Hearn. 'It looked crooked because of the score from my friend Harry Gibbs, who was from Brentwood. People get suspicious, but it wasn't crooked, that's for sure. It was a tough fight to score because there really weren't many clear, concussive punches,' Hearn told me. 'But boxing is a business – Eubank is in the ring with me afterwards and asked me what a draw meant. And I told him, it means we get to do it again. It was a great night for boxing, a great atmosphere. Frankly, I could have made a case for either man. I'm just glad I called it a draw, because it made it look crooked.'

At a press conference later, Benn finally spoke about the decision. It appeared 'the Dark Destroyer' wasn't playing any more and it was also clear that he did think something underhand had happened, with the blame on Hearn. 'I hold one man responsible for this. I don't mean Don King or Frank Warren. Chris has got away with a few things like this.' When informed of Benn's remarks, Hearn responded by saying, 'The officials were appointed by the WBC. I don't have any power over these things. I wish I did.'

By appearing to be so enraged, Benn was allowing Eubank to play the role of gentleman with gloves and the WBO champion did not fail. 'I will fight him again. I feel I own a part of his WBC title and he owns a part of my WBO title. I'm giving Nigel Benn the proper respect. I take my hat off to him. I feel I fought as well as I could. I didn't think he would be that formidable. I thought he would have deteriorated in the three years since the last fight. I thought I would box more. I thought I would knock him out, I thought his legs would go. But he was very strong, very durable and took some good shots from me. It was the sort of fight which perhaps nobody deserved to win. I told him this was pugilism at the highest level and he should conduct himself better.' And, again, that was at the crux of why Benn did not like Eubank. No one told Benn how to behave and certainly not someone who he had just fought to a standstill. Eubank was dangling the carrot about a third fight because he could already sense how much money he could make. How much he was being paid was also important to Benn, but you sensed that it didn't matter as much as revenge.

Eubank would never make any strong claim immediately afterwards that he deserved to win and would admit that he had underestimated Benn. But he did know that a draw suited him and Hearn. Under the original terms of the contract that was signed, the winner and loser would be contracted to Don King. But there was no provision for a draw, which meant both boxers were free to do as they chose. Given that Eubank had always feared working for King and that he might end up becoming the piece of meat that he so despised seeing happen in boxing, it was the right result. He decided to stay with Hearn and the Matchroom stable. Unsurprisingly, Benn would opt for a future with the King/Warren axis, his distrust of Hearn having now peaked. 'We were never close,' says Hearn. 'Nigel always felt I was a Eubank man.' But there were regrets: 'We never got a third fight'. Rival promotions, and that's what Hearn and Warren were, seldom work together. The major reason is usually 'options' – what will happen if their fighter loses? Benn paid a high price when he lost to Eubank, because there was no provision for an immediate rematch. After the second fight, there was nothing in writing that compelled either man to fight the other again.

If Benn had stayed with Hearn, it would have been simple to make a third fight. In fact, the promoter believes it would have had a long-term effect on boxing. 'It would have launched pay-per-view in this country.' Of course, pay-per-view was a phenomenon that the British public had heard about but were yet to experience. In years to come, Sky would ask their subscribers to pay more for certain fights, initially for bouts in America before it became the norm for high-profile domestic clashes. Pay-per-view would not happen on terrestrial television, but then Hearn was already thinking of taking Eubank off free-to-air and to Sky, where the reduction in his exposure would be balanced by significantly better purses. But he did not have Benn with him. And he was obviously not prepared to let Eubank fight on other promotions.

The debate about who had won continued for a few more days. The majority of ringside reports gave Benn the nod, but by no more than a point. One such journalist was John

Rodda of the *Guardian*, who, while siding with the WBC champion, added a caveat: 'Benn was the more aggressive and more varied fighter and he took the points on my card because he was catching so many of Eubank's shots and Eubank never matched his work-rate. Eubank, though, could be the smarter man and the silkiness in the way he moved from point to point suggested in the first half-dozen rounds that he was just too well equipped for Benn.'

In the *Independent*, the veteran Ken Jones gave it to Eubank by that one-point margin, awarding him both of the last two rounds. 'There was none of the ferocity that marked their first meeting in Birmingham three years ago, the impression being that both have improved enough since then to expose each other's limitations. Becoming less reckless, Benn is better able to pace a contest, but still punches off-balance and often missed badly, as did Eubank.'

ITV broadcast a programme the following week which showed the fight in full and asked Barry McGuigan to score the fight. The Irishman had gone for a draw on the night and did so again under the spotlight. With him were Nunn, King and Warren, the latter saying he believed Benn had won. The show highlighted one thing – it was a rivalry that people still bought into and that still divided them. You could not love them both. So, surely, a third fight had to happen. There had been plenty of people who believed the drawn outcome was the convenient result which facilitated a third fight. The public were mildly interested to see what happened when either man fought the hard-hitting Henry Wharton, but the most obvious domestic match was still a third Benn–Eubank bout. But in 1994, something happened that all but guaranteed that it would never happen.

Chris Eubank signed a deal with BSkyB, who were keen to add a marquee name to their expanding boxing portfolio, which already included Lennox Lewis. The key to their strategy was that they could offer more air time to Hearn's other fighters. The promoter had been seething with ITV since a week after Old Trafford, when they pulled the plug on coverage of Eamonn Loughran's WBO welterweight title challenge. 'I've attracted the third biggest viewing figures for sport with Benn and Eubank at Old Trafford, and then a week later they drop me. If they think they can come in and just pick up Benn–Eubank III they will have to think again. This has made a difference, they will have to go to the market place with everybody else. I felt sorry for the people in Ulster and in England not to have the benefit of live coverage. It's a shame on ITV for doing what they did. They are supposed to provide a service to all of us. Their decision not to show this fight is nothing short of disgraceful.' With Eubank on satellite television and Benn still on terrestrial – he would end up on Sky, but only in the final stages of his career – a third fight now looked impossible. And the appetite for it disappeared – people had waited so long for the rematch they weren't interested in another game of cat and mouse.

After years of losing money in boxing, Hearn was at last starting to turn a tidy profit – and with BSkyB's better terms and dedicated coverage, it made sense to accept their buck, even if fewer people would see the top man from now on. In the end, they'd all leave the screens and with that went boxing's profile. Boxing was now a niche sport. Along with Eubank, Benn, Lennox Lewis, Prince Naseem Hamed, Joe Calzaghe and others would all end up fighting on satellite television, despite having begun their careers on terrestrial.

No one could blame them – that was where the money was. But terrestrial television had proved during the latter part of the 1970s and the 1980s that it could make sports stars. From the likes of the swashbuckling Ian Botham to the staid Steve Davis, personalities were created who became part of the national consciousness. Boxing was no different; even after all the arguments about its place in a civilised society, it delivered men like Eubank, Benn and Watson who demanded attention from the viewer. People would moan when they left our licence-fee funded screens, but not many were prepared to pay the money to follow them elsewhere. And so began the era when the boxing fan's love could be equated with how much he was prepared to spend – in the twenty-first century, you can watch all the boxing you like, but it can cost you up to £100 a month, around 7 per cent of the average national monthly wage. The last major foray into boxing by a terrestrial television channel came in 2000, when the BBC signed Olympic gold medallist Audley Harrison to a ten-fight deal while also purchasing rights in overseas bouts. But it was too late. A generation of fans had missed what was so special about the sport and those who were ambivalent about it weren't likely to be persuaded to invest their time in boxing as they watched Harrison plod his way through a series of undemanding prime-time assignments. By the time Harrison's deal came to an end, there weren't many new fans and even fewer who were prepared to watch the big man fail on other channels.

By now, the nation's obsession with football had reached epidemic proportions. It was hard to see what place boxing now had in the nation's sporting conscience. The amateur game was, like many Olympic sports, benefiting from increased funding with so much resting on London 2012. And there had been proof that stars could be created by satellite television, a prime example being Ricky Hatton, whose entire career had been away from terrestrial television. But he was the exception. And explaining the sport to newcomers was becoming harder and harder. Why were there so many world champions?

Nigel Benn was asked recently if he still watched boxing. 'Yeah, but it's all different now' was his response. Whether he meant because there were too many titles or because it was harder to watch thanks to the number of channels that showed it was unclear. Twenty years after he and Chris Eubank traded punches for the last time, Carl Froch and George Groves met in a bout that drew comparisons with the classic battle in Birmingham in 1990. There was dislike aplenty between Froch and Groves in the build-up, including a manufactured head-to-head confrontation on Sky that had many thinking back to when Benn and Eubank signed contracts in the presence of Hearn, Mendy and Nick Owen. The fight itself lived up to its billing, with underdog Groves flooring the more experienced Froch before wilting in the ninth round. But the comparisons ended when you compared the audiences for the two fights – while upwards of twelve million watched Benn and Eubank's first contest, considerably less than a million watched Froch–Groves, which was sold as a pay-per-view event. Had Benn, Eubank and Watson been born into this era, it's likely their stardom would have been diminished, with every title defence sold on a pay-per-view basis, the consumer forced to make a choice based on finance rather than violence. Viewing figures for boxing at the Olympics, when it is still free-to-air, are favourable enough to make one believe that the sport's basic appeal remains intact. But until a promoter or fighter decides that they prefer profile to profit, the vast majority of professional boxers will remain figures of mystery and myth for a society whose Saturday night entertainment is now based around a cycle of talent shows and reality television.

And so we were and are left with the memories of when the sport was a commodity that defined our lives. That knowledge that when you went to work on a Monday morning, it wasn't just the football scores you talked about. Did you see the big fight? You bet. My generation had these three men. We were too young for Ali, Frazier and Foreman and so we put all our energies into Benn, Eubank and Watson. They gave us their all and, because of them, we bought into the sport, its pain, its glory, its nastiness and its hype.

Act VI

Chris Eubank would carry on defending his WBO super middleweight title for another two years. In that time, he displayed some of the qualities for which he had become renowned. His first bout after the draw with Benn was against the durable German southpaw Graciano Rocchigiani in Berlin. Eubank fought hard that night and although some thought it hadn't been enough to win the decision, the judges voted unanimously in his favour. Later in 1994, he signed that deal with Sky Sports. The pattern of facing unremarkable opponents continued, despite the fact that he was on a £10 million guarantee while contracted to the broadcasters – the likes of Mauricio Amaral, Sam Storey and Dan Schommer would have been decent competition if Eubank hadn't been a world champion of some standing. There would also be an example of his ability to box to a plan, and with some style, when he took on fellow Englishman Henry Wharton a couple of weeks before Christmas 1994. Eubank was masterful that evening, keeping the heavy-handed Wharton at bay with movement and punching, winning on points and without any controversy over the scoring.

It would be the last world title fight that Eubank would win. In March 1995, Eubank fought the tough Irishman Steve Collins in Ireland. The hometown man ignored the Eubank mystique by listening to his own music through some headphones while the champion walked in to the strains of Tina Turner. The sight of Collins, in his corner, eyes shut, as Eubank strutted, was as memorable as anything else about the fight. Eubank was already concerned at Collins using a hypnotist and had even suggested that promoter Barry Hearn should call the fight off. In the ring, the challenger pressed the champion throughout, making sure he always had the last word in their exchanges and even flooring Eubank in the eighth round with a body punch – not for the first time, the Brighton man exclaimed that he'd slipped, but his fall had been down to poor balance and footwork. Eubank's only glimmer of hope came in the tenth round, when he floored Collins with a heavy right hand. But the years of neglecting his roadwork and devoting himself to creating a persona to amuse the public seemed to catch up with him that night; the energy required to chase Collins down and hurt him just wasn't there. The bout would go the full twelve rounds but for the first time since he'd turned professional ten years earlier, Eubank would hear the other man's name read out as victor.

Eubank would have a couple of easy knockout wins before the obvious rematch with Collins, later that year. This time there were no knockdowns and, although the bout was undeniably closer, another defeat followed. Eubank immediately announced his retirement from the sport, but within thirteen months he was back. During a memorable phone-in programme on Channel 5, he admitted he needed 'a platform' and that he knew nothing else and also missed the limelight. There would be three more defeats for Eubank before he retired again, this time permanently. He'd take a bout with Joe Calzaghe for the vacant WBO super middleweight belt – his old title – and would lose a unanimous points decision, having been floored twice. The Welshman's speed and superior work rate were too much that day, added to the fact that Eubank had accepted the bout on a fortnight's notice, having prepared for a fight at the light heavyweight limit. That was in 1997; the following year he'd twice take on British cruiserweight Carl Thompson for the WBO title – both were brutal contests, which he'd lose firstly on points and then in the rematch, the ringside doctor would decide that Eubank's left eye was so badly swollen, he was not in condition to continue after the ninth round. In both contests, he'd enjoyed vociferous backing from the crowd – the irony being that only now, as a man clearly past his best, resembling the pug he had always professed he didn't want to be, was Eubank truly loved and cherished by the majority. Because people felt sorry for him.

The stoppage against Thompson on 18 July 1998 would represent the last outing of Chris Eubank's professional career. Just as bizarre was the hollow feeling among all those who had waited for so long to see him take a beating and now realised the emotion they felt wasn't triumph but admiration. Because despite all the strutting and pontificating and all the slurs about the sport from which he drew his income, Eubank displayed one thing in every one of his fifty-two contests – the heart of a warrior. Those who had waited for years to see him walk away from battle were denied so frequently that, in the end, they had to re-evaluate and then admire that man they had so despised.

In 2001, he was a contestant on *Celebrity Big Brother* and suffered the indignity of being the first contestant to be evicted, even before Vanessa Feltz. The following year, he was the focus of a documentary in which he was followed by the television presenter Louis Theroux. Among the many highlights were Eubank refusing to admit to drinking alcohol, even though the programme had paid one of his bar bills, and the sight of the former champion driving through Brighton in a Peterbilt truck. When pressed on how he earned money, now that his primary source of income had disappeared, Eubank declined to answer. Whatever those business interests were that he mentioned to Theroux without being specific, they failed to yield fruit. In 2005, he was declared bankrupt, having run up a tax bill of £1.3 million, which he was unable to pay. Out went the mansion in Brighton, as did his wife of fifteen years, Karron. In 2010, Eubank returned to public life as a designer of suits for a company named Cad & The Dandy. Apart from the money, which was as welcome as it had ever been in his life, Eubank now had a piece of the limelight again. In an interview with Alan Hubbard of the *Independent*, he alluded to how the estimated ten million that he had earned had disappeared.

'How did a man like me end up in a position like that? If you trust people, you will lose your money. Period. I learned the hard way. I've always had something much more than money, which is respect. When I was champion, people looked into my heart and some said, "We may not like Mr Eubank, but we respect him. He fights beyond the call of duty and he never quits".'

It represented some of the most honest offerings from boxing's most prolific mouth. In another interview three years later, Eubank also admitted that the love of the good life and a lack of financial prudence were the root of his problems. He could never see value in the phrase 'less is more'. What was also apparent was his desire to be a player again. Amazingly, despite all the derision he had heaped on boxing, his son, Christopher, had set his sights on emulating his father's career. Eubank senior resisted his son's ambitions until it became apparent that he could no longer keep the young tyro at bay. At his insistence, the teenager was sent to Las Vegas to learn the sport the hard way, just as his father had done nearly thirty years earlier. At the time of writing, Eubank junior is an unbeaten super middleweight boxer with a bright future. Faster and fitter than his dad, he lacks only the concussive punch that helped his father get out of many perilous situations. His skills are not in question – gym gossip became frenzied in 2012 when Eubank junior apparently handled 2008 Olympic gold medallist James DeGale in a sparring session in east London and wasn't asked to come back. Eubank junior comes as a package – if you want to interview him, you speak to Dad as well. Just like his father before him, he is being trained by Ronnie Davies. And just like his dad, he walks the streets handing out signed pictures of himself to unsuspecting passers-by.

I first spoke to Chris Eubank in 1994, when I was a work experience 'kid' at *Boxing News*. He had rung the office to berate the editor, Harry Mullan, for his reporting of the Graciano Rocchigiani contest. Mullan took the call and spent nearly an hour discussing why he had written that he believed Eubank had been fortunate to win the decision. Mullan, a gently spoken Irishman who inspired many within boxing because of his genuine love for the sport and its participants, later told me that it wasn't unusual for Eubank to call in but he also added that it was hard not to like him. I spent the next two years chasing an interview with him, to be told on each occasion by his public relations representative, Shaa Wasmund, that he did not do 'boxing' interviews, because he did not want to publicise the sport. By the time I became a boxing writer, Eubank's career was over and I had no need to speak to him, aside from occasionally calling him to ask his opinion on a forthcoming super middleweight contest. Anytime I did speak to him, he would ask how I got his number and then put the phone down, reminding me not to call him again.

When agreeing to write this book, I called him once again, and he politely asked me to contact his agents and make a proposal. That was summarily rejected, without explanation, despite a reasonable financial offer. I called him directly one more time, enthused by how helpful virtually everyone else had been with their time. Once again, I was left holding a phone with an empty line. Sadly, his trainer Ronnie Davies, out of respect for his former employer, also refused to cooperate. However, a great many other people have spoken to me about him and it is their insights, along with my own opinions, which have helped shape the view of Eubank that you've read.

What is beyond debate is the courage, defiance and

charisma that together were the guaranteed currency of his ring career. He won forty-five of his fifty-two bouts, relying on his durability as much as he did skill. Although he ended with three consecutive defeats, all to British fighters, it remains pertinent that he was never beaten by Benn or Watson. What Eubank will never truly admit to is how much he enjoyed himself at his peak. He may have believed sincerely that boxing was a 'mug's game' but it was his mug that was on the receiving end of a staggering amount of punishment. And even now, as he prepares for his fifties, he still seeks a return to combat. In 2012, he met Benn to discuss a potential third contest, albeit outside of the auspices of the British Boxing Board of Control. The offer to his former foe was within the region of £2 million, but was rejected. All the evidence presented either on television or radio is that Eubank has retained his faculties and has exhibited no signs of the ring wars. It is to be hoped that living vicariously through his eldest son is enough to satisfy that craving for the spotlight. Perhaps the most appropriate words I heard about him came from trainer Jimmy Tibbs, who in five attempts, could never help a fighter sufficiently enough to beat Eubank. 'He was good for the game.' In whatever guise he appeared, whether it was as challenger or champion, there would be either entertainment or something different. You never knew.

Despite the inevitable linking of his name to Eubank and Watson and those glory days, Nigel Benn's career had heights still to reach. He would give Eubank the blueprint to defeat Henry Wharton in February 1994, displaying a skill and poise rarely associated with him before or even after. It was a victory that trainer Tibbs still raves about, the night the brawler turned boxer. After a comprehensive points victory over the Yorkshireman and another points win, this time over the Paraguayan Juan Carlos Giménez, Benn faced the ultimate challenge. With an unpaid tax bill hanging over his head and his private life as traumatic as always (his marriage to Sharron was coming to a bitter end), he agreed to fight the dangerous Gerald McClellan for three-quarters of a million pounds, rather than the less threatening Michael Nunn for half a million pounds less. The American was regarded as the most ferocious puncher in the sport, having stopped his last fourteen opponents, usually in the first two or three rounds. No one had anything complimentary to say about McClellan outside the ring – in his spare time he 'nurtured' pit bulls – and everyone agreed that he was a wrecking machine. It was impossible to find anyone who gave Benn, now thirty-one, a chance. He had split from Jimmy Tibbs – 'I never once had a disagreement with Nigel, but it was other people putting things in his head,' were Tibbs's words – and was now trained by Kevin Saunders, who tolerated Benn's distaste for sparring by honing his skills on the pads.

On a night of tension and excitement in London's Docklands, Benn was knocked out of the ring within the opening minute, hurt by a fuselage of punches from McClellan. Pushed back into the squared circle by Gary Newbon, Benn managed to survive the round and then stage a remarkable fight back, repeatedly rocking his opponent with hooks and right hands. Down again in the eighth, Benn once again got up and hit back harder. In the tenth, McClellan, who appeared to have struggled with his breathing from the early stages, twice, voluntarily it seemed, sought the canvas to escape Benn's fury. The second time, he didn't get up. Moments after the referee awarded victory to the Englishman, McClellan slipped into unconsciousness, having suffered a serious brain injury. Both he and Benn spent that night in hospital. The winner had paid a heavy price, urinating blood and suffering from severe exhaustion. At one point that evening, Benn visited McClellan's room and kissed him on the forehead; such humanity was generally overlooked in favour of his response to a question put to him at the same hospital about the plight of McClellan: 'Rather him than me.'

As a consequence of the regulations put in place at British rings following Michael Watson's injuries, McClellan received the best possible medical care available. Even so, his recovery has been slow. He remains without sight, memory recollection and is wheelchair-bound, cared for by his sisters, Lisa and Sandra, in his native city of Freeport, Illinois. Ten years ago I spoke to Lisa, whose love of boxing had not diminished despite her brother's plight; what was clear was her disdain for many involved in the sport, who she claimed had turned their backs on someone who had paid the ultimate price for his ring endeavours.

Naturally, McClellan's injuries overshadowed the performance of Benn that night. In time it has become recognised as one of the best by a British fighter, especially given the start and the level of opposition. Every fighter, trainer or promoter I spoke to went to great pains to point out that what Benn did that night was probably beyond most of his compatriots. It also took an immense toll on him, physically and emotionally. He'd defend his WBC title successfully two more times, but the end was nearing. In February 1996, he lost a points decision to the one man he always struggled with, 'Sugar Boy' Malinga. There were two more fights that year, both stoppage losses to Steve Collins. He was booed out of the ring after the second fight, having retired in his corner after six rounds. The fire that separated Benn from his contemporaries had gone out. After a career of just less than ten years, which included forty-eight fights, it was time to call it a day.

Most fighters struggle to cope with life after their careers end because the addiction to fame, the spotlight and love of performing are hard to replace. That wasn't the case with Nigel Benn. Retirement forced him to evaluate his life and the path of destruction he'd chosen, in and out of the ring. The affairs continued, as did the drug use, until it became obvious to him that his life was beyond his control. He attempted suicide in south London in 2001, attaching a hose to the exhaust of his car, and says the reason he failed was that the hose slipped from the exhaust three times. It would take him a long time to come to terms with the life he'd been leading. Sanctuary came in the form of Christianity, touring Britain and spreading the word, with the help of his wife, Carolyne. Having based himself in Mallorca for much of his post-boxing life, he emigrated to Australia in 2013.

Before that, he'd face demons in the form of a meeting with Gerald McClellan. Benn hadn't seen him since the immediate aftermath of their battle. He'd be the target of accusations from the McClellan camp, notably that he had used anabolic steroids in preparation for that fight, a charge without truth. In 2007, Benn and an array of figures from boxing helped raise a sizeable amount of money to aid McClellan, who has no income to fund the care he requires on a daily basis.

In doing so, Benn came face to face with the man he had injured. For someone who had always worn his heart on his sleeve, keeping calm or stoic for Benn was impossible. Tears flowed at the sight of the once proud warrior now wheelchair-bound, asking for Benn to identify himself.

There were other moments captured on camera which would surprise those who'd followed his career. He participated in *I'm a Celebrity, Get Me Out of Here!* in 2002 and became the second person to be eliminated; in 2008, in a series of televised segments in conversation with a psychiatrist there was more soul-baring, particularly about the night he tried to take his life and also about his feelings concerning the loss of his brother at such a young age. There was also a gladiator-type contest with Eubank, which saw the pair theatrically threaten each other for five days during training, before engaging in combat using plastic swords and shields. For the record, Benn won, but no one's pride was hurt. At the end of it, Eubank was left to wonder whether his rival would ever stop loathing him. Benn says of Eubank and Watson that he has 'love for both of them' because they made him what he is today, an ordained minister in Sydney, Australia. There is no bling about Benn now and while the intimidating stare remains, as much because of the darkness of his eyes, there is now an unmistakable warmth and generosity of spirit. 'He'll always be the dark destroyer,' says long-time friend and agent Kevin Lueshing, who thinks that Benn is now as close to peace as he's ever known. That much became obvious when he met up with Eubank shortly before emigrating to Australia. The pair embraced before admitting they had needed each other to become who they were. Some say the rivalry is still there and maybe it always will lurk beneath the surface. But the better part of their relationship is formed by respect. They brought out the best and worst of each other.

It would be wrong to suggest that Michael Watson's recovery from life-threatening injuries continued without moments of self-doubt. He was feet away when Gerald McClellan slumped into a state of darkness. Incredibly, it wasn't that which prompted him to reconsider what he was trying to achieve, but the stark reminder that what Benn – to whom he had grown closer since their encounter – achieved that night was beyond him. Nevertheless, Watson had plans for the future. In 2002, when a testimonial in his honour raised around £180,000, his doctor, Peter Hamlyn suggested he try completing the London Marathon. At that stage of his life, Watson could walk just 400 yards and that was an ask. Now, he was intent on walking more than 110 times that distance and he only had about four months to get his battered body into condition to do so. No one who knew anything about him should have doubted his ability to finish the race, which he started on a Sunday and finished the following Saturday. In all £200,000 was raised, not for Watson, but for the Brain and Spine Foundation. A man who would be considered disabled in any form of life, had put his body on the line to raise money for charity. Of Watson's achievement over those six days Hamlyn would say: 'He was an inspiration to me throughout it, as he has been to all those who have met him. He is a noble man, who, unbowed by a burden which even now would extinguish most of us, took his long walk not for himself but for others less fortunate.' His former promoter Barry Hearn, whose eyes light up at the mention of Watson's name, told me: 'He does all this charity work 'cos he says he wants to help people less fortunate than himself! I say to him, "Michael have you fucking seen yourself!"' To this day, Watson continues to talk to people in an effort to help them turn their lives around or to help them find faith as they recover from similar traumas. The effort used to debilitate him, but now he can overcome a lot of the fatigue that is a natural consequence of what he has been through. He sleeps from ten in the evening to ten in the morning and still makes the occasional trip to the gym, hitting the light bag and hanging out with some younger boxers just starting out.

More than twenty years after that tragic night at White Hart Lane that rendered him immobile and totally reliant on medical assistance, Michael Watson is now self-sufficient enough to eat on his own and go to the toilet by himself, not to mention plan for yet another go at the London Marathon, before he retires from public life when he turns fifty in 2015. He still harbours regrets that his ring career never quite reaped the dividends of his peers, although there is no bitterness about the night that ended his career. He speaks of Benn with warmth. Of Eubank, he says only that his former rival 'doesn't know who he is. He's lost.' For how he managed to effect such an incredible change in his own life, he has the most simple of reasons:

'I just love life.'

It is said that Sugar Ray Leonard understood the magnitude of situations in the ring better than virtually anyone and could get himself out of trouble in Houdini-esque fashion. Chris Eubank never inhabited a fistic journey comparable to the American, except that he knew better than most how to escape danger. It was an instinct honed, I suspect, from hours on the street as a youth, dodging police or rival gangs. And it also related to his ego – having told the world he was the best, he surely could not fail them when asked to prove it. But, my how he battled – against Benn on that first fight when he should have been pulled out given the blood he lost, against Watson in the second fight when he had prepared himself for defeat from the midway point and in those epic fights with the bigger, stronger and heavier Carl Thompson.

Having avoided defeat to fighters from his own country for so long, it was ironic that he would end his career with three consecutive losses to fellow Brits. And the fact that he undoubtedly outstayed his welcome in the ring convinced many of us that, in fact, he was not nearly as smart as he thought he was. The problem, by that stage, was that he had spent so long ignoring advice from everyone that no one was ever going to tell him to get out. Or, conversely, was the gravy train so rich that no one wanted it to stop?

Like Watson, the ring was his theatre, his place of expression. But it wasn't that he wanted to show you how skilled he was. More a case of 'look at where I am'. His magnificently sculpted physique masked his limitations and the fact that his training regimes were not of the spartan. And there was a bit of insecurity that some never wanted to try and expose. The youngest of a brood of brothers, Eubank never stopped trying to prove himself in the eyes of his siblings, two of whom boxed and not nearly as successfully as him. And he admits that, even with all he achieved, he still could not earn their respect. The criticism from newspapers and commentators always hurt him as well and he never stopped trying to prove, through chat show appearances and constant mentions of the charity work that he did, what a good guy he was. Plenty would vouch for that and plenty would also say that they were happy for him to be whoever he wanted to be as long as he did it on his own time.

If other boxers were jealous of him and the extraordinary publicity he enjoyed, they would eventually realise one thing: when faced with the opportunity for greatness, as in the first Benn bout and the Watson rematch, he seized the moment. There will never be anyone like him again, because sportsmen in this day and age are treated like politicians, their every utterance scrutinised to the point where their advisers tell them to say nothing at all. Like him or loathe him, he was different and he demanded attention, 'a boxer with an opinion'.

Eubank may well have achieved similar levels of notoriety and fame without Nigel Benn, but having him there helped. Their rivalry seemed natural enough as long as Benn remained combustible and Eubank aloof. People told and still tell stories of what could have happened when the pair would accidentally collide but the rivalry did not need myths or misdirection to take it to a higher place. From the moment the pair signed a contract on television, with the snarls and impassive stares as genuine as the punches they would exchange, their rivalry captivated the nation. On the surface, their approaches to the sport seemed so different, but, in the ring, it always came down to a battle of wills. On one occasion, Eubank's was greater and on the other there was nothing to choose between the two.

The temptation to portray Benn as little more than a

one-dimensional brawler was easy for at his peak he conveyed and displayed violence in a way that no British fighter has done since. Because of the success of another destructive brawler in Mike Tyson, the style was very much in vogue. And while Benn was never quite at the level of the American, he could, at his best, be just as exciting. The style spoke for so much of society as well – the anger, the violence, the hate and the success, all of which existed in the Thatcher era and for some time after. But the frequency with which he changed trainers suggested someone who knew his limitations and would do anything to improve. What he couldn't do was beat either of his domestic rivals.

Like Eubank, he enjoyed certain theatrical aspects of his ring life. It was sometimes hard to work out whether he was showman or ring assassin. That lack of clarity perhaps explains why one former promoter, who enjoyed his time with Benn, would say 'he can be anything he wants to be, depending on the situation'.

The man who held a mirror out to both them was Watson. In beating Benn, he showed the world how one-dimensional 'the Dark Destroyer' actually was. And in his two fights with Eubank he demonstrated that he was the superior boxer, while also taking him to another level. It is tempting to label Watson as a throwback, the kind of boxer who learned his trade quietly and shunned the limelight, believing that his skills spoke better than his mouth. But Watson, in fact, humanised both his rivals. The hate and anger that was so much a part of Benn's psychological make-up disappeared when he was near Watson. He never had much desire for a rematch with his fellow Londoner and, as years passed, they developed a friendship that was quite unique in boxing.

Watson's impact on Eubank was to remind him that very few can control the sport. Up until their second fight, it had always been fun for Eubank. But in first promising to hurt an opponent and then doing so to such a dreadful extent, Eubank found that hardly anyone gets to leave the ring mentally unscathed.

Boxing rivalries don't generally come in threes – many world champions of recent vintage only fight once a year, not enough to build that tension and drama. So revisiting Eubank, Benn and Watson and seeing the map of their conflict, which involved upsets, wars, tragedy and controversy, all packed into four and a half years, is a reminder of a time when disputes, conflicts and tantrums were all condensed into one good scrap on a Saturday or Sunday, televised live for your viewing pleasure. And with the trio made up of a prancer, a bully and a straight man, it's hard to believe it will ever happen again.

Acknowledgements

This book would have been impossible to write without the help of a great many people, who gave of their time willingly and were incredibly helpful. Thanks go to, in no particular order, Ambrose Mendy, Kevin Lueshing, Nigel Benn, Mike Costello, Frank Warren, Frank Maloney, Jane Couch, Colin Hart, Barry Hearn, John Wischhusen, Jim McDonnell, Leonard Ballack, Michael Watson, Jimmy Tibbs, David Brenner, Jim Rosenthal, Clive Bernath, Jim Evans, Steve Farhood, Geraldine Davies, Gary Newbon, Nick Owen, Paul Fairweather, Glyn Leach, James Cook, Suzanne Pakarian, Colin McMillan, Trevor East, Herol Graham and Bruce Trampler.

I am eternally grateful to Alice Everett of Addenbrooke's Hospital for patiently explaining to me the intricacies of brain injuries and how an individual can bring himself back to the condition Michael Watson is now in.

I foolishly believed before I began the process of writing this book that I could remember everything as it happened during my late teens and early twenties. That turned out not to be the case and I relied on the following books to help me put into order the events as they happened. *Nigel Benn*, an autobiography published by Blake; *Eubank: The Autobiography*, published by CollinsWillows; *Michael Watson's Story: The Biggest Fight*, published by Sphere; and *Bomber: Behind the Laughter*, Herol Graham's revealing autobiography, written with Stuart Wilkin and published by TH Media. Also invaluable were *Fighting Words*, by Harry Mullan; *War, Baby: The Glamour of Violence*, by Kevin Mitchell; *Dark Trade: Lost in Boxing*, by Donald McRae; and *Twenty & Out: A Life in Boxing*, the autobiography of Mickey Duff.

As always, I am indebted to the people who have tolerated me for so long. My mother and father, who allowed their hyperactive child to stay up late and watch John Conteh in the late seventies. My brother Raj, who listened to my ramblings from as long as I can remember, and Trev, who still listens and offers insights I wish I had. Of course, no one helps more than those around me now. To my handsome and talented sons, Raf and Ruben, thanks for the laughs and smiles and for being so bloody awesome (sorry for swearing, boys). And as for my wife Laura, there are no words left to describe your wonder. And patience.

And a big thank you to Robin Harvie at Aurum, who came to me a while ago and discussed this project and the best way to approach it. And to Richard Collins and Alison Anderson, whose editing have made this book a lot more readable.

I should also say a thank you to Charlotte, Jessica and Lucy at Quarto for a variety of things it would take too long to list!

Back in 1992, Andrew Forrester suggested to me that it was time for us to go to fights, rather than watch them on TV and stuff our faces with fast food. So began a six-year period when these two public schoolboys travelled the country, watching Benn, Eubank, Lennox, Naz and the rest. And it was a blast. We lost Andy in 1998 and not a day has passed since that I haven't expected him to come through the door and tell me he has tickets for the next big one.

Miss you, fella.

Index